The Complete Learn Italian For Adult

Beginners Book (3 in 1)

Master Reading, Writing, and Speaking Italian With This Simple 3 Step Process

Worldwide Nomad

FREE GIFT

Inside this gift you'll find:

Online Pronunciation Course: Easily perfect pronunciation through an online video course for audio learners

TO CLAIM BONUS

Scan the QR Code below

OR

Visit the link below:

https://worldwidenomadbooks.com/Italian-opt-in

Index

Italian Grammar Workbook and Textbook For *Beginners*

Learn Italian With Essential, Easy to Understand Lessons

Worldwide Nomad

Introduction

Welcome to "Un Assaggio d'Italia"

In this comprehensive guide, you're about to embark on an exciting journey of learning the Italian language from scratch to the B1 level of proficiency. Learning a new language is a thrilling adventure, and we're here to guide you every step of the way.

Why Learn Italian?

Learning a new language opens the door to exciting opportunities and enriches your life in many ways. Here are some compelling reasons to embark on the journey of learning Italian:

- Cultural Riches: Italy boasts a rich cultural heritage, from Renaissance art to world-famous cuisine. Learning Italian allows you to immerse yourself in this captivating culture.
- Travel Adventures: Italy is a top tourist destination with its historic cities, stunning coastlines, and picturesque villages. Speaking Italian enhances your travel experience and enables you to connect with locals on a deeper level.
- Career Opportunities: Italian is the language of business and industry in various fields, including fashion, design, and automotive. Proficiency in Italian can open doors to international job opportunities.
- Personal Growth: Learning a new language challenges your brain and enhances cognitive skills. It boosts self-confidence as you overcome linguistic barriers and connect with people from diverse backgrounds.
- Global Communication: Italian is one of the most widely spoken languages globally, making it a valuable asset for communication in both personal and professional settings.

Overview of the Italian Language and Its Importance

Italian, often regarded as the language of art and romance, belongs to the Romance language family, along with French, Spanish, and Portuguese. It is the official language of Italy and also holds official status in Switzerland, San Marino, and Vatican City. Italian's musicality and expressive nature make it a delight to learn and speak. The Italian language is known for its clear pronunciation and phonetic consistency. This book will guide you through the Italian alphabet, pronunciation, and essential grammar rules. You will gradually build your vocabulary and language skills, enabling you to communicate effectively in various situations.

Structure of the Book

"Italiano da Zero a B1" is structured into units, each designed to provide you with a well-rounded understanding of both the language and the culture of Italy. Here's an overview of what each unit will cover:

- Language: You'll learn essential grammar, vocabulary, and language skills specific to different contexts, progressively building your proficiency.

- Culture: Discover the rich and diverse culture of Italy, from its regions and daily life to its cuisine, social norms, and more.
- Training: Apply what you've learned through practical exercises and activities, including listening exercises, role-plays, and quizzes to reinforce your knowledge.

By the end of this book, you will have acquired the language skills and cultural insights needed to reach a B1 level of proficiency in Italian. Remember, learning a new language is an exciting journey, and this book is your trusted companion along the way.

Let's embark on this adventure together and delve into the beauty of the Italian language and culture! Godetevi il viaggio! (Enjoy the ride!)

UNIT 1

Language:

- The alphabet

The Italian alphabet, a derivative of Latin, includes 21 standard letters, augmented by 5 additional letters (j, k, w, x, y) mainly found in English loan words. This amalgamation results in a total of 26 letters. Italian is renowned for its consistent pronunciation, where each letter maintains a specific sound, significantly easing the learning process for new speakers.

- The Vowels

Italian vowels have a straightforward and clear pronunciation:
  - A: Always pronounced like the 'a' in "father", as in "amore" (love).
  - E: Can sound like the 'e' in "bed", (e.g., "pesce" - fish), or like the 'e' in "they", as in "bene" (well).
  - I: Pronounced like 'ee' in "see", as in "isola" (island).
  - O: Can be like 'o' in "pot", as in "otto" (eight), or 'o' in "go", as in "oro" (gold).
  - U: Similar to 'oo' in "food", as in "uva" (grape).

- The Consonants: C and G

Most Italian consonants are pronounced similarly to their English counterparts, but there are some exceptions. Here are a few notable ones

  - C: Before 'a', 'o', 'u', or consonants (e.g., "casa"), it's pronounced like 'k'. Your tongue should be positioned towards the back of the mouth, not touching the roof. Before 'e' or 'i' (e.g., "cena"), it sounds like 'ch' in "church", where the tongue curves upwards, touching the roof of the mouth near the front teeth.
  - G: Before 'a', 'o', 'u', or consonants (e.g., "gatto"), it's pronounced hard, like 'g' in "go". The tongue should be near the back of the mouth, slightly touching the soft palate. Before 'e' or 'i' (e.g., "giorno"), it's soft, like 'j' in "gem", with the tongue positioned closer to the front of the mouth, creating a softer sound.
  - The "GN" sound in Italian, as in "gnocchi", is not quite the same as the 'ny' in "canyon". It requires more pressure from the tongue against the palate. To achieve this, place the middle of your tongue against the roof of your mouth and push firmly, creating a resonant, nasal sound.
  - SC is pronounced like 'sk' in "school" before 'a', 'o', 'u', or consonants (e.g., "scuola" - school), but like 'sh' in "she" before 'e' or 'i' (e.g., "pesce").

- Accents and Stress

Accents: Italian uses acute (é) and grave (è) accents to modify vowel sounds. While "è" is pronounced like 'e' in "bet", "é" resembles 'ay' in "say". Interestingly, the use of these accents may not always be distinct to native Italian speakers, as regional variations often influence their pronunciation.

Stress: Unlike accents, stress in Italian words is consistently recognized and correctly used by native speakers. Stress can change the meaning of words, as seen with "àncora" (anchor) vs "ancóra" (still, yet). Correctly placing stress in spoken Italian is crucial for clear and accurate communication.

Grammar:

- The Present Tense of "Essere" (to be)

"Essere" is an irregular verb, meaning it does not follow the typical conjugation patterns of regular Italian verbs. Here's how it conjugates in the present tense:

Io sono [ee-oh SOH-noh]	I am	"Io sono felice" (I am happy)
Tu sei [too SEH-ee]	You are (sing.)	"Tu sei mio amico" (You are my friend)
Lui/Lei è [loo-ee/lay EH]	He/She is	"Lei è intelligente" (She is intelligent)
Noi siamo [noh-ee SEE-ah-moh]	We are	"Noi siamo studenti" (We are students)
Voi siete [voh-ee SEE-eh-teh]	You are (plural)	"Voi siete gentili" (You are kind)
Loro sono [LOH-roh SOH-noh]	They are	"Loro sono insegnanti" (They are teachers)

- Usage and Examples
  - Identifying People and Things: "Essere" is used to identify people and things. For example, "Lei è un medico" (She is a doctor).
  - Describing Characteristics: It helps in describing the characteristics of a subject. For instance, "Il cielo è blu" (The sky is blue).
  - Expressing Location: "Essere" is used for stating where someone or something is located, like "Noi siamo a casa" (We are at home).
  - Forming Compound Tenses: It serves as an auxiliary verb in compound tenses. For example, "Io sono stato a Roma" (I have been to Rome).
  - Implying Conditions or Emotions: It's often used to express conditions or emotions, such as "Tu sei triste" (You are sad).

- Common Mistakes to Avoid
  - Misusing "Essere" with Professions: In Italian, articles are generally not used with professions. Correct: "Lui è ingegnere" (He is an engineer); Incorrect: "Lui è un ingegnere".

- ○ Confusing "Essere" with "Stare": While "essere" is used for permanent states, "stare" implies temporary states or locations. For example, "Io sto bene" (I am well) vs. "Io sono contento" (I am happy).

Training:

Exercise 1: Fill in the Vowels

Fill in the blanks with the appropriate vowel (A, E, I, O, U).

_m_re
p_sc_
c_s_
c_n_
sc__l_

Exercise 2: Word Matching

Match the Italian word to its English translation.

Ciao - [Hello, Book, Red]
Amico - [Friend, Apple, House]
Casa - [Car, House, Cat]
Blu - [Blue, Tree, Goodbye]
Gatto - [Dog, Cat, Table]

Exercise 3: Consonant Recognition

Indicate if 'c' or 'g' in the following words is hard (H) or soft (S).

Gatto ( )
Cena ( )
Casa ( )
Giorno ( )

Exercise 4: Accent Identification

Circle the words with accents.

Words: perché, cane, è, sé, libro

Exercise 5: Conjugating "Essere" - Fill in the Blanks

Fill in the blanks with the correct form of "essere".

Io _____ felice.
Tu _____ mio amico.
Loro _____ insegnanti.
Noi _____ a casa.
Lei _____ intelligente.

Exercise 6: True or False – Basic Greetings

Indicate whether each statement is true or false.

"Buonasera" means "Good morning."
"Ciao" can be used for both "Hello" and "Goodbye."
"Mi chiamo" means "My name is."
"Come ti chiami?" means "How old are you?"

Exercise 7: Link the Regions with Their Capitals

Draw a line to connect each region with its capital.

Tuscany - [Florence, Milan, Rome]
Lombardy - [Florence, Milan, Rome]
Lazio - [Florence, Milan, Rome]
Veneto - [Florence, Milan, Venice]

Exercise 8: Cultural Etiquette - Choose the Right Option

Choose the correct option for each situation.

In Italy, when meeting someone for the first time, you should:
A) Hug them
B) Shake hands
C) Wave from a distance

If you are invited to an Italian home, it is customary to:
A) Bring a small gift
B) Arrive exactly on time
C) Avoid eating everything on your plate

UNIT 2

Language:

- Numbers 1-100
  - ○ 1-10: The Foundations

In Italian, the numbers from 1 to 10 are the building blocks for forming higher numbers. It's important to become comfortable with these foundational numbers first. Here they are:

Italian	English	Pronunciation
Uno	One	[OO-noh]
Due	Two	[DOO-eh]
Tre	Three	[tray]
Quattro	Four	[KWAHT-tro]
Cinque	Five	[CHEEN-kweh]
Sei	Six	[say]
Sette	Seven	[SET-teh]
Otto	Eight	[OHT-toh]
Nove	Nine	[NOH-veh]
Dieci	Ten	[DYEH-chee]

Practice pronouncing these numbers with the help of the pronunciation guides, paying attention to the vowels and consonants you've already learned.

  - ○ 11-20: Unique Formations

Moving on, numbers 11 through 20 in Italian have their own unique formations. Pay special attention to '17' (diciassette), '18' (diciotto), and '19' (diciannove), as they slightly deviate from the pattern:

Italian	English	Pronunciation
Undici	Eleven	[oon-DEE-chee]
Dodici	Twelve	[doh-DEE-chee]
Tredici	Thirteen	[tray-DEE-chee]
Quattordici	Fourteen	[kwah-TTOR-dee-chee]
Quindici	Fifteen	[kween-DEE-chee]
Sedici	Sixteen	[say-DEE-chee]
Diciassette	Seventeen	[dee-chahs-SET-teh]
Diciotto	Eighteen	[dee-CHOHT-toh]
Diciannove	Nineteen	[dee-chahn-NOH-veh]
Venti	Twenty	[VEN-tee]

Notice the prefix "dici" in 17, 18, and 19, which is a contraction of "dieci" (ten).

- ◦ 21 and Beyond: Combining Units

For numbers 21 and beyond, Italian combines smaller units. For example, 21 is "ventuno" (twenty-one), and 22 is "ventidue" (twenty-two). This pattern continues with the other tens:

Italian	English	Pronunciation
Ventuno	21	[ven-TOO-noh]
Ventidue	22	[ven-tee-DOO-eh]
Trenta	30	[TREN-tah]
Trentuno	31	[tren-TOO-noh]
Quaranta	40	[kwa-RAN-tah]
Quarantuno	41	[kwa-ran-TOO-noh]
Cinquanta	50	[cheen-KWAN-tah]
Sessanta	60	[ses-SAN-tah]
Settanta	70	[set-TAN-tah]
Ottanta	80	[oht-TAN-tah]
Novanta	90	[noh-VAN-tah]
Cento	100	[CHEN-toh]

- ◦ Tens and Hundreds: Common Errors

In this part, focus on tens (30, 40, 50, etc.) and hundreds (100, 200, 300, etc.). Be aware of common errors, such as confusing '16' (sedici) with '60' (sessanta). Learning to differentiate these sounds is crucial.

- • Days of the Week, Months, and Seasons
  - ◦ Days of the Week

In Italian, the days of the week are:

Italian	English	Pronunciation
Lunedì	Monday	loo-neh-DEE
Martedì	Tuesday	mar-teh-DEE
Mercoledì	Wednesday	mehr-koh-leh-DEE
Giovedì	Thursday	joh-veh-DEE
Venerdì	Friday	veh-ner-DEE
Sabato	Saturday	SAH-bah-toh
Domenica	Sunday	doh-MEH-nee-kah

Cultural note: In Italy, 'Domenica' is traditionally a day of rest, where many businesses are closed, and families spend time together.

- ◦ Months

The months in Italian are:

Italian	English	Pronunciation
Gennaio	January	jen-NAH-yoh
Febbraio	February	feb-BRAH-yoh
Marzo	March	MAR-tsoh
Aprile	April	ah-PREE-leh
Maggio	May	MAJ-joh
Giugno	June	JOON-yoh
Luglio	July	LOOL-yoh
Agosto	August	ah-GOHS-toh
Settembre	September	set-TEM-breh
Ottobre	October	ot-TOH-breh
Novembre	November	no-VEHM-breh
Dicembre	December	dee-CHEM-breh

- ◦ The four seasons in Italian are:

Italian	English	Pronunciation
Primavera	Spring	pree-mah-VEH-rah
Estate	Summer	eh-STAH-teh
Autunno	Autumn/Fall	ow-TOON-noh
Inverno	Winter	een-VEHR-noh

Grammar:

- ◦ Present Tense of Regular Verbs

In Italian, mastering verb conjugation is essential for effective communication and does need a different approach based on the verb group and the person who performs the action, as you have probably already noticed with the verb "to be". Verbs are divided into three main groups according to their infinitive endings: -ARE, -ERE, and -IRE. Each group follows a specific pattern in the present tense.

- ◦ ARE Verbs

-ARE verbs are the most common in Italian. To conjugate these verbs, remove the -are ending and add the appropriate endings based on the subject.

For example, let's take the verb "Parlare" (to speak):

Italian	English	
Io parlo	I speak	
Tu parli	You speak	informal
Lui/Lei parla	He/She speaks	
Noi parliamo	We speak	
Voi parlate	You speak	formal or plural
Loro parlano	They speak	

Other examples of regular -ARE verbs include "Amare" (to love), "Giocare" (to play), and "Cantare" (to sing).

- ◦ ERE Verbs

-ERE verbs form the second-largest group. Conjugation involves removing the -ere ending and adding new endings.

Consider "Vedere" (to see) as an example:

Italian	English	
Io vedo	I see	
Tu vedi	You see	informal
Lui/Lei vede	He/She sees	
Noi vediamo	We see	
Voi vedete	You see	formal or plural
Loro vedono	They see	

More regular -ERE verbs include "Leggere" (to read), "Credere" (to believe), and "Correre" (to run).

- ◦ IRE Verbs

-IRE verbs are the smallest group. They follow a similar pattern to the other two, but many of the irregular verbs, which do not follow a specific rule, belong to the -IRE group. However, regular -IRE verbs follow a conjugation like -ARE and -ERE ones.

Take "Dormire" (to sleep) for example:

Italian	English	
Io dormo	I sleep	
Tu dormi	You sleep	informal
Lui/Lei dorme	He/She sleeps	
Noi dormiamo	We sleep	
Voi dormite	You sleep	formal or plural
Loro dormono	They sleep	

Other regular -IRE verbs include "Aprire" (to open), "Sentire" (to hear), and "Offrire" (to offer).

  ◦ Additional Notes

Pay attention to the pronouns used with each verb form. The pronoun indicates who is performing the action, but unlike English, each person has a different form of the verb and therefore you might sometime face a verb without subject pronoun, that is because they can be tacitly implied and you can guess it from the conjugation of the verb.

Some verbs might slightly change their stem in the conjugation process, especially in the -IRE group. For example, "Capire" (to understand) becomes "Io capisco."

Context is key when choosing the correct verb form. Consider the subject and the action being performed to select the appropriate conjugation.

Training:

Exercise 1: Fill in the Blanks - Numbers 1-10

Fill in the blanks with the correct Italian number:

___ (Two)
___ (Five)
___ (Eight)
___ (Ten)
___ (One)

Exercise 2: Match the Number to its Italian Name

Match the following numbers with their correct Italian names:

14 - A. Sedici
19 - B. Quattordici

16 - C. Diciannove

Exercise 3: Days of the Week Ordering

Order the days of the week in Italian starting from Monday:

Venerdì
Mercoledì
Domenica
Lunedì
Martedì
Giovedì
Sabato

Exercise 4: Translate the Months

Translate the following months into Italian:

January
April
July
October

Exercise 5: Complete the Sentence - Basic Vocabulary

Choose the correct Italian word to complete each sentence:

"___ costa?" (How much does it cost?)
"Dove è il ___?" (Where is the bathroom?)
"Mi chiamo ___." (My name is...)

Exercise 6: Verb Conjugation - ARE Verbs

Conjugate the verb "Giocare" (to play) in the present tense:

Io ___ (I play)
Tu ___ (You play, informal)
Loro ___ (They play)

Exercise 7: Identify the Meal

Identify the Italian term for each meal:

Breakfast
Lunch
Dinner

Exercise 8: Cultural Understanding

Match the Italian holiday/festival with its description:

Natale - A. Festivities before Lent
Carnevale - B. Christmas
Pasqua - C. Easter

UNIT 3

Grammar:

- Articles (definite and indefinite):

In Italian, articles are small but mighty words that precede nouns. They indicate the gender (masculine/feminine) and number (singular/plural) of the noun and sometimes its initial letter. Mastering their use is crucial for proper Italian communication.

- Definite Articles:
  Definite articles are used to talk about specific items. Italian has a variety: 'il', 'lo', 'la', 'i', 'gli', 'le'. The use depends on the gender, number, and the first letter of the noun following it.

Article	Gender	Number	Usage	Example	Translation
il	masculine	singular	nouns starting with most consonants	il pane	the bread
lo	masculine	singular	nouns beginning with s + consonant, z, ps, gn	lo zucchero	the sugar
la	feminine	singular	all nouns	la pasta	the pasta
i	masculine	plural	nouns starting with most consonants	i pomodori	the tomatoes
gli	masculine	plural	nouns starting with vowels, s+consonant, z , ps, gn	gli spaghetti	the spaghetti
le	feminine	plural	all nouns	le mele	the apples

- Indefinite Articles:
  Indefinite articles, used for unspecified items, are simpler.

Article	Gender	Number	Usage	Example	Translation
un	masculine	singular	all nouns	un libro	a book
una	feminine	singular	all nouns	una mela	an apple
uno	masculine	singular	nouns beginning with s + consonant, z, ps, gn	uno zaino	a backpack

- Usage and Examples:
  Practice is key to mastering articles. Use 'il' when talking about a specific known item, like 'il caffè' (the coffee) you drink every morning. Use 'un' when it's about any item, like

  'Un caffè' (a coffee) when ordering without specifying which one.

- Mistakes to Avoid:

Don't use 'il' or 'la' when a general statement is intended. For example, "Amo il caffè" (I love the coffee) implies a specific coffee, while "Amo caffè" (I love coffee) is more general. Remember the special cases for 'lo' and 'gli'. Forgetting these can confuse the listener, as in using 'il zucchero' instead of 'lo zucchero.'

- The Elided Article: " l + apostrophe "
  In addition to 'il', 'lo', 'la', 'i', 'gli', and 'le', there's another important definite article in Italian: the elided article " l' ". This article is used for both masculine and feminine singular nouns and is applied when the noun begins with a vowel. It's a contraction of sorts, designed to make pronunciation smoother.

- " L' " is used in front of both masculine and feminine singular nouns starting with a vowel. It ensures a smoother flow of speech by avoiding the awkward pause between the article and the noun.

- Examples:
  "L'amico" (The friend - masculine) - Here, 'l'amico' is used instead of 'il amico' for ease of pronunciation.
  "L'arancia" (The orange - feminine) - Similarly, 'l'arancia' is used instead of 'la arancia.'

- Mistakes to Avoid with " L' ":
  Do not use ' l' ' with nouns that start with consonants. It is exclusively for nouns beginning with vowels.
  Remember to use ' l' ' regardless of whether the noun is masculine or feminine, as long as it starts with a vowel.

Training:

Exercise 1

Fill in the blanks with the correct article:

___ pizza è deliziosa. (The pizza is delicious.)
Ho visto ___ cane in strada. (I saw a dog on the street.)
Dove è ___ zucchero? (Where is the sugar?)
___ uomini mangiano ___ arance. (The men eat the oranges.)
___ amica di Maria è molto simpatica. (Maria's friend is very nice.)
Vorrei ___ birra e ___ acqua minerale, per favore. (I would like a beer and a mineral water, please.)
___ bambini giocano nel parco. (The children are playing in the park.)
Ho comprato ___ libro interessante ieri. (I bought an interesting book yesterday.)

Exercise 2

Translate the following menu items into English, paying attention to the use of articles:

Il pollo arrosto
Una insalata mista
Le lasagne al forno
Un gelato alla vaniglia
Gli antipasti misti
La pasta al pesto
I calamari fritti
L'espresso italiano

Exercise 3

Read the sentences and identify the incorrect use of articles:

"La ragazza hanno un gatto." (The girl have a cat.)
"Ho ordinato il pasta al ristorante." (I ordered the pasta at the restaurant.)
"Vorrei un acqua frizzante." (I would like a sparkling water.)
"Gli uva è dolce." (The grape is sweet.)
"Maria ha visitato lo Francia l'anno scorso." (Maria visited France last year.)
"Ho visto l'elefante allo zoo." (I saw an elephant at the zoo.)
"Il studenti studiano italiano." (The students study Italian.)
"Un amici di Paolo sono qui." (A friends of Paolo are here.)

UNIT 4

Grammar:

"Ci sono" and "C'è"

Ci sono (there are): [Chee soh-no].
C'è (there is): [Cheh].

• Comprehensive Usage

"Ci sono" and "C'è" are used to indicate the presence or existence of people or things. "C'è" is used for singular nouns, while "ci sono" is for plural. For example, "C'è una stazione vicino" (There is a station nearby) and "Ci sono molti treni oggi" (There are many trains today).

• Common Mistakes to Avoid

A common error learners make is mismatching the subject's number with "ci sono" and

Remember, "C'è" should only be used with singular nouns and "ci sono" with plural. For instance, "C'è un autobus" (There is a bus) but "Ci sono autobus" (There are buses). This mistake can lead to confusion and misunderstanding, so practice is key.

• Constructing Sentences

When constructing sentences with "ci sono" and "C'è", place them at the beginning. For example:

"C'è un ristorante buono qui vicino" (There is a good restaurant nearby).

"Ci sono tre camere libere nell'albergo" (There are three free rooms in the hotel).

• Exceptions and Special Cases

Certain expressions use "c'è" and "ci sono" in idiomatic ways, such as "C'è bisogno di" (There is a need for) and "Ci sono volte in cui" (There are times when). These expressions don't always follow the standard rule but are commonly used in everyday language.

Articulate Prepositions

The "preposizioni articolate" in Italian, are a combination of simple prepositions and definite articles. They are fundamental in connecting different parts of a sentence and are widely used in everyday Italian. Understanding their usage is crucial for anyone learning Italian.

• Simple Prepositions

The main simple prepositions in Italian are: di (of), a (to, at), da (from, by), in (in), con (with), su (on), per (for), and tra/fra (between/among).

- Definite Articles

As we have learned in Unit 3, Italian definite articles vary according to the gender (masculine/feminine) and number (singular/plural) of the noun they precede.

- Combining Prepositions with Articles

Articulate prepositions are formed by merging a preposition and a definite article. For example, "di" + "il" becomes "del", "a" + "la" becomes "alla", and so on. Here's a comprehensive list:

Combining

Preposition + Article	Italian Example	English Translation	Pronunciation
di + il	Il sapore del formaggio	The taste of the cheese	[del for-mah-joh]
di + lo	L'arte dello scrittore	The art of the writer	[del-lo skree-toh-reh]
di + la	La porta della casa	The door of the house	[del-lah kah-zah]
di + i	I colori dei fiori	The colors of the flowers	[day fee-o-ree]
di + gli	Il suono degli uccelli	The sound of the birds	[de-lyee oo-chel-lee]
di + le	Le foglie delle piante	The leaves of the plants	[del-leh pee-ahn-teh]
a + il	Vado al mercato	I go to the market	[al mer-kah-toh]
a + lo	Mi dirigo allo stadio	I head to the stadium	[al-lo stah-dee-oh]
a + la	Andiamo alla spiaggia	We go to the beach	[al-lah spee-ah-jah]
a + i	Parlo ai bambini	I speak to the children	[ah-e bam-bee-nee]
a + gli	Dò da mangiare agli animali	I feed the animals	[ahl-lyee ah-nee-mah-lee]
a + le	Le chiavi sono alle donne	The keys are with the women	[al-leh dohn-neh]
da + il	Torno dal dottore	I return from the doctor	[dal doh-toh-reh]
da + lo	Arrivo dallo zio	I arrive from the uncle	[dal-lo tsee-oh]
da + la	La lettera dalla nonna	The letter from the grandmother	[dal-lah non-nah]
da + i	I consigli dai genitori	The advice from the parents	[dah-ee jeh-nee-toh-ree]
da + gli	Un regalo dagli amici	A gift from the friends	[dahl-lyee ah-mee-chee]

da + le	Le storie dalle insegnanti	The stories from the teachers	[dahl-leh een-sehn-tahn-tee]
in + il	Nel libro	In the book	[nel lee-broh]
in + lo	Nello spazio	In the space	[nel-lo spah-tsee-oh]
in + la	Nella scatola	In the box	[nel-lah ska-toh-lah]
in + i	Nei giorni feriali	On weekdays	[nay jee-ohr-nee feh-ree-ah-lee]
in + gli	Negli Stati Uniti	In the United States	[neh-glee stah-tee oo-nee-tee]
in + le	Nelle strade	In the streets	[nel-le strah-deh]
su + il	Sul tavolo	On the table	[sool tah-voh-loh]
su + lo	Sullo schermo	On the screen	[sool-lo sker-moh]
su + la	Sulla sedia	On the chair	[sool-lah seh-dee-ah]
su + i	Sui muri	On the walls	[soo-ee moo-ree]
su + gli	Sugli alberi	On the trees	[soo-glee ahl-beh-ree]
su + le	Sulle pagine	On the pages	[sool-leh pah-jeen-eh]

- Usage in Sentences

Preposition + Article	Italian Example	English Translation
Del	Il libro del ragazzo	The boy's book
Alla	Vado alla scuola	I go to the school
Dalla	Vengo dalla biblioteca	I come from the library
Nel	Il gatto è nel cesto	The cat is in the basket
Sul	Il libro è sul tavolo	The book is on the table

- Common Mistakes and Tips
  - Agreement in Gender and Number
    One of the most common mistakes is the incorrect agreement of the preposition with the noun's gender and number. Always ensure that the article matches the noun it refers to.

  - When Not to Use Articulate Prepositions
    In some cases, such as with names of cities, simple prepositions are used instead of articulate ones: "Vado a Roma" (I go to Rome), not "Vado alla Roma".

Training:

Exercise 1

Complete the following sentences with the appropriate articulate preposition:

Vado ____ scuola.
Il libro ____ ragazzo è interessante.
Ho visto un gatto ____ cesto.
Lei viene ____ stazione.

Exercise 2

Translate the following sentences from English to Italian:

I go to the market.
The cat is on the chair.
There are many trees in the park.
The book of the teacher.

Exercise 3

Decide whether these sentences correctly use "ci sono" and "c'è":

Ci sono un cane nel parco. (True/False)
C'è molte macchine in strada. (True/False)
C'è un ristorante buono qui vicino. (True/False)
Ci sono una penna sul tavolo. (True/False)

Exercise 4

Match the Italian sentences with their English translations:

Dove si trova la stazione?
Vado alla spiaggia.
C'è un treno alle 10.
Il suono degli uccelli.

a. There is a train at 10.
b. I go to the beach.
c. The sound of the birds.
d. Where is the station?

Exercise 5

Create sentences using the following phrases:

Nel libro
Alla fermata dell'autobus
Sullo schermo
Degli amici

Exercise 6

Identify and correct the mistakes in the following sentences:

Vado al Roma.
La chiavi sono sulle tavolo.
Ci sono una bella piazza in città.
C'è molte persone qui.

Exercise 7

Choose the correct articulate preposition to complete each sentence:

Il regalo è ___ zio. (del/dello)
Ho comprato una bici ___ negozio. (della/dal)
Lavoro ___ ufficio. (nell'/nella)
Il cane dorme ___ letto. (sul/sulla)

Exercise 8

Choose between "c'è" or "ci sono" to complete the sentences:

___ una lettera per te sulla scrivania.
___ molti libri interessanti in biblioteca.
___ un telefono nella borsa?
___ tre finestre in questa stanza.

UNIT 5

Grammar:

- Prepositions of Place
  Italian prepositions of place include di, a, da, in, su, con, per, and tra/fra. Here's how you can use them:

Preposition	Meaning	Example	Phonetic
Di	of from	Il libro di Maria	[dee]: eel LEE-broh dee Mah-REE-ah
A	to at in	Vado a Roma	[ah]: VAH-doh ah ROH-mah
Da	from by	Vengo da Milano	[dah]: VEN-goh dah Mee-LAH-noh
In	in to	Abito in Italia	[een]: ah-BEE-toh een ee-TAH-lee-ah
Su	on above	Il libro è su la tavola	[soo]: eel LEE-broh eh soo lah tah-VOH-lah
Con	with	Vado al cinema con gli amici	[kohn]: VAH-doh ahl CHEE-nah-mah kohn glee ah-MEE-chee
Per	through for	Passo per il parco	[pehr]: PAHS-soh pehr eel PAR-koh
Tra/Fra	between among	Il parco è tra la scuola e il museo	[trah/frah]: eel PAR-koh eh trah/frah lah SKWOH-lah eh eel moo-ZAY-oh

- Prepositions of Time
  For time, the prepositions a, in, di, da, per, and tra/fra are commonly used:

Preposition	Meaning	Example	Phonetic
A	at in	A mezzogiorno	[ah]: ah metz-zoh-JOR-noh
In	in	In estate	[een]: een eh-STAH-teh
Di	of in	Di mattina	[dee]: dee mah-TEEN-ah
Da	since for	Studio italiano da tre anni	[dah]: STOO-dyoh ee-tah-LEE-ah-noh dah treh AN-nee
Per	for	Vado in vacanza per due settimane	[pehr]: VAH-doh een vah-KAHN-tsah pehr doo-eh sett-ee-MAH-neh
Tra/Fra	in	Tra una settimana	[trah/frah]: trah OO-nah sett-ee-MAH-nah

The verb "avere" is fundamental in Italian. It's used in its literal sense (to possess) and also in many idiomatic expressions. This section explains its conjugation and use.

- Conjugation of "Avere"

Io ho	I have	[EE-oh oh]
Tu hai	You have	[TOO eye]

Lui/Lei ha	He/She has	[LOO-ee/LAY ah]
Noi abbiamo	We have	[NOY ahb-BYAH-moh]
Voi avete	You all have	[VOY ah-VEH-teh]
Loro hanno	They have	[LOH-roh AHN-noh]

- Pronunciation Focus: "Ho" vs "O"

The pronunciation of "ho" ([oh] with a glottal stop) and "o" ([oh] without a glottal stop) is a common challenge. To master this, practice saying "ho" with a slight emphasis at the beginning, as if starting the sound from the back of your throat.

- Idiomatic Expressions

Expression	Meaning	Phonetic
Ho fame.	I am hungry.	[Oh FAH-meh]
Ha freddo.	He/She is cold.	[Ah FREHD-doh]
Abbiamo fretta.	We are in a hurry.	[Ahb-BYAH-moh FREHT-tah]
Ho sete.	I am thirsty.	[Oh SEH-teh]
Abbiamo sonno.	We are sleepy.	[Ahb-BYAH-moh SOHN-noh]
Hai ragione.	You are right.	[Eye rah-JOH-neh]
Hanno paura.	They are afraid.	[AHN-noh POW-rah]
Ho freddo.	I am cold.	[Oh FREHD-doh]
Ho caldo.	I am hot.	[Oh KAHL-doh]
Ha bisogno di aiuto.	He/She needs help.	[Ah bee-ZOH-nyoh dee ah-YOO-toh]
Abbiamo fretta.	We are in a hurry. (Duplicate)	[Ahb-BYAH-moh FREHT-tah]
Hai voglia di...?	Do you feel like...?	[Eye VOHL-yah dee...?]
Ho voglia di gelato.	I feel like having ice cream.	[Oh VOHL-yah dee jeh-LAH-toh]
Hanno voglia di viaggiare.	They feel like traveling.	[AHN-noh VOHL-yah dee vyah-JAH-reh]
Ha mal di stomaco.	He/She has a stomachache.	[Ah MAHL dee STOH-mah-koh]
Abbiamo tempo.	We have time.	[Ahb-BYAH-moh TEHM-poh]
Hai pazienza.	You have patience.	[Eye pah-TSYEN-tsah]

These expressions show how "avere" is not just used to denote possession but also to express feelings and states of being, which is a distinctive feature of the Italian language.

- Using "Avere" in Context

Understanding the context in which "avere" is used is crucial. It's often employed where English would use the verb "to be," especially in expressing age, hunger, thirst, and other conditions or feelings. For example, "Ho vent'anni" literally means "I have twenty years," but it translates to "I am twenty years old."

- Cultural Insight

In Italian conversation, sharing personal information such as age, feelings, or plans is common and expected. Using "avere" correctly can help you participate in these exchanges more naturally.

Training:

Exercise 1: Translation Practice

Translate the following sentences from English to Italian:

a. "Hello, what's your name?"
b. "I am from London."
c. "I like listening to music."
d. "Do you want to go to the beach tomorrow?"
e. "I am surprised to see you here."

Exercise 2: Fill in the Blanks

Complete the following sentences with appropriate Italian words or phrases:

a. "_____, come ti chiami?"
b. "Sono di _____, ma vivo a Roma."
c. "Ti va di andare a _____ stasera?"
d. "Ho _____ di andare in vacanza."
e. "Quanti anni _____?"

Exercise 3: Matching Exercise

Match the Italian phrases to their English translations:

a. "Che hobby hai?" - (1) "I am happy."
b. "Sono triste." - (2) "What hobbies do you have?"
c. "Mi dispiace." - (3) "I'm sorry."
d. "Sono felice." - (4) "I am sad."

Exercise 4: Fill in the Blanks

Fill in the blanks with the correct Italian word or phrase:

a. "Quando sono triste, mi piace _____." (When I am sad, I like to _____.)
b. "Se hai freddo, posso prestare il mio _____." (If you are cold, I can lend my _____.)
c. "In estate, spesso _____ sete." (In the summer, I often _____ thirsty.)
d. "Ogni mattina, _____ alle sette." (Every morning, I wake up at _____.)
e. "Non vedo l'ora di _____ al parco domani!" (I can't wait to _____ in the park tomorrow!)

Exercise 5: Conjugation Exercise

Conjugate the verb "avere" in the present tense for each person (io, tu, lui/lei, noi, voi, loro) and translate each form into English.

Exercise 6: Matching Exercise

Match the Italian sentences to their correct translations:

a. "Sono di Roma." - (1) "I feel so-so."
b. "Mi sento cosí cosí." - (2) "I am from Rome."
c. "Vuoi andare al cinema stasera?" - (3) "Do you want to go to the cinema tonight?"
d. "Ho vent'anni." - (4) "I am twenty years old."
e. "Abbiamo tempo per un caffè?" - (5) "Do we have time for a coffee?"

Exercise 7: Find the Mistake

Identify and correct the mistake in each Italian sentence:

a. "Hai fratello o sorella?" (Correct: "Hai fratelli o sorelle?")
b. "Noi avemo sonno." (Correct: "Noi abbiamo sonno.")
c. "Ti piace la musica?" - Response: "Si, mi piaci." (Correct Response: "Sì, mi piace.")
d. "Loro hanno seta e fame." (Correct: "Loro hanno sete e fame.")
e. "Sono felici perché ho trovato il mio gatto." (Correct: "Sono felice perché ho trovato il mio gatto.")

Exercise 8: Fill in the Blanks

Complete the sentences using the correct form of "avere":

a. "Io _____ una bicicletta nuova." (I have a new bicycle.)
b. "Tu _____ ragione su questo argomento." (You are right about this topic.)
c. "Lui _____ un appuntamento alle tre." (He has an appointment at three.)
d. "Noi _____ fretta stamattina." (We are in a hurry this morning.)
e. "Voi _____ i compiti da fare?" (Do you all have homework to do?)
f. "Loro _____ molte idee per la festa." (They have many ideas for the party.)

UNIT 6

Grammar:

- Negative Forms in Italian:
  - The Cornerstone of Negation: "Non" [non]
    The word "non" [non] precedes the verb to negate a sentence in Italian. This fundamental rule is your first step toward constructing clear and precise negative statements.

Type	Italian	Pronunciation	English
Affirmative	Io parlo italiano.	EE-oh PAR-loh ee-tah-LYAH-no	I speak Italian.
Negative	Io non parlo italiano.	EE-oh non PAR-loh ee-tah-LYAH-no	I do not speak Italian.
Affirmative	Lui ha un libro.	LOO-ee ah oon LEE-broh	He has a book.
Negative	Lui non ha un libro.	LOO-ee non ah oon LEE-broh	He does not have a book.

  - Expressing the Void: "Non... Nessuno" [non... ness-OO-no] and "Non... Niente/Nulla" [non... NYEN-teh/NOO-lah]

    To articulate the absence of entities or objects, "non" pairs with "nessuno" for persons and "niente" or "nulla" for inanimate objects or concepts, emphasizing a complete lack of presence or existence.

    Example with "nessuno": "Non vedo nessuno." [non VEH-doh ness-OO-no] (I see nobody/I don't see anyone.)

    Example with "niente/nulla": "Non ho niente/nulla." [non oh NYEN-teh/NOO-lah] (I don't have anything.)

  - Specific Negations: "Non... Mai" [non... my] and "Non... Più" [non... pyoo]

    To navigate through time in your negations, whether never having done something or ceasing to continue an action, "non... mai" and "non... più" come into play.

    Example with "mai": "Non sono mai stato in Italia." [non SO-no my STAH-toh in ee-TAH-lyah] (I have never been to Italy.)

    Example with "più": "Non lavoro più qui." [non LAH-vo-roh pyoo kwee] (I no longer work here.)

  - Double Negatives

In Italian, using double negatives doesn't create confusion but rather reinforces the negation. This linguistic feature is a staple in the Italian language, showcasing the flexibility and depth of negation.

Example: "Non ho visto nessuno." [non oh VEE-stoh ness-OO-no] (I didn't see anyone.)

- ○ Negation with Infinitives: The Subtle "Non"

  When an infinitive verb is influenced by another verb, negation is smoothly introduced by "non" positioned before the infinitive, crafting nuanced sentences that reflect intention or preference.

  Example: "Preferisco non parlare." [preh-feh-REES-koh non pahr-LAH-reh] (I prefer not to speak.)

- Adjectives and Agreement (Gender and Number)

Italian adjectives agree in gender (masculine/feminine) and number (singular/plural) with the nouns they describe.

- Regular Adjectives:

Gender	Number	Italian	Pronunciation	English
Masculine	Singular	alto (ends in -o)	ahl-toh	tall
Feminine	Singular	alta (change -o to -a)	ahl-tah	tall
Masculine	Plural	alti (change -o to -i)	ahl-tee	tall
Feminine	Plural	alte (change -a to -e)	ahl-teh	tall

- Irregular Adjectives Ending in -e:

These adjectives have the same form for masculine and feminine singular.

Singular: e.g., gentile [jen-TEE-leh] - kind

Plural: add -i for both masculine and feminine (e.g., gentili [jen-TEE-lee] - kind)

- Position of Adjectives:

Most adjectives in Italian follow the noun they modify, unlike English.

Example: una casa grande [OO-nah KAH-sah GRAHN-deh] - a big house (literally "a house big").

- Agreement in Complex Sentences:

Adjectives must agree in gender and number with every noun they describe.

Example: Il gatto nero e la gatta nera [eel GAHT-toh NEH-roh eh lah GAHT-tah NEH-rah] - The black cat (male) and the black cat (female).

- Usage and Examples

    ○ Describing People and Things:

Example: Marco è alto e simpatico. [MAHR-koh eh AHL-toh eh seem-PAH-tee-koh] - Marco is tall and nice.

    ○ Describing Situations:

Example: La cena è stata deliziosa. [lah CHEH-nah eh STAH-tah deh-LEE-tsyoh-sah] - The dinner was delicious.

- Common Mistakes to Avoid

    ○ Incorrect Gender Agreement:

Incorrect: Una scarpa bellO. [OO-nah SKAHR-pah behl-LOH]

Correct: Una scarpa bellA. [OO-nah SKAHR-pah behl-LAH]

    ○ Incorrect Number Agreement:

Incorrect: Due gatti nerO. [doo-eh GAHT-tee neh-ROH]

Correct: Due gatti nerI. [doo-eh GAHT-tee neh-REE]

Adjective Position:

Remember that most adjectives follow the noun in Italian.

- Direct Object Pronouns:

In Italian, direct object pronouns are essential for replacing nouns that are the direct recipients of an action, thereby streamlining communication and avoiding repetitiveness. These pronouns differ based on the number (singular or plural) and gender (masculine or feminine) of the noun they replace.

- ◦ Singular Forms:
  lo for masculine singular objects, particularly before consonants such as z, s + another consonant, gn, ps, x, and y.
  la for feminine singular objects.
  l' for both masculine and feminine objects preceding a vowel sound.

- ◦ Plural Forms:
  li for masculine plural objects.
  le for feminine plural objects.

- ◦ Enclitic and Proclitic Placement:
  Direct object pronouns can be placed before the verb (proclitic) or attached to the end of the verb (enclitic). The placement affects the flow and emphasis of a sentence, and understanding when to use each form is crucial for sounding native.
  Proclitic placement (before the verb) is standard in most sentences, especially with conjugated verbs: Lo vedo. (I see him.)
  Enclitic placement (attached to the verb) is typical with infinitives, gerunds, and imperative forms: Voglio vederlo. (I want to see him.), Sto vedendolo. (I am seeing him.), Guardalo! (Look at him!)

- ◦ Usage with Modal Verbs:
  When combined with modal verbs (potere, volere, dovere), direct object pronouns can either precede the modal verb or attach to the infinitive that follows. This flexibility allows for variations in emphasis and style: Lo voglio vedere. or Voglio vederlo. Both structures are correct, but the choice between them can reflect different nuances and personal preferences.

- ◦ Native Speaker Preferences:
  The choice between enclitic and proclitic forms largely depends on the verb tense, mood, and the sentence's overall rhythm. Native speakers tend to use the proclitic form in everyday speech for simplicity and clarity, especially in negative sentences or with modal verbs. However, the enclitic form is favored for adding emphasis or in poetic and literary contexts, as well as with infinitives and imperatives to maintain a fluid sentence structure.

- ◦ Indirect Object Pronouns
  In Italian, indirect object pronouns are words that replace the name of the person to whom the action of the verb is directed. These pronouns help avoid repetition and make sentences more fluid. Here's a list of the indirect object pronouns:

Italian	Pronunciation	English
Mi	mee	to me
Ti	tee	to you (singular, informal)
Gli	lee	to him

Le	leh	to her / to you (formal)
Ci	chee	to us
Vi	vee	to you (plural)
Gli	lee	to them (masculine and feminine)

- ○ Placement
  Indirect object pronouns generally precede the verb, except in the imperative affirmative form, where they follow and attach to the verb.

- ○ Examples:
  Mi dai il libro? (Are you giving me the book?) - [Mee dye eel LEE-broh?]

  Dammelo! (Give it to me!) - [DAM-meh-loh!]

  Usage with Different Verbs

  Indirect object pronouns are commonly used with verbs that involve giving, saying, asking, and similar actions. Some frequently encountered verbs include "dare" (to give) - [DAH-reh], "dire" (to say) - [DEE-reh], "mandare" (to send) - [man-DAH-reh], and "offrire" (to offer) - [of-FREE-reh].

- ○ Example:
  Le scrivo una lettera. (I write her a letter.) - [Leh SCREE-voh OO-na let-TEH-rah.]

- ○ Proclitic and Enclitic Positioning
  Understanding the positioning of indirect object pronouns involves distinguishing between proclitic and enclitic positions.

  Proclitic Position: This is when the indirect object pronoun is placed before the verb. It's the standard position in most sentences, especially in declarative ones.

  Example: Mi ha chiamato. (He/She called me.) - [Mee ah key-AH-mah-toh.]

  Enclitic Position: In this case, the pronoun is attached to the end of the verb. This positioning is typical in affirmative commands, infinitives, and gerunds.

  Example: Dammi il libro. (Give me the book.) - [DAM-mee eel LEE-broh.]

- ○ Which Option is Preferred by Natives?
  Natives tend to use both positions, but preferences can be context-dependent. In everyday conversation, the proclitic position is more common due to its straightforwardness and simplicity. However, the enclitic position has a nuanced role, particularly in giving

commands or when using modal verbs and infinitives, adding a layer of sophistication or emphasis to the sentence.

For example, in a more formal or literary context, you might hear "Dirmelo potresti?" (Could you tell it to me?) - [Deer-MEH-loh poh-TRES-tee?] where the enclitic position adds a touch of formality. In contrast, in everyday speech, "Puoi dirmelo?" (Can you tell it to me?) - [PWAWY deer-MEH-loh?] with a proclitic pronoun is more common.

○ Special Considerations
With "piacere": The indirect object pronoun changes according to who likes something, not according to what is liked. For instance, "Mi piace la pizza" (I like pizza) - [Mee PYAH-cheh lah PEE-tsah].

With "essere": When used with the verb "essere" - [EH-seh-reh], the indirect object pronoun must agree in gender and number with the subject. This is often seen in passive constructions.

Reflexive Verbs: Some verbs automatically include an indirect object pronoun as part of their reflexive form, indicating that the action is performed by and directed towards the subject.

• Possessive Adjectives

Possessive adjectives in Italian come before the noun they modify and are always accompanied by an article, except in certain cases with family members. The possessive adjectives must agree in gender and number with the noun they refer to. Here's how they change:

Possessive	Relation	Italian Example	Pronunciation	English Example
Mio	My	il mio libro la mia casa	eel MEE-oh LEE-broh lah MEE-ah KAH-sah	my book my house
Tuo	Your (singular, informal)	il tuo amico la tua amica	eel TOO-oh ah-MEE-koh lah TOO-ah ah-MEE-kah	your friend (m/f)
Suo	His/Her/Its/Your (formal)	il suo lavoro la sua auto	eel SWOH lah-VOH-roh lah SWAH OW-toh	his/her/your job car
Nostro	Our	il nostro giardino la nostra casa	eel NOH-stroh jahr-DEE-noh lah NOH-strah KAH-sah	our garden house
Vostro	Your (plural)	il vostro insegnante la vostra insegnante	eel VOH-stroh een-sehn-YAHN-teh lah VOH-strah een-sehn-YAHN-teh	your teacher (m/f)

| Loro | Their | il loro appartamento la loro macchina | eel LOH-roh ah-pahr-tah-MEN-toh lah LOH-roh MAK-kee-nah | their apartment car |

Note: When referring to singular family members, the definite article is typically omitted (e.g., "mio padre" - [MEE-oh PAH-dreh], "my father", instead of "il mio padre"), but it is used in the plural (e.g., "i miei genitori" - [ee MEE-ey jeh-nee-TOH-ree], "my parents").

- Possessive Pronouns

Possessive pronouns in Italian replace the noun and must also agree in gender and number with the noun being replaced. They are used with the definite article, again except for singular family members where the article is usually omitted.

Possessive	Italian Example	Pronunciation	English Example
Mio	Il libro è mio	Eel LEE-broh eh MEE-oh	The book is mine
Tuo	La macchina è tua	Lah MAK-kee-nah eh TOO-ah	The car is yours
Suo	La casa è sua	Lah KAH-sah eh SWAH	The house is his/hers/yours
Nostro	Il giardino è nostro	Eel jahr-DEE-noh eh NOH-stroh	The garden is ours
Vostro	L'appartamento è vostro	Lah-pahr-tah-MEN-toh eh VOH-stroh	The apartment is yours
Loro	La decisione è loro	Lah deh-chee-ZYOH-neh eh LOH-roh	The decision is theirs

- Demonstrative Adjectives

Demonstrative adjectives are used to modify nouns and agree with the nouns they describe in both gender and number.

Italian	Pronunciation	English	Note
Questo	KWES-toh	This	singular masculine
Questa	KWES-tah	This	singular feminine
Questi	KWES-tee	These	plural masculine
Queste	KWES-teh	These	plural feminine

Use "questo" and "questa" for objects that are close to the speaker. For example:

Questo libro (KWES-toh LEE-broh) - This book
Questa penna (KWES-tah PEH-nnah) - This pen

For objects that are a bit further away but still relatively close, use "questi" and "queste" to refer to plural masculine and feminine nouns, respectively.

Questi libri (KWES-tee LEE-bree) - These books
Queste penne (KWES-teh PEH-nneh) - These pens

Italian	Pronunciation	English	Note
Quello	KWEL-loh	That	singular masculine
Quella	KWEL-lah	That	singular feminine
Quelli	KWEL-lee	Those	plural masculine
Quelle	KWEL-leh	Those	plural feminine

"Quello" and its forms are used for objects that are farther away from the speaker.

Quello zaino (KWEL-loh ZAI-noh) - That backpack
Quella sedia (KWEL-lah SEH-diah) - That chair
Quelli studenti (KWEL-lee stoo-DEN-tee) - Those students
Quelle case (KWEL-leh KA-seh) - Those houses
Note: The forms "quello" and "quella" change slightly before a noun starting with a vowel, s + consonant, z, gn, ps, and x, similar to the definite articles. "Quello" becomes "quell'" before vowels, and "quella" follows the same rule. For example:

Quell'amico (KWEL-lah-MEE-koh) - That friend (m)
Quell'ora (KWEL-loh-rah) - That hour

○ Demonstrative Pronouns
Demonstrative pronouns stand in place of a noun and also agree in gender and number with the noun they replace. They are identical in form to demonstrative adjectives but are used without the noun. In English, these would be "this one," "that one," "these," and "those."

To emphasize the object or person being referred to, Italians often use "questo" for "this one" and "quello" for "that one," in their respective forms without repeating the noun.

Italian	English	Gender
Questo	This one	masculine
Questa	This one	feminine
Questi	These	masculine
Queste	These	feminine
Quello	That one	masculine
Quella	That one	feminine

| Quelli | Those | masculine |
| Quelle | Those | femin |

For example:
Preferisci questo o quello? (preh-feh-REE-shee KWES-toh oh KWEL-loh?) - Do you prefer this one or that one?
Queste sono le mie preferite. (KWES-teh SO-noh leh mee-EH preh-feh-REE-teh) - These are my favorites.
Tra quelle penne, quale scegli? (trah KWEL-leh PEH-nneh, KWAI-leh SHEHL-yee?) - Among those pens, which one do you choose?

Training:

Exercise 1

Complete the sentences using "non" to negate them.

(Io) _____ parlo francese.
(Tu) _____ hai il cane.
(Lui) _____ vede il film.
(Noi) _____ mangiamo carne.
(Voi) _____ leggete quel libro.
(Lei) _____ capisce la domanda.
(Essi) _____ giocano a calcio.
(Io) _____ bevo caffè.

Exercise 2

Select the correct word to complete each sentence.

Non vedo _____ (nessuno/niente).
Non abbiamo _____ (nessuno/niente) da fare.
Non c'è _____ (nessuno/niente) qui.
Non ho ricevuto _____ (nessuno/niente) messaggi.
Non conosco _____ (nessuno/niente) in questa città.
Non trovo _____ (nessuno/niente) nel cassetto.
Non ho visto _____ (nessuno/niente) interessante.
Non ho parlato con _____ (nessuno/niente) oggi.

Exercise 3

Match each adjective with its appropriate noun, considering gender and number.

Bambino (alto, alte, alti, alta)
Scarpe (vecchio, vecchia, vecchie, vecchi)
Gatto (nero, nera, neri, nere)
Libri (interessante, interessanti)
Casa (grande, grandi)
Amica (simpatico, simpatica, simpatici, simpatiche)
Studenti (gentile, gentili)
Città (bello, bella, belli, belle)

Exercise 4

Identify and correct the adjective to agree with the noun.

Una scuola grande (Correct: _____)
I gatti bianca (Correct: _____)
Le ragazze simpatico (Correct: _____)
Un libro interessanti (Correct: _____)
Le case piccolo (Correct: _____)
Un'amica gentile (Correct: _____)
I ragazzi alto (Correct: _____)
Le penne nuovo (Correct: _____)

Exercise 5

Replace the direct object in the sentence with the correct pronoun.

(Io) vedo il film. (Io) _____ vedo.
(Tu) leggi il libro. (Tu) _____ leggi.
(Lui) mangia la pizza. (Lui) _____ mangia.
(Noi) abbiamo le chiavi. (Noi) _____ abbiamo.
(Voi) scrivete le lettere. (Voi) _____ scrivete.
(Lei) compra i fiori. (Lei) _____ compra.
(Essi) vedono il cane. (Essi) _____ vedono.
(Io) ascolto la musica. (Io) _____ ascolto.

Exercise 6

Choose the correct pronoun to complete each sentence.

_____ (Mi/Ti) dai il libro?
Posso chiedere un favore a _____ (ti/te)?
Ho comprato un regalo per _____ (loro/lei).
Vuoi parlare con _____ (ci/voi)?
Devo inviare una mail a _____ (gli/le).
Racconta la storia a _____ (me/te).
Mandiamo un messaggio a _____ (loro/lei).
Chiedo scusa a _____ (ti/te).

Exercise 7

Complete each sentence with the appropriate possessive adjective.

Questa è _____ (mio/tuo) macchina.
Ho perso _____ (mio/tuo) chiavi.
_____ (Suo/Nostro) insegnante è molto bravo.
Dove sono _____ (loro/vostro) libri?
_____ (Mia/Tua) sorella arriva domani.
_____ (Loro/Nostro) giardino è bellissimo.
_____ (Tuo/Mio) amico chiama.
_____ (Sua/Loro) decisione è finale.

Exercise 8

Select "questo" or "quello" to correctly complete the sentences.

Preferisci _____ (questo/quello) gelato o _____ (questo/quello) torta?

_____ (Questo/Quello) libro è interessante, ma _____ (questo/quello) è noioso.

Guarda _____ (questo/quello) cane! È così carino.

Non mi piace _____ (questo/quello) film; preferisco _____ (questo/quello) abbiamo visto ieri.

_____ (Questo/Quello) maglione è troppo grande per me.

_____ (Questo/Quello) esercizi sono più facili di _____ (questo/quello) di ieri.

Hai letto _____ (questo/quello) articolo sul giornale?

_____ (Questo/Quello) penne scrivono meglio di _____ (questo/quello).

UNIT 7

Grammar:

- Question Words and Forming Questions

The question words in Italian, much like in English, are essential for constructing questions.

Italian Word	English Translation	Pronunciation
Chi?	Who?	kee
Che cosa? or Cosa?	What?	keh KOH-sah or KOH-sah
Dove?	Where?	DOH-veh
Quando?	When?	KWAN-doh
Perché?	Why?	pehr-KEH
Come?	How?	KOH-meh
Quanto?	How much/How many?	KWAN-toh

These question words are used to ask specific questions about people, places, times, reasons, methods, and quantities.

- ◦ Forming Questions
  In Italian, there are several ways to form questions, ranging from simple intonation changes in statements to the use of specific question structures. Here's a detailed exploration:

  Rising Intonation: One of the simplest ways to ask a question in Italian is by changing the intonation of a statement. The pitch of the voice rises at the end of the sentence, turning a statement into a question. For example, the statement "Tu sei italiano" ([too seh ee-tah-lee-AH-noh]; You are Italian) can become a question by simply raising your intonation at the end: "Tu sei italiano?" (Are you Italian?).

- ◦ Using Question Words: When seeking specific information, use the question words listed above at the beginning of your sentence. For instance:

  "Dove vivi?" ([DOH-veh VEE-vee]; Where do you live?)

  "Che cosa fai?" ([keh KOH-sah fah-EE]; What are you doing?)

  "Quando arriva il treno?" ([KWAN-doh ah-REE-vah eel TREH-noh]; When does the train arrive?)

- ◦ Inversion: While less common compared to English, inversion can be used in Italian, especially in more formal contexts. This involves reversing the order of the subject and the verb, often accompanied by a question word. For example, "Quando arriva il treno?" could be formally stated as "Quando il treno arriva?" though this structure is more stylistic than necessary for everyday conversation.

- ◦ Using "Non" for Yes/No Questions: In Italian, forming a yes/no question can also involve using "non" (no) in the question to prompt confirmation or denial. This is somewhat akin to tag questions in English. For example, "Non è vero?" ([non eh VE-roh]; Isn't it true?) or "Non hai fame?" ([non eye FAH-meh]; Aren't you hungry?).

- ◦ Special Note on "Quanto"
  "Quanto" ([KWAN-toh]) varies in form to agree with the gender and number of the noun it refers to. It changes as follows:

Italian Word	Gender Usage
Quanto?	for masculine singular
Quanta?	for feminine singular
Quanti?	for masculine plural
Quante?	for feminine plural

For example:
"Quanto costa?" ([KWAN-toh KOH-stah]; How much does it cost?) for singular, undetermined gender items.
"Quante persone ci sono?" ([KWAN-teh pehr-SOH-neh chee SOH-noh]; How many people are there?) for plural, feminine.

- • Expressing Likes and Dislikes with "Piacere"
  The Italian verb "piacere" ([pyah-CHAY-ray]) is used to express likes and dislikes, and it operates quite differently from its English counterpart "to like."

- • The Basics of "Piacere"
  "Piacere" literally translates to "to please," so when you say "Mi piace" ([mee PYAH-chay]), it means "It pleases me" rather than "I like." This distinction is important because the subject of the sentence is the thing that pleases you, not yourself.

- • Conjugation of "Piacere"
"Piacere" is conjugated according to what is liked. The singular form "piace" is used for a single object or activity, while the plural form "piacciono" ([pyah-CHOH-noh]) is for multiple objects or activities.

Number	Italian Sentence	English Translation	Pronunciation
Singulag	Mi piace il gelato.	I like ice cream.	mee PYAH-chay eel jeh-LAH-toh
Plural	Mi piacciono i libri.	I like books.	mee pyah-CHOH-noh ee LEE-bree

- Indirect Object Pronouns with "Piacere"

The person who likes something is indicated by an indirect object pronoun, not the subject pronoun as in English. Here are the indirect object pronouns used with "piacere":

Italian Word	English Translation	Pronunciation
Mi	to me	mee
Ti	to you (singular informal)	tee
Gli/Le	to him/her	lyee/lay
Ci	to us	chee
Vi	to you (plural or formal)	vee
Gli	to them	lyee

Expressing Dislikes with "Piacere"

To express dislike, you simply put "non" before the indirect object pronoun:

Non mi piace il freddo. ([nohn mee PYAH-chay eel FREHD-doh]) - I don't like the cold. Non ci piacciono i compiti. ([nohn chee pyah-CHOH-noh ee kohm-PEE-tee]) - We don't like homework.

Emphasizing and Specifying Likes or Dislikes

To emphasize or specify what you like or dislike, you can use "molto" ([MOHL-toh]) for "very much" or "per niente" ([pehr NYEN-teh]) for "not at all":

Mi piace molto viaggiare. ([mee PYAH-chay MOHL-toh vyah-JAH-ray]) - I really like to travel.

Non mi piace per niente il calcio. ([nohn mee PYAH-chay pehr NYEN-teh eel KAL-cho]) - I don't like soccer at all.

"Piacere" with Infinitive Verbs

When talking about activities, "piacere" is often used with infinitive verbs:

Mi piace leggere. ([mee PYAH-chay LEH-jjeh-ray]) - I like to read.

Ti piace cucinare? ([tee PYAH-chay koo-chee-NAH-ray]) - Do you like to cook?

- Advanced Usage

For more advanced expressions involving "piacere," such as expressing likes or dislikes towards actions or situations, the verb can be conjugated in different tenses. However, at the A2 level, focus on mastering the present tense usage, as outlined above.

- Practice and Application
Understanding and practicing the use of "piacere" will greatly enhance your ability to communicate your preferences in Italian. Pay special attention to the indirect object pronouns and the distinction between "piace" and "piacciono." Try to incorporate these structures into your spoken and written Italian to express your likes and dislikes more naturally.

- Modal Verbs "Potere," "Volere," and "Dovere"

Modal verbs in Italian, just like in English, are used to indicate ability, intention, or necessity. They are essential in both academic and business contexts.

- Potere (Can/May)
Present Tense Conjugation:
  - Io posso
  - Tu puoi
  - Lui/Lei può
  - Noi possiamo
  - Voi potete
  - Loro possono

"Potere" is used to express the ability to do something or to ask for permission. In English, this translates to both "can" and "may." For example, "Posso usare il computer?" can mean both "Can I use the computer?" and "May I use the computer?"

- Volere (Want)
Present Tense Conjugation:
  - Io voglio
  - Tu vuoi
  - Lui/Lei vuole
  - Noi vogliamo
  - Voi volete
  - Loro vogliono

"Volere" is used to express a desire or a wish. It's straightforward in its usage, similar to the English "want." For example, "Voglio imparare l'italiano" (I want to learn Italian).

- Dovere (Must/Have to)
Present Tense Conjugation:
  - Io devo
  - Tu devi
  - Lui/Lei deve
  - Noi dobbiamo
  - Voi dovete
  - Loro devono

"Dovere" indicates a necessity or obligation, akin to "must" or "have to" in English. For instance, "Devo finire il mio lavoro oggi" (I must finish my work today).

Nuances and Comparisons with English
Understanding the nuances of these modal verbs and their comparisons with English usage is crucial for effective communication.

Kind Use of "Potere"
In Italian, "potere" is often used to make polite requests. For example, "Potrei avere un caffè?" (May I have a coffee?), which is softer than directly saying "Voglio un caffè" (I want a coffee).

- Equivalences and Differences in Usage

  ○ "Potere" as "Can" and "May":

In English, "can" is used for ability and "may" for permission. Italian uses "potere" for both. For instance, "Puoi parlare italiano?" can mean "Can you speak Italian?" (ability) and "May you speak Italian?" (permission).

  ○ "Volere" and Directness:

In English, expressing desires can be softened using phrases like "would like to." Italian often uses "volere" directly, but it can sometimes sound blunt. For politeness, phrases like "Vorrei" (I would like) are used instead of "Voglio" (I want).

  ○ "Dovere" and Obligation:

While "dovere" translates to "must" or "have to," it's important to note that in English, "must" often implies a strong necessity, whereas "have to" suggests a requirement, possibly from an external source. In Italian, "devo" encompasses both senses.

Contextual Application
Understanding the context in which these verbs are used is important. For example, in a workplace setting, using "potere" can be a polite way to inquire about possibilities, like "Posso parlare con il direttore?" (May I speak with the director?). In an academic context, "dovere" indicates assignments or deadlines, such as "Devo consegnare la tesi entro venerdì" (I have to submit the thesis by Friday).

- Combining Modal Verbs with Other Verbs

Modal verbs are often used in conjunction with other verbs. The structure typically involves the modal verb in its conjugated form followed by an infinitive verb. For example:

"Posso studiare?" (Can I study?)

"Voglio imparare l'italiano." (I want to learn Italian.)

"Devo lavorare domani." (I must work tomorrow.)

The infinitive verb remains unchanged regardless of the subject, making this structure a key component of Italian sentence construction.

Training:

Exercise 1

Complete the sentences with the correct question word from the list: Chi, Dove, Quando, Perché, Come, Quanto.

_____ è il tuo attore preferito?
_____ posso trovare un buon ristorante qui vicino?
_____ inizia la lezione?
_____ vuoi andare in vacanza quest'anno?
_____ ti chiami?
_____ è alta la Torre Eiffel?
_____ ci vuole per arrivare a Roma in treno?
_____ fai questo fine settimana?

Exercise 2

Match the Italian question words with their English meanings.

Come - ( ) What
Perché - ( ) When
Quanto - ( ) How
Dove - ( ) Why
Chi - ( ) Where
Cosa - ( ) Who
Quando - ( ) How much/How many

Exercise 3

Choose the correct form of "Quanto" to complete each question.

_____ tempo abbiamo per completare il progetto? (Quanto/Quanta)
_____ zucchero metti nel caffè? (Quanto/Quanta)

_____ ragazzi vengono alla festa? (Quanti/Quante)
_____ sorelle hai? (Quanti/Quante)
_____ costa la maglietta? (Quanto/Quanta)
_____ pagine deve avere il saggio? (Quanti/Quante)
_____ distanza c'è tra Milano e Venezia? (Quanto/Quanta)
_____ persone hanno confermato la loro presenza? (Quanti/Quante)

Exercise 4

Identify and correct the mistake in each sentence.

Chi sono andato al cinema?
Quando tu fai colazione?
Dove è il mio telefono?
Perché non ti piace mangiare fuori?
Come si dice "book" in italiano?
Quanto costa sono questi scarpe?
Cosa fai stasera?
Chi è il tuo migliore amico?

Exercise 5

Complete the sentences with the correct form of "piacere" (piace/piacciono).

A Maria _____ la pasta.
A noi _____ guardare film d'azione.
A te _____ i fiori?
A loro _____ leggere libri di avventura.
A me non _____
il freddo in inverno.
6. A voi _____ le vacanze al mare?

A Giorgio _____ giocare a calcio.
A me _____ molto i dolci italiani.

Exercise 6

Fill in the blank with the correct modal verb: potere, volere, dovere.

Lui _____ visitare il museo domani.
Noi _____ studiare per l'esame.
Voi _____ andare al concerto stasera?
Lei _____ parlare con il professore dopo la lezione.

Io _____ prendere in prestito il tuo libro?
Tu _____ lavorare fino a tardi oggi?
Elisa e Marco _____ comprare una nuova casa.
Voi _____ assistere alla riunione domani?

Exercise 7

Translate the sentences to Italian, using the correct question word or modal verb.

How many languages can you speak?
When do we have to submit the report?
What do you want for your birthday?
Why are they going to Italy?
Where can I buy tickets?
Who wants to go to the beach?
How can I learn Italian quickly?
Why don't you like coffee?

Exercise 8

Transform the statement into a yes/no question by using "non."

Lei sa cucinare.
Abbiamo tempo per vedere un film.
Loro sono felici qui.
Tu hai letto questo libro.
Noi possiamo arrivare presto.
Voi avete un cane.
Lei capisce l'inglese.
Io devo andare ora.

UNIT 8

Grammar:

• Reflexive Verbs

To conjugate reflexive verbs in the present tense, you must first remove the "si" from the infinitive to find the stem and then add the appropriate reflexive pronouns (mi, ti, si, ci, vi, si) before the verb. These pronouns correspond to "myself," "yourself," "himself/herself/itself," "ourselves," "yourselves," and "themselves," respectively.

Example: Lavarsi (to wash oneself)

Italian	English	Phonetic
Io mi lavo	I wash myself	EE-oh mee LAH-voh
Tu ti lavi	You wash yourself	TOO tee LAH-vee
Lui/Lei si lava	He/She washes himself/herself	LOO-ee/lay see LAH-vah
Noi ci laviamo	We wash ourselves	NOY chee lah-VEE-ah-moh
Voi vi lavate	You all wash yourselves	VOY vee lah-VAH-teh
Loro si lavano	They wash themselves	LOH-roh see lah-VAH-noh

Pronunciation Guide

When pronouncing reflexive verbs, emphasize the reflexive pronoun and the stem's first syllable. The reflexive pronouns "mi," "ti," "si," "ci," "vi," and the verb endings should flow smoothly together.

Reflexive Verbs in Daily Routine

Reflexive verbs are often used to talk about daily routines. Here are some common reflexive verbs related to daily activities:

Italian	English	Phonetic
Alzarsi	to get up	ahl-ZAHR-see
Vestirsi	to get dressed	vehs-TEER-see
Svegliarsi	to wake up	sveh-LYAR-see
Addormentarsi	to fall asleep	ahd-dohr-men-TAHR-see

Pronouns and Reflexive Verbs

The placement of reflexive pronouns changes with different tenses and moods, but they always precede the verb in the present tense. In compound tenses like the passato prossimo, the reflexive pronoun precedes the auxiliary verb "essere" and the past participle must agree in gender and number with the subject.

Example: Svegliarsi (to wake up)
Io mi sono svegliato/a (I woke up) - [EE-oh mee SOH-noh svehl-YAH-toh/ah]

Lei si è svegliata (She woke up) - [lay see eh svehl-YAH-tah]

Reflexive vs. Non-Reflexive Verbs
Some verbs can be reflexive or non-reflexive depending on the context. For example, "lavare" means "to wash" and "lavarsi" means "to wash oneself." The difference in meaning is reflected in the use of the reflexive pronoun.

Negative Forms
To make a reflexive verb negative, place "non" before the reflexive pronoun.

Example: Non mi lavo (I do not wash myself) - [nohn mee LAH-voh]

Imperative Form
Reflexive verbs in the imperative mood require the reflexive pronoun to follow the verb and are attached as a suffix. For negative commands, "non" precedes the verb, and the reflexive pronoun returns to its position before the verb.

Example: Lavati! (Wash yourself!) - [lah-VAH-tee]

Non ti lavare! (Do not wash yourself!) - [nohn tee lah-VAH-reh]

- Imperative Form (Commands)
The imperative mood is used to give orders, instructions, advice, or suggestions. In Italian, the form of the imperative changes according to the person you are speaking to (tu, Lei, voi, noi) and whether the command is positive or negative.

Formation of the Imperative
Tu Form (Informal Singular You)

For -are verbs, drop the final -e of the present tense: Parlare (to speak) becomes "Parla!" ([PAHR-lah]) - Speak!

For -ere and -ire verbs, drop the final -e of the present tense: Prendere (to take) becomes "Prendi!" ([PREHN-dee]) - Take!; Aprire (to open) becomes "Apri!" ([AH-pree]) - Open!

Lei Form (Formal Singular You)

Use the third-person singular present tense form: Parlare becomes "Parli!" ([PAHR-lee]) - Speak (formally)!

Add the word "Lei" for clarity or emphasis: "Parli, Lei!" - Speak, please!

Noi Form (We)
Use the first-person plural present tense form: Mangiare (to eat) becomes "Mangiamo!" ([mahn-JAH-moh]) - Let's eat!

Voi Form (Informal Plural You)
Use the second-person plural present tense form without any changes: Parlare becomes "Parlate!" ([pahr-LAH-teh]) - Speak (you all)!

Negative Commands
To form negative commands, simply place "non" ([nohn]) before the verb. For example:

Tu form	"Non parlare!"	Don't speak!	nohn PAHR-lah-reh
Lei form	"Non parli!"	Don't speak (formally)!	nohn PAHR-lee
Noi form	"Non mangiamo!"	Let's not eat!	nohn mahn-JAH-moh
Voi form	"Non parlate!"	Don't speak (you all)!	nohn pahr-LAH-teh

Irregular Verbs
Some verbs have irregular imperative forms, especially in the "tu" and "noi" forms. Here are a few common irregular verbs:

Essere (to be): Sii	Be! (tu form)	SEE
Essere (to be): Siamo	Let's be! (noi form)	SYAH-moh
Avere (to have): Abbi	Have! (tu form)	AHB-bee
Avere (to have): Abbiamo	Let's have! (noi form)	ahb-BYAH-moh
Fare (to do/make): Fai	Do! (tu form)	fah-EE
Fare (to do/make): Facciamo	Let's do! (noi form)	fah-CHAH-moh
Dare (to give): Dai	Give! (tu form)	dah-EE
Dare (to give): Diamo	Let's give! (noi form)	DYAH-moh
Andare (to go): Vai	Go! (tu form)	vah-EE
Andare (to go): Andiamo	Let's go! (noi form)	ahn-DYAH-moh

Pronouns with Commands
When using direct, indirect, or reflexive pronouns with affirmative commands, attach them to the end of the verb, forming a single word. For example:

Parlami!	Talk to me! (Parlare + mi)	PAHR-lah-mee
Dimmi!	Tell me! (Dire + mi)	DEE-mee
Lavati!	Wash yourself! (Lavare + ti)	lah-VAH-tee

For negative commands, place the pronoun before the verb:
"Non mi parlare!" ([nohn mee PAHR-lah-reh]) - Don't talk to me!

- Basic Conjuctions

In Italian, conjunctions are vital for constructing coherent sentences and expressing complex ideas smoothly.

Italian Conjunction	English Equivalent(s)	Phonetic
E	And	eh
E is the Italian equivalent of "and" in English. It is used to join two or more nouns, verbs, adjectives, or sentences that are related or in sequence., EE-oh eh MEE-oh frah-TEHL-loh		
Ma	But	mah
Ma contrasts information or introduces an exception. It is similar to "but" in English., SOH-noh STAHN-koh, mah FEH-lee-che		
O	Or	oh
O offers a choice or alternative between two or more elements. It is used in the same way as "or" in English., VWOH-ee teh oh kahf-FEH?		
Perché	Because	pehr-KEH
Perché is used to explain reasons or causes. It translates to "because" in English., STOO-dyoh ee-tah-LYAH-noh pehr-KEH mee PYAH-che		
Quindi	So, Therefore	KWEEN-dee
Quindi indicates a consequence or result. It is often used in the sense of "so" or "therefore.", EH TAHR-dee, KWEEN-dee doh-BBYAH-moh ahn-DAH-reh		
Anche	Also, Too	AHN-keh
Anche adds information in addition to what has already been mentioned. It translates to "also" or "too.", lay PAHR-lah ee-tah-LYAH-noh eh AHN-keh frahn-CHEH-seh		
Ovvero	Or rather, That is	oh-VEHR-roh
Ovvero is used to clarify or specify something previously mentioned. It can be translated as "or rather" or "that is.", doh-VREHM-moh een-kohn-TRAHR-chee AHL-leh treh, oh-VEHR-roh DOH-poh PRAHN-zoh		
Dunque	So, Thus	DOON-kweh
Dunque is similar to "quindi," indicating a conclusion or inference. It can be translated as "so" or "thus.", non ah ree-SPOHS-toh, DOON-kweh non vehr-RAH		
Se	If	seh
Se introduces a condition or hypothesis. It is the equivalent of "if" in English., seh PYOH-veh, reh-STYAH-moh ah KAH-sah		
Però	However	pehr-OH
Però is used to introduce a contrast or exception, similar to "however" in English., EH KA-roh, pehr-OH dee BWOH-nah kwah-lee-TAH		
Nonostante	Despite, In spite of	nohn-oh-STAHN-teh
Nonostante introduces an exception or contradiction. It translates to "despite" or "in spite of.", nohn-oh-STAHN-teh lah PYOH-jah, SYAH-moh ooh-SHEE-tee		
Finché	Until	feen-KEH

Finché indicates a time limit or duration. It means "until.", ah-speht-teh-ROH feen-KEH nohn TOHR-nee		
Benché	Although, Even though	BEHN-keh
Benché is used to introduce a concession, similar to "although" or "even though.", BEHN-keh SEE-ah dee-FEE-chee-leh, loh fah-ROH		
Siccome	Since, As	SEEK-koh-meh
Siccome introduces a reason or cause, similar to "since" or "as" in English., SEEK-koh-meh PYOH-veh, prehn-DYAH-moh lom-BREHL-loh		
Mentre	While	MEHN-treh
Mentre indicates simultaneity or contrast in actions. It translates to "while.", MEHN-treh STOO-dyah-voh, ah-skohl-TAH-voh MOO-see-kah		
Così	So, In this way	koh-SEE
Così suggests manner or consequence, often translated as "so" or "in this way.", ah spyeh-GAH-toh koh-SEE BEH-neh keh oh kah-PEE-toh TOOT-toh		

Training:

Exercise 1

Fill in the blanks with the correct reflexive pronouns (mi, ti, si, ci, vi, si) based on the subject.

Io ___ alzo alle 6 ogni mattina.
Tu ___ lavi le mani prima di mangiare.
Lei ___ pettina i capelli dopo la doccia.
Noi ___ addormentiamo dopo mezzanotte.
Voi ___ svegliate presto durante la settimana.
Loro ___ vestono in fretta per la scuola.
Marco ___ rilassa nel weekend.
Le ragazze ___ truccano prima di uscire.

Exercise 2: Match the Verb with Its Reflexive Form

Connect each infinitive verb with its correct reflexive form.

Lavare - A. Addormentarsi
Vestire - B. Alzarsi
Svegliare - C. Vestirsi
Addormentare - D. Lavarsi
Truccare - E. Svegliarsi
Rilassare - F. Truccarsi
Alzare - G. Rilassarsi
Preparare - H. Prepararsi

Exercise 3

Select the correct imperative form of the verb given the subject.

(Tu) Dormire - A. Dormi! B. Dorma! C. Dormiamo!
(Noi) Partire - A. Partiamo! B. Partite! C. Parti!
(Voi) Stare - A. Stai! B. State! C. Stiamo!
(Tu) Venire - A. Vieni! B. Venite! C. Veniamo!
(Noi) Fare - A. Fai! B. Fate! C. Facciamo!
(Tu) Dire - A. Dici! B. Dite! C. Diamo!
(Voi) Avere - A. Avete! B. Abbiamo! C. Avere!
(Tu) Andare - A. Vai! B. Andiamo! C. Vanno!

Exercise 4

Identify and correct the mistake in each sentence.

Loro si svegliano presto ogni mattina. (Correct: Loro si svegliano presto ogni mattina.)

Tu ti vesti dopo aver fatto la doccia. (Correct: Tu ti vesti dopo aver fatto la doccia.)

Noi ci laviamo le mani prima di pranzare. (Correct: Noi ci laviamo le mani prima di pranzare.)

Voi vi rilassate nel fine settimana. (Correct: Voi vi rilassate nel fine settimana.)

Lei si addormenta leggendo un libro. (Correct: Lei si addormenta leggendo un libro.)

Io mi preparo velocemente la mattina. (Correct: Io mi preparo velocemente la mattina.)

Lui si trucca prima di uscire. (Correct: Lui si trucca prima di uscire.)

Noi ci alziamo tardi la domenica. (Correct: Noi ci alziamo tardi la domenica.)

Exercise 5

Fill in the blanks with the correct conjunction (e, ma, o, perché, quindi, anche, ovvero, dunque, se, però, nonostante, finché, benché, siccome, mentre, così).

Vorrei andare al cinema, ___ piove.
Mangio la pizza ___ mi piace molto.
Lavoro il sabato, ___ la domenica riposo.
Studia italiano ___ vuole viaggiare in Italia.
Ha freddo, ___ mette un maglione.
Vieni alla festa ___ no?

Parla sia inglese ___ spagnolo.
___ ha fatto tardi, non usciremo.

Exercise 6

Conjugate the reflexive verb in parentheses in the present tense to complete the sentence.

Io ___ (vestirsi) rapidamente ogni mattina.
Tu ___ (lavarsi) prima di andare a letto.
Lei ___ (truccarsi) per la cena fuori.
Noi ___ (rilassarsi) dopo il lavoro.
Voi ___ (prepararsi) per l'esame domani.
Loro ___ (svegliarsi) all'alba.
Marco ___ (allenarsi) in palestra.
Le ragazze ___ (divertirsi) al concerto.

Exercise 7

Transform the sentence into its negative form by placing "non" correctly.

Io mi lavo → Non mi lavo.
Tu ti vesti → Non ti vesti.
Lei si trucca → Non si trucca.
Noi ci rilassiamo → Non ci rilassiamo.
Voi vi preparate → Non vi preparate.
Loro si svegliano → Non si svegliano.
Marco si allena → Non si allena.
Le ragazze si divertono → Non si divertono.

Exercise 8

Given a verb in the imperative mood, place the pronoun correctly for an affirmative or negative command.

Parlare (tu, affirmative) + lo = Parlalo!
Non mangiare (tu, negative) + la = Non la mangiare!
Scrivere (noi, affirmative) + le = Scriviamole!
Non prendere (voi, negative) + li = Non li prendete!
Leggere (tu, affirmative) + lo = Leggilo!
Non vendere (tu, negative) + la = Non la vendere!
Aprire (noi, affirmative) + lo = Apriamolo!
Non chiudere (voi, negative) + le = Non le chiudete!

UNIT 9

Grammar:

- Frequency Adverbs
  Frequency adverbs describe how often something happens. They can be specific (giving an exact frequency) or vague (giving a general idea of frequency). In Italian, just as in English, they are placed directly before the main verb or at the beginning or end of the sentence for emphasis.

  List of Common Frequency Adverbs

Italian	Phonetic	English
Sempre	SEHM-preh	Always
Mai	MAI	Never
Spesso	SPEHS-so	Often
Di solito	dee SOH-lee-toh	Usually
A volte	ah VOHL-teh	Sometimes
Raramente	rah-rah-MEHN-teh	Rarely
Quasi mai	KWAH-see mai	Hardly ever

Position in a Sentence
The placement of frequency adverbs can slightly change the emphasis of the sentence but generally does not alter its meaning. Here are some examples to illustrate their placement:

Sempre - "Io sempre studio dopo cena." (I always study after dinner.)
Mai - "Lui non va mai al cinema." (He never goes to the cinema.)
Spesso - "Spesso vado in palestra." (I go to the gym often.)
Note: When using "mai" in a sentence, it usually requires the negation "non" to precede the verb, forming a negative statement.

Using Frequency Adverbs with "Essere" and "Avere"
When using frequency adverbs with the verbs "essere" (to be) and "avere" (to have), the adverb typically comes after the verb.

Essere - "Sono spesso felice." (I am often happy.)
Avere - "Hai mai avuto paura?" (Have you ever been scared?)

Expressing General Frequency
For less specific frequencies, Italian uses phrases that can be adapted with various adverbs to suit the context. Some examples include:

Ogni tanto (OHN-yee TAHN-toh) - Now and then

Una volta alla settimana (OO-nah VOHL-tah AH-lah seh-tih-MAH-nah) - Once a week
Due volte al mese (DOO-eh VOHL-teh ahl MEH-seh) - Twice a month
Comparing Frequency
Comparative and superlative forms of frequency adverbs are also useful. For example:

Più spesso (pyoo SPEHS-soh) - More often
Il più spesso possibile (eel pyoo SPEHS-soh poh-SEE-bee-leh) - As often as possible
Meno spesso (MEH-noh SPEHS-soh) - Less often

• Using "Qualche," "Molto," and Other Quantifiers
Quantifiers in Italian are essential for expressing amounts, whether it be the quantity of objects, the degree of an adjective, or the frequency of an action.

1. "Qualche" ([KWAL-keh]) - Some/Few
"Qualche" is a unique quantifier in Italian used to indicate a small, indefinite quantity, equivalent to "some" or "a few" in English. Despite referring to a plural quantity, "qualche" is always followed by a singular noun.

Examples:
Qualche libro ([KWAL-keh LEE-broh]) - Some books
Qualche giorno ([KWAL-keh jee-OR-noh]) - A few days
Note that "qualche" does not change form; it remains the same regardless of the gender and number of the noun it precedes.

2. "Molto" ([MOL-toh]) - Much/Many
"Molto" is a versatile quantifier used to express a large quantity or degree. It can mean "much" when used with uncountable nouns or "many" with countable nouns. Unlike "qualche", "molto" agrees in gender and number with the noun it modifies.

Singular:

Molto zucchero ([MOL-toh ZOOK-keh-roh]) - Much sugar
Molta pazienza ([MOL-tah pa-TSYEN-tsah]) - Much patience
Plural:

Molti libri ([MOL-tee LEE-bree]) - Many books
Molte persone ([MOL-teh per-SOH-neh]) - Many people
3. "Poco" ([POH-koh]) - Little/Few
"Poco" mirrors "molto" but indicates a small amount or degree. It also agrees in gender and number with the noun it accompanies.

Singular:

Poco tempo ([POH-koh TEM-poh]) - Little time

Poca acqua ([POH-kah AHK-kwah]) - Little water
Plural:

Pochi amici ([POH-kee ah-MEE-chee]) - Few friends
Poche idee ([POH-keh EE-deh]) - Few ideas
4. "Tanto" ([TAN-toh]) - So Much/So Many
"Tanto" is used similarly to "molto" but often with a nuance of intensity or comparison. It agrees in gender and number with the noun it modifies.

Singular:

Tanto amore ([TAN-toh ah-MOH-reh]) - So much love
Tanta energia ([TAN-tah eh-NER-jee-ah]) - So much energy
Plural:

Tanti problemi ([TAN-tee pro-BLEH-mee]) - So many problems
Tante soluzioni ([TAN-teh soh-loo-TSYOH-nee]) - So many solutions
5. "Troppo" ([TROP-poh]) - Too Much/Too Many
"Troppo" is used to express an excess quantity or degree and agrees in gender and number.

Singular:

Troppo rumore ([TROP-poh roo-MOH-reh]) - Too much noise
Troppa fretta ([TROP-pah FRET-tah]) - Too much hurry
Plural:

Troppi compiti ([TROP-pee KOM-pee-tee]) - Too many assignments
Troppe opzioni ([TROP-peh op-TSYOH-nee]) - Too many options
6. "Ogni" ([OHN-yee]) - Every
"Ogni" indicates each individual item of a group and is used with singular nouns. It does not agree in gender or number because it always remains the same.

Examples:
Ogni giorno ([OHN-yee jee-OR-noh]) - Every day
Ogni volta ([OHN-yee VOL-tah]) - Every time
7. "Alcuni/Alcune" ([al-KOO-nee/al-KOO-neh]) - Some/Several
"Alcuni" (masculine) and "alcune" (feminine) are used with plural nouns to indicate an indefinite but not minimal quantity, similar to "some" or "several" in English.

Masculine:
Alcuni studenti ([al-KOO-nee stoo-DEN-tee]) - Some (male or mixed) students
Feminine:
Alcune idee ([al-KOO-neh EE-deh]) - Some ideas

- **Common Phrasal Verbs**

Italian phrasal verbs can be challenging because the addition of a preposition to a verb can completely change its meaning. For example, "pensare" (to think) can become "pensare a" (to think about) or "pensare di" (to intend to), each with distinct uses and meanings.

Pronunciation Guide

When learning Italian phrasal verbs, pronunciation is key. Italian pronunciation is more consistent than English, so once you've mastered the basic sounds, you'll find it easier to pronounce new words correctly. Remember, stress is essential in Italian and can sometimes fall on the preposition, altering the meaning of the verb.

Common Italian Phrasal Verbs

Let's explore some of the most common Italian phrasal verbs. These verbs are not only frequently used in daily conversation but also enhance your ability to express complex ideas more naturally.

Italian Phrase	Phonetic	English	Example in Italian	Example in English
Andare via	ahn-DAH-reh VEE-ah	to leave, to go away	Devo andare via ora.	I have to leave now.
Fare fuori	FAH-reh FWOH-ree	to finish off, to kill	Hanno fatto fuori tutto il cibo.	They finished off all the food.
Tornare indietro	tor-NAH-reh in-DYEH-tro	to go back, to return	Dobbiamo tornare indietro, ho dimenticato le chiavi.	We need to go back; I forgot the keys.
Venire fuori	veh-NEE-reh FWOH-ree	to come out, to emerge	La verità verrà fuori.	The truth will come out.
Mettere su	meh-TEH-reh soo	to put on (weight), to start (an activity)	Ha messo su cinque chili quest'inverno.	He put on five kilos this winter.
Passare a	pah-SAH-reh ah	to stop by, to switch to	Passerò a prenderti alle 8. È ora di passare a energie rinnovabili.	I'll stop by to pick you up at 8. It's time to switch to renewable energies.
Pensare a	pen-SAH-reh ah	to think about	Pensa sempre a sua madre.	He always thinks about his mother.
Pensare di	pen-SAH-reh dee	to intend to, to think of doing something	Penso di andare in vacanza a giugno.	I intend to go on vacation in June.
Guardare a	gwahr-DAH-reh ah	to look at, to consider	Guarda a questo problema da un'altra prospettiva.	Look at this problem from another perspective.

Rimanere su	ree-MAH-neh soo	to stay on (a topic), to insist on	Rimaniamo su questo argomento per ora.	Let's stay on this topic for now.

- Italian Past Tense: Passato Prossimo vs. Imperfetto

  - Passato Prossimo (Past Perfect)
  Passato prossimo is a compound tense that expresses actions or events that have been completed in the past and have definitive beginnings and ends. It is formed with the auxiliary verbs "avere" (to have) or "essere" (to be) plus the past participle of the main verb.

  Formation:

  Avere (ah-VEH-reh) + Past Participle (for most verbs)
  Essere (EH-sser-reh) + Past Participle (for verbs of movement and reflexive verbs)

  The choice between "avere" and "essere" as the auxiliary verb depends on the main verb's transitivity and other factors, including movement and reflexive verbs typically using "essere."

  Usage:
  To describe actions that occurred at a specific point in the past: "Ieri ho mangiato la pizza" ([YEH-ree oh MAHN-jah-toh lah PEE-tzah]) - Yesterday, I ate pizza.

  For actions that are completed and have no direct relation to the present: "L'anno scorso sono andato in Italia" ([LAHN-noh SKOR-soh SOH-noh ahn-DAH-toh een ee-TAH-lyah]) - Last year, I went to Italy.

  - Imperfetto (Imperfect)
  Imperfetto is a simple tense that describes past actions or states of being that were ongoing, habitual, or not completed at a specific moment in the past. It conveys a sense of continuity or habitual action in the past.

  Formation:
  The imperfetto is formed by adding specific endings to the stem of the verb, which vary according to the conjugation (-ARE, -ERE, -IRE).

  Usage:
  To describe ongoing, habitual actions in the past: "Da bambino, giocavo sempre fuori" ([Dah BAM-bee-noh, joh-CAH-voh SEM-preh FWOH-ree]) - As a child, I always played outside.

For setting the scene or describing the background in narratives: "Era una notte buia e tempestosa" ([EH-rah OO-nah NOH-tteh BWOY-ah eh tem-peh-STOH-sah]) - It was a dark and stormy night.

To express age, weather, time, and feelings in the past: "Avevo freddo" ([ah-VEH-voh FREHD-doh]) - I was cold.

Key Differences and When to Use
Completion vs. Continuation: Passato prossimo is used for actions that have a clear beginning and end, while imperfetto is for ongoing actions or states without a specific endpoint.

Specific Time vs. Habitual Action: Use passato prossimo for actions at a specific time, and imperfetto for habitual or repeated actions.

Narrative Background vs. Main Events: Imperfetto sets the scene or describes conditions (time, weather, age, feelings), whereas passato prossimo narrates specific events or actions that move the narrative forward.

Examples
Passato Prossimo: "Ieri ho visto un film interessante" ([YEH-ree oh VEES-toh oon feelm een-teh-RES-sahn-teh]) - Yesterday, I saw an interesting movie.

Imperfetto: "Quando ero piccolo, leggevo molto" ([KWAHN-doh EH-roh PEEK-koh-loh, LEHJ-jeh-voh MOHL-toh]) - When I was little, I used to read a lot.

Practice Tips
Listen and Read: Pay attention to the context in which verbs in the past tense are used in Italian songs, movies, and literature.

Contextual Practice: Try to describe your daily routine in the past using both tenses to get a feel for their different uses.

Writing Exercises: Write short paragraphs about specific events using passato prossimo and about habitual actions or scenes using imperfetto.

Training:

Exercise 1

Fill in the blanks with the correct frequency adverb from the list: sempre, mai, spesso, di solito, a volte, raramente, quasi mai.

Io ___ mangio la pizza il sabato.
Loro ___ vanno in vacanza una volta all'anno.
Lei ___ legge prima di dormire.
Tu ___ fai colazione al bar?
Noi ___ guardiamo film italiani per imparare la lingua.
Voi ___ lavorate fino a tardi?
Marco ___ si dimentica le chiavi di casa.
Gli studenti ___ arrivano in ritardo alla prima lezione.

Exercise 2

Match each Italian quantifier with its English equivalent.

Molto - ___
Qualche - ___
Poco - ___
Tanto - ___
Troppo - ___
Ogni - ___
Alcuni - ___
Pochi - ___

Exercise 3

Identify and correct the mistake in each sentence. Each sentence contains an error with the use of a quantifier or a frequency adverb.

Abbiamo mangiato troppo dolci ieri sera.
Ogni giorno, prendo qualche tazza di caffè.
Lei ha molti pazienza con i suoi studenti.
Questo mese, vado al cinema pochi volte.
Lui ha letto troppi libro durante le vacanze.
Noi facciamo spesso errore quando parliamo italiano.
Lei compra qualche scarpe ogni mese.
Loro hanno visto molti film la settimana scorsa.

Exercise 4

Choose the correct form of "molto", "poco", "tanto", or "troppo" to complete each sentence based on context.

Questa città ha ___ parchi. (molti/pochi)
In estate, bevo ___ acqua. (molta/poca)

Abbiamo ___ tempo per visitare il museo. (molto/poco)
Ci sono ___ negozi aperti la domenica. (molti/pochi)
Ho ___ lavoro da fare oggi. (molto/poco)
Quest'anno ho viaggiato ___ volte. (molte/poche)
In inverno, vedo ___ il sole. (molto/poco)
Lei ha ___ amici in città. (molti/pochi)

Exercise 5

Select the correct preposition to complete each phrasal verb.

Non riesco a smettere di pensare ___ quella conversazione. (a/di)
Oggi devo passare ___ prendere i libri in biblioteca. (a/da)
Abbiamo deciso di andare ___ senza di lui. (via/su)
Loro vogliono mettere ___ una nuova attività. (su/giu)
Dovremmo fare ___ questi vecchi mobili. (fuori/su)
È importante guardare ___ i dettagli. (a/da)
Penso ___ invitare molti amici alla festa. (a/di)
Voglio venire ___ con una soluzione entro stasera. (fuori/su)

Exercise 6

Choose the correct tense for each verb in parentheses. Decide between passato prossimo and imperfetto.

Quando ero piccolo, (andare) ___ spesso al mare.
L'anno scorso, (visitare) ___ Parigi in primavera.
Da giovane, (suonare) ___ la chitarra ogni giorno.
(Avere) ___ una bella esperienza al concerto.
Mio nonno (raccontare) ___ storie incredibili.
(Essere) ___ molto felice di vederti ieri.
(Fare) ___ un viaggio meraviglioso l'estate scorsa.
(Giocare) ___ a calcio con gli amici ogni weekend.

Exercise 7

Fill in the blanks with the correct phrasal verb from the list: andare via, fare fuori, tornare indietro, venire fuori.

Ogni mattina, ___ un po' di esercizio fisico.
Ieri, ___ finito di leggere quel libro.
La scorsa notte, ___ molto tardi a causa del lavoro.
La settimana scorsa, ___ al cinema da sola.

Durante la festa, ___ troppo cibo.
Quest'estate, ___ in montagna per una settimana.
L'anno scorso, ___ a nuotare ogni giorno.
A Natale, ___ regali a tutti i miei amici.

Exercise 8

Select the correct form of the quantifier to agree with the noun in each sentence.

Desidero ___ (molto/molta) cioccolata.
Ci sono ___ (pochi/poche) biscotti nella scatola.
Ho comprato ___ (qualche/alcuni) regali per la festa.
___ (Ogni/Ogni) settimana vado al mercato.
Abbiamo ___ (troppo/troppa) lavoro da fare.
Ci sono ___ (molti/molte) studenti in classe oggi.
Lei ha ___ (poco/poca) interesse per il cinema.
Durante l'estate, mangio ___ (tanti/tante) gelati.

UNIT 10

Grammar:

- Simple Comparatives and Superlatives
The structure to form comparatives is quite simple and similar to English, but with some nuances.

Equality - To express equality in Italian, we use the structure "tanto... quanto" (as... as) or "così... come" (as... as).

Esempio (Example): Maria è tanto intelligente quanto Luca (Maria is as intelligent as Luca) - [MAH-ree-ah EH TAHN-toh een-tehl-LEE-jehn-teh KWAHN-toh LOO-kah].

Inferiority - To express inferiority, Italian uses "meno... di" (less... than) or "meno... che" (less... than), depending on the following word.

Esempio: Questo libro è meno interessante di quello (This book is less interesting than that one) - [KWEH-stoh LEE-broh eh MEH-noh een-teh-ress-AHN-teh dee KWEHL-loh].

Superiority - Superiority is expressed with "più... di" (more... than) or "più... che" (more... than). The choice between "di" and "che" follows the same rule as for inferiority.

Esempio: La pizza è più buona di pasta (Pizza is more delicious than pasta) - [lah PEE-tsah EH pyoo BWOH-nah dee PAH-stah].

Superlative Forms
Superlatives in Italian express the highest degree of a quality within a group or of all possible groups. They are formed by placing "il/la/i/le più" (the most) or "il/la/i/le meno" (the least) before the adjective. The definite article agrees in gender and number with the noun it modifies.

Absolute Superlative - Unlike English, Italian can also express a very high degree of a quality without comparing it to other elements, using the suffixes "-issimo/a/i/e" attached to the adjective.

Esempio: Fortissimo (Very strong) - [for-TEE-see-moh].

Relative Superlative - This form compares a quality of one element against all others in the same category.

Esempio: Marco è il ragazzo più alto della classe (Marco is the tallest boy in the class) - [MAR-koh EH eel rah-GAH-tzoh pyoo AHL-toh DEL-lah KLAH-sse].

Important Notes
Pronunciation Guide: Remember that in Italian, every letter in a word is usually pronounced, and stress can fall on different syllables, which is crucial for proper pronunciation.

Irregular Forms: Some adjectives have irregular comparative and superlative forms, like "buono" (good), which becomes "migliore" (better) for comparatives and "il migliore" (the best) for superlatives. Another example is "cattivo" (bad), which becomes "peggiore" (worse) and "il peggiore" (the worst).

Esempio: Questo è il migliore libro di sempre (This is the best book ever) - [KWEH-stoh EH eel meel-YOH-reh LEE-broh dee SEM-preh].

Agreement: Always ensure that the adjective agrees in gender (masculine/feminine) and number (singular/plural) with the noun it modifies.

- Formation and Use of the Gerund
The gerund in Italian, known as "il gerundio," is a verb form that ends in -ando for -are verbs and -endo for -ere and -ire verbs. It corresponds to the English "-ing" form used in gerunds (e.g., "speaking") and present participles (e.g., "I am speaking"). This versatile form is used to express actions that are happening simultaneously or actions that are dependent on another action.

Formation of the Gerund
To form the gerund in Italian, you need to follow these simple rules based on the verb's conjugation:

-ARE Verbs: Drop the -are ending and add -ando. For example, Parlare (to speak) becomes Parlando ([par-LAHN-doh]).

-ERE and -IRE Verbs: Drop the -ere or -ire ending and add -endo. For example, Leggere (to read) becomes Leggendo ([leh-JEN-doh]), and Partire (to leave) becomes Partendo ([par-TEN-doh]).

Use of the Gerund
The Italian gerund can be used in several contexts:

To Indicate an Action Happening Simultaneously with Another: It's commonly used with the verb "stare" to form a continuous tense, similar to the English present continuous.

Stare + Gerund: "Sto mangiando" ([STOH man-JAN-doh]) - "I am eating."

As a Verbal Adverb to Describe How an Action is Performed: When used this way, the gerund modifies the verb, providing additional information about the action.

"Leggendo velocemente, ha finito il libro in una sera." ([LEHJ-jen-doh veh-loh-CHAY-men-teh, ah FEEN-ee-toh eel LEE-broh in OO-nah SEH-rah]) - "Reading quickly, he finished the book in one evening."

To Express a Cause or Reason: The gerund can indicate the reason behind an action.

"Cadendo, si è fatto male." ([kah-DEN-doh, see eh FAH-toh MAH-leh]) - "Falling, he hurt himself."

With Prepositions: When preceded by a preposition, the gerund can express various nuances, such as time, manner, or condition.

"Prima di uscire, controlla le finestre." ([PREE-mah dee oo-SHEE-reh, kon-TROH-lah leh feen-ES-treh]) - "Before going out, check the windows."

Key Points to Remember
The gerund in Italian does not change according to gender or number. It remains the same regardless of the subject.

When used with "stare" to form the continuous tense, it conveys an action that is currently happening or was happening at a specific time in the past or future.

Unlike English, the Italian gerund cannot stand alone as a noun.

- **Partitive Article**
  In Italian language, the partitive article is used to express an undefined quantity of something, equivalent to the English words "some" or "any."

Formation of the Partitive Article
The partitive article in Italian is formed by combining the preposition "di" ([dee]) with the definite article (il, lo, l', la, i, gli, le), which corresponds to the noun's gender and number. The choice of the definite article is determined by the same rules that apply to its usage with nouns.

Here are the forms the partitive article can take:

Number	Gender	Article	When to Use It	English Translation	Pronunciation
Singular	Masculine	del	il nouns	of the	del
Singular	Masculine	dello	lo nouns	of the	DEHL-lo
Singular	Masculine	dell'	before a vowel	of the	del
Singular	Feminine	della	la nouns	of the	DEHL-lah
Singular	Feminine	dell'	before a vowel	of the	del
Plural	Masculine	dei	i nouns	of the	day
Plural	Masculine	degli	gli nouns	of the	DEH-lyee
Plural	Feminine	delle	le nouns	of the	DEHL-leh

Usage of the Partitive Article

The partitive article is used in various contexts to indicate an unspecified quantity of something. Some common situations include:

Talking about food and drink: When ordering or talking about food and beverages without specifying the exact amount.

Vorrei del pane. ([vo-REE dehl PAH-neh]) - I would like some bread.

Prendiamo della birra? ([pren-DAH-moh DEHL-lah BEER-rah]) - Shall we have some beer?

Discussing quantities: When the quantity of an item is not specified or is indefinite.

Hai degli amici? ([eye DEH-lyee ah-MEE-chee]) - Do you have any friends?

Ci sono delle mele in frigo. ([chee SOH-noh DEHL-leh MEH-leh in FREE-goh]) - There are some apples in the fridge.

Expressing the existence of something in a general sense:

C'è dell'acqua? ([cheh DEHL-lah-KWAH]) - Is there any water?

When Not to Use the Partitive Article

It's important to note that the partitive article is not used with adjectives that imply an indefinite quantity by themselves, such as "molto" ([MOHL-toh]) for "much" or "many," or "poco" ([POH-koh]) for "little" or "few." In these cases, the adjective already conveys the sense of an unspecified quantity.

- Using "Ci" and "Ne"
  These two pronouns are used frequently in everyday conversation, and their functions are varied and essential to grasp.

"Ci" - [CHEE]

"Ci" has multiple uses in Italian, making it a versatile pronoun in the language. It can represent a place, a concept, or be part of idiomatic expressions.

As a replacement for a place or location: "Ci" can substitute phrases introduced by "a," "in," "su," etc., meaning "there" or "here."

"Vai al mare questo weekend?" - "Are you going to the sea this weekend?"

"Sì, ci vado." - "Yes, I am going there." - [SEE VAH-doh]

In reflexive and reciprocal verbs: It often means "ourselves," "each other," and is used to indicate an action that refers back to the subject.

"Ci vediamo domani!" - "We'll see each other tomorrow!" - [CHEE veh-DYAH-moh DOH-mah-nee]

With expressions of feeling or being: It replaces phrases like "about it" or "on it."

"Pensi spesso a Roma?" - "Do you often think about Rome?"

"Sì, ci penso spesso." - "Yes, I think about it often." - [SEE PEN-soh SPEHS-soh]

To mean "us": When used with verbs like "incontrare" (to meet), "ci" can mean "us."

"Incontrerai ci al cinema?" - "Will you meet us at the cinema?" - [een-kohn-trah-RAI CHEE ahl CHEE-neh-mah]

Pronunciation Tips for "Ci"

The "c" in "ci" is pronounced as [CH], similar to the "ch" sound in "cheese."

Emphasize the short, sharp sound, keeping it light and quick.

"Ne" - [NEH]

"Ne" is used to indicate a part of something, quantity, or to replace phrases introduced by "di," "da," "in," "su," etc. It often translates to "of it," "about it," "from there," or "some" in English.

To indicate a part or quantity: When talking about a quantity of something, "ne" is used to avoid repetition.

"Vuoi delle mele?" - "Do you want some apples?"

"Sì, ne voglio due." - "Yes, I want two of them." - [NEH VOH-lyoh DOO-eh]

To replace phrases introduced by "di": It can replace phrases that would require the use of "of" in English, often when talking about possession or origin.

"Quanti libri hai letto di questo autore?" - "How many books have you read by this author?"

"Ne ho letti cinque." - "I have read five of them." - [NEH oh LEHT-tee CHEEN-kweh]

With verbs that require "di": When verbs are followed by an infinitive that requires "di," "ne" can be used to refer back to something previously mentioned.

"Parliamo della festa? Sì, ne parliamo." - "Shall we talk about the party? Yes, let's talk about it." - [NEH pahr-LYAH-moh]

Pronunciation Tips for "Ne"

The "ne" sound is like the "ne" in "net" but with a more emphasized "eh" sound.

Ensure the "n" is clear and the "e" is pronounced as a short, sharp "eh."

Understanding "Ci" and "Ne" Through Examples

Mastering "ci" and "ne" involves practice and exposure. Their usage can be nuanced, but understanding their core functions will significantly enhance your ability to express complex ideas in Italian. Here are a few more examples to illustrate their use:

Ci: "Non ci credo!" - "I don't believe it!" - [non CHEE KREH-doh]

Ne: "Quante penne hai? Ne ho solo una." - "How many pens do you have? I have only one of them." - [KWAHN-teh PEH-neh eye? NEH oh SOH-loh OO-nah]

Training:

Exercise 1

Complete the sentences using the correct form of "più... di," "meno... di," "tanto... quanto," or "così... come."

Il caffè è _____ amaro _____ il tè.
Questo film è _____ interessante _____ quello che abbiamo visto ieri.
Luca corre _____ veloce _____ Matteo.
Il gatto è _____ intelligente _____ il cane.
La bicicletta è _____ costosa _____ la moto.
Questo libro è _____ noioso _____ quello.
Lei è _____ bella _____ sua cugina.
L'appartamento è _____ grande _____ la casa.

Exercise 2

Select the correct superlative form to complete each sentence.

È la torta _____ buona che abbia mai mangiato. (più/meno)
Questo. è il museo _____ visitato della città. (più/meno)
Sono le scarpe _____ comode che ho. (più/meno)

È l'insegnante _____ apprezzato dagli studenti. (più/meno)
Questa è la strada _____ corta per arrivare al parco. (più/meno)
Sono i fiori _____ belli del giardino. (più/meno)
È il lavoro _____ stressante che abbia mai avuto. (più/meno)
Questo è il periodo _____ caldo dell'anno. (più/meno)

Exercise 3

Connect each infinitive verb with its correct gerund form.

Mangiare - A. Partendo
Scrivere - B. Leggendo
Leggere - C. Scrivendo
Partire - D. Mangiando
Dormire - E. Dormendo
Sentire - F. Sentendo
Capire - G. Capendo
Finire - H. Finendo

Exercise 4

Identify and correct the mistake in each sentence.

Questi libri sono meno interessanti di quelli.
La macchina è più veloce di bicicletta.
Sto leggendo il giornale con leggendo attentamente.
Lei ha meno amici di me.
Questo è il più piccolo di quella stanza.
Ci penso spesso a quella vacanza.
Vorrei del uva dal mercato.
Sto ascoltando alla musica mentre lavoro.

Exercise 5

Fill in each blank with either "ci" or "ne."

Quante persone _____ vengono stasera?
_____ sono stato l'anno scorso e mi è piaciuto molto.
Quanti dolci hai fatto? _____ ho preparati quattro.
Non _____ credo, sembra impossibile.
_____ hai parlato con tuo fratello?
Quante mele vuoi? _____ vorrei un paio.
_____ vado ogni domenica per rilassarmi.

Vorresti della cioccolata? Sì, _____ prendo un pezzetto.

Exercise 6

Choose the correct partitive article to complete each sentence.

Posso avere _____ (del/della) latte?
Ho comprato _____ (degli/delle) occhiali nuovi.
Vorrei _____ (dei/delle) pomodori per l'insalata.
Hai bisogno di _____ (del/della) aiuto?
Ci sono _____ (dei/delle) libri sul tavolo che potrebbero interessarti.
Vorrei _____ (degli/delle) informazioni sul corso.
Serve ancora _____ (del/della) farina per la torta?
Posso offrirti _____ (dei/delle) biscotti?

Exercise 7

Select how the gerund is used in each sentence.

"Correndo, ho visto un vecchio amico."
A. Action happening simultaneously
B. As a verbal adverb
C. To express a cause or reason
"Studiando ogni giorno, ha superato l'esame."

A. Action happening simultaneously
B. As a verbal adverb
C. To express a cause or reason
"Cantando sotto la doccia, si sente felice."

A. Action happening simultaneously
B. As a verbal adverb
C. To express a cause or reason
"Risparmiando, potremo comprare una nuova auto."

A. Action happening simultaneously
B. As a verbal adverb
C. To express a cause or reason
"Viaggiando, ho imparato molte lingue."

A. Action happening simultaneously
B. As a verbal adverb
C. To express a cause or reason

"Piangendo, ha espresso il suo dolore."

A. Action happening simultaneously
B. As a verbal adverb
C. To express a cause or reason
"Ascoltando musica, fa i compiti più velocemente."

A. Action happening simultaneously
B. As a verbal adverb
C. To express a cause or reason
"Parlando troppo velocemente, a volte non si viene capiti."

A. Action happening simultaneously
B. As a verbal adverb
C. To express a cause or reason

Exercise 8

Match the sentence beginnings with their correct endings based on the usage of comparatives, superlatives, gerund, partitive article, "ci," and "ne."

Vorrei delle fragole, _____
A. e ne ho visto uno bellissimo.
Questo parco è più bello di quello, _____
B. quindi ci andiamo domani.

Sto imparando a suonare la chitarra, _____
C. e ci esercito ogni giorno.

Ci sono molte stelle stasera, _____
D. e ne vorrei un chilo.

Marco è il più alto della classe, _____
E. perché ci piace di più.

Ho letto molti libri quest'anno, _____
F. quindi ne ho bisogno di nuovi.

Questo è il periodo meno freddo dell'anno, _____
G. quindi ci vestiamo più leggeri.

Vorrei del pane, _____
H. e ne compro sempre qui.

UNIT 11

Grammar:

- Basic Expressions of Time
Before:
To express "before" in Italian, you can use the word "prima di." This is often followed by an infinitive verb or a noun.

Examples:
I eat breakfast before going to work. (Io) mangio la colazione prima di andare al lavoro.
He arrived before the meeting. (Lui) è arrivato prima della riunione.
After:
To convey "after" in Italian, the term "dopo" is commonly used. Similar to "prima di," it can be followed by an infinitive verb or a noun.

Examples:
We'll have dinner after watching the movie. (Noi) ceniamo dopo aver visto il film.

She always calls her parents after finishing work. (Lei) chiama sempre i suoi genitori dopo aver finito il lavoro.

During:
In Italian, "during" can be translated as "durante." This word is employed similarly to its English counterpart, usually followed by a noun.

Examples:
I read a book during my break. (Io) leggo un libro durante la pausa.

They talked during the entire journey. (Loro) hanno parlato durante tutto il viaggio.

Temporal Prepositions:
Italian uses prepositions to denote temporal relationships. Some common ones include "da," "per," and "tra/fra."

"Da" is used to indicate starting points in time, similar to "since" or "from."

Example: I've been studying Italian since last year. (Io) studio l'italiano da l'anno scorso.

"Per" signifies duration, akin to "for."

Example: He slept for two hours. (Lui) ha dormito per due ore.

"Tra" or "fra" denotes a time frame or a period in between two points.

Example: We'll meet in two weeks. Ci incontreremo tra/fra due settimane.

Note: When using temporal expressions in Italian, it's essential to pay attention to gender and number agreement when necessary.

Prima di (Before) - [PREE-mah dee]
Dopo (After) - [DOH-poh]
Durante (During) - [doo-RAHN-teh]
Da (Since/From) - [dah]
Per (For) - [pehr]
Tra/Fra (Between) - [trah/frah]

- Needs and Wants
  Expressing Needs

In Italian, expressing needs often involves the verb "avere bisogno di" ([AH-veh-re bee-ZOH-nyoh dee]) which translates to "to need" in English. This structure is useful for expressing a need for both tangible objects and abstract concepts.

Structure: Subject + avere bisogno di + [noun/infinitive verb]

Io ho bisogno di acqua. ([EE-oh oh bee-ZOH-nyoh dee] AH-kwah) - I need water.

Tu hai bisogno di riposare. ([TOO ah-ee bee-ZOH-nyoh dee] ree-poh-SAH-reh) - You need to rest.

Expressing Wants
To express wants, the verb "volere" ([voh-LEH-reh]) is used, which means "to want."

Structure: Subject + volere + [noun/infinitive verb]

Io voglio un caffè. ([EE-oh VOHL-yoh] oon kahf-FEH) - I want a coffee.

Noi vogliamo viaggiare. ([NOY VOHL-yah-moh] vyahd-JAH-reh) - We want to travel.

Polite Requests
For more polite requests or to soften the tone, you can use "vorrei" ([voh-RAY-ee]), which is the conditional form of "volere" and translates to "I would like."

Vorrei un bicchiere d'acqua. ([voh-RAY-ee] oon bee-KYEH-reh dahk-WAH) - I would like a glass of water.

Expressing Necessity
The verb "dovere" ([DOH-veh-reh]) is used to express necessity or must, which can also indicate a strong need or obligation.

Structure: Subject + dovere + infinitive verb

Devo studiare stasera. ([DEH-voh stoo-DYAH-reh] stah-SEH-rah) - I must study tonight.

Using "Bisogna"

"Bisogna" ([bee-ZOH-nyah]) is an impersonal form used to express a general need or necessity, similar to "one must" or "it is necessary."

Bisogna mangiare sano. ([bee-ZOH-nyah] mahn-JAH-reh SAH-noh) - One must eat healthily.

Practice Sentences

Ho bisogno di imparare l'italiano per il mio viaggio. ([OH bee-ZOH-nyoh dee] eem-pah-RAH-reh lee-tah-LYAH-noh pehr eel MEE-oh VYAH-joh) - I need to learn Italian for my trip.

Vorrei visitare il Colosseo. ([voh-RAY-ee vee-zee-TAH-reh eel Kohl-LOH-seh-oh) - I would like to visit the Colosseum.

Dobbiamo trovare un hotel. ([dohb-BYAH-moh] troh-TAH-reh oon oh-TEL) - We need to find a hotel.

- Ability, Possibility, Permission

  "Potere," "volere," and "dovere" are essential for communicating what you can, want, or must do, and they play a crucial role in everyday conversations.

The Modal Verbs "Potere," "Volere," and "Dovere"

Potere (to be able to/can)
Pronunciation: [poh-TEH-reh]
Potere is used to express ability or possibility. It's equivalent to "can" or "may" in English.
Conjugation in the Present Tense:

Italian	Phonetic	English
Io posso	EE-oh POH-sso	I can
Tu puoi	TOO pwoy	You can (informal)
Lui/Lei può	loo-EE/lay PWÒ	He/She can
Noi possiamo	NOY pohs-SYAH-moh	We can
Voi potete	VOY poh-TEH-teh	You all can
Loro possono	LOH-roh poh-SOH-noh	They can

Examples:
Posso parlare italiano. [POH-sso par-LAH-reh ee-tah-LYAH-noh] - I can speak Italian.

Puoi venire domani? [PWOY veh-NEE-reh doh-MAH-nee?] - Can you come tomorrow?

Volere (to want)
Pronunciation: [voh-LEH-reh]
Volere is used to express a desire or wish.
Conjugation in the Present Tense:

Italian	Phonetic	English
Io voglio	EE-oh VOHL-yoh	I want
Tu vuoi	TOO vwoy	You want (informal)
Lui/Lei vuole	loo-EE/lay VWOH-leh	He/She wants
Noi vogliamo	NOY VOHL-yah-moh	We want
Voi volete	VOY voh-LEH-teh	You all want
Loro vogliono	LOH-roh VOHL-yoh-noh	They want

Examples:
Voglio imparare l'italiano. [VOHL-yoh eem-pah-RAH-reh lee-tah-LYAH-noh] - I want to learn Italian.

Vuoi mangiare qualcosa? [VWOY man-JAH-reh kwahl-KOH-sah?] - Do you want to eat something?

Dovere (to have to/must)
Pronunciation: [doh-VEH-reh]
Dovere expresses necessity or obligation.
Conjugation in the Present Tense:

Italian	Phonetic	English
Io devo	EE-oh DEH-voh	I must
Tu devi	TOO DEH-vee	You must (informal)
Lui/Lei deve	loo-EE/lay DEH-veh	He/She must
Noi dobbiamo	NOY dohb-BYAH-moh	We must
Voi dovete	VOY doh-VEH-teh	You all must
Loro devono	LOH-roh DEH-voh-noh	They must

Examples:
Devo studiare italiano ogni giorno. [DEH-voh stoo-DYAH-reh ee-tah-LYAH-noh OH-nyee johr-noh] - I must study Italian every day.

Devi finire i compiti. [DEH-vee fee-NEE-reh ee kom-PEE-tee] - You must finish the homework.

Expressing Permission
To ask for permission in Italian, "potere" is commonly used in the form of a question.

Examples:
Posso usare il bagno? [POH-sso oo-ZAH-reh eel BAH-nyoh?] - May I use the bathroom?

Posso entrare? [POH-sso en-TRAH-reh?] - Can I come in?

Expressing Ability
Besides "potere," expressing ability in Italian can also be done using "sapere" [sah-PEH-reh] in the context of knowing how to do something.

Conjugation in the Present Tense:

Italian	Phonetic	English
Io so	EE-oh soh	I know
Tu sai	TOO say	You know (informal)
Lui/Lei sa	loo-EE/lay sah	He/She knows
Noi sappiamo	NOY sap-PYAH-moh	We know
Voi sapete	VOY sah-PEH-teh	You all know
Loro sanno	LOH-roh SAH-noh	They know

Example:
So nuotare. [SOH nwOH-tah-reh] - I know how to swim.

Expressing Possibility
Possibility can be expressed using "potere" to indicate that something might happen or be true.

Example:
Può piovere domani. [PWÒ pee-OH-veh-reh doh-MAH-nee] - It might rain tomorrow.

Training:

Exercise 1

Fill in the blanks with "prima di," "dopo," or "durante."

_____ mangiare, mi lavo le mani.
Leggiamo un libro _____ la pausa.
_____ aver finito i compiti, guardo la TV.
_____ partire, facciamo i bagagli.
Vado a correre _____ cena.

_____ la lezione, prendo appunti.
Si rilassa _____ lavorare.
_____ andare a dormire, leggo sempre.

Exercise 2

Match the sentences with their English translation.

Italian:

Ho bisogno di bere acqua.
Vuoi venire al cinema con me?
Dobbiamo svegliarci presto domani.
Posso usare il tuo telefono?
Devo finire questo lavoro entro oggi.
Vorrei un po' di gelato.
Può piovere più tardi.
Studiamo italiano da tre mesi.

English:

A. I need to drink water.
B. Do you want to come to the cinema with me?
C. We need to wake up early tomorrow.
D. May I use your phone?
E. I need to finish this work by today.
F. I would like some ice cream.
G. It might rain later.
H. We have been studying Italian for three months.

Exercise 3

Choose the correct word: "da," "per," or "tra/fra."
Studierò in Italia _____ un anno.
Ci vediamo _____ due ore.
Vivo qui _____ 2015.
Leggo _____ l'intera serata.
Andremo in vacanza _____ una settimana.
Lavoro qui _____ dicembre.
Cammineremo _____ tre chilometri.
Parlo con te _____ mezz'ora.

Exercise 4

Correct the mistake in each sentence.

Ho bisogno di riposare dopo di lavoro.
Voglio un caffè durante il mattina.
Devo studiare italiano per due anni.
Posso venire da te tra cinque minuti.
Vorrei andare al parco per il pomeriggio.
Dobbiamo finire il progetto da lunedì.
Può essere freddo durante dicembre.
Sono in Italia da tre giorni.

Exercise 5

Translate the following sentences into Italian.

I have been learning Italian since January.
We will meet in three days.
She needs to rest for an hour.
Can I enter?
I must study tonight.
They want to travel next year.
It is necessary to eat healthy.
I know how to cook.

Exercise 6

Fill in the blanks with the correct form of "potere," "volere," or "dovere."

Io _____ (volere) mangiare qualcosa.
Tu _____ (potere) aiutarmi?
Lui _____ (dovere) finire il lavoro entro domani.
Noi _____ (volere) vedere quel film.
Voi _____ (potere) venire alla festa?
Loro _____ (dovere) svegliarsi presto.
_____ (Potere) io avere un po' d'acqua?
Tu _____ (volere) imparare l'italiano?

Exercise 7

Connect the expressions with their correct usage.

Expressions: 1. avere bisogno di, 2. volere, 3. dovere, 4. potere, 5. sapere
Usage: A. obligation, B. desire, C. permission or ability, D. need, E. ability or knowledge

Exercise 8

Find and highlight the modal verb in each sentence.

Devo andare al supermercato oggi.
Vuoi venire a pranzo con noi?
Posso chiederti un favore?
Lei sa parlare tre lingue.
Vogliamo partire alle nove.
Devi completare questi documenti.
Possono giocare fuori dopo i compiti.
Sapete dove si trova la stazione?

UNIT 12

Grammar:

- Direct and Indirect Speech
  In Italian, as in English, we often find ourselves reporting the words spoken by others. This can be done in two ways: using direct speech or indirect speech.

  Direct Speech (Discorso Diretto)
  Direct speech is when we quote the exact words spoken by someone else. In Italian, like in English, direct speech is enclosed in quotation marks. However, Italian punctuation and capitalization rules can differ slightly.

  How to Formulate Direct Speech in Italian
  When quoting directly, you'll use the following structure:

  Quotation Marks: Italian uses angular quotation marks (« »), also known as chevrons or guillemets, but you may also see the double quotes (" ") used in informal contexts or digital communication.

  Capitalization: The first letter of the quoted sentence is capitalized.

  Punctuation: The punctuation mark (comma, period, question mark, etc.) is placed inside the quotation marks.

  Example:
  Marco said, "I am tired." becomes Marco ha detto, «Sono stanco.» ([MAR-koh ah DEHT-toh, "SOH-noh STAHN-koh"]).

  Indirect Speech (Discorso Indiretto)
  Indirect speech involves paraphrasing what someone else said without quoting their exact words. This requires adjustments to the sentence structure, verb tense, and pronouns to fit the context of the report.

  Converting Direct to Indirect Speech
  To convert direct speech into indirect speech, follow these steps:

  Introduction Phrase: Use a verb like "dire" (to say) or "raccontare" (to tell) in the past tense, depending on the context.

  Change in Pronouns: Adjust pronouns from the first or second person to the third person.

  Tense Shift: Often, the verb tense will shift back (e.g., present to imperfect).

  No Quotation Marks: Indirect speech does not use quotation marks.

Example:
Direct: Marco said, "I am tired." becomes Indirect: Marco said that he was tired. In Italian: Marco ha detto che era stanco ([MAR-koh ah DEHT-toh keh EH-rah STAHN-koh]).

Important Note on Tense Shift
The tense shift in indirect speech follows a pattern known as the "sequence of tenses." Here's a simplified guide:

Present to Imperfect: "I am tired" becomes "he was tired" (sono stanco → era stanco).

Simple Past to Pluperfect: "I went" becomes "he had gone" (sono andato → era andato).

Future to Conditional: "I will go" becomes "he would go" (andrò → andrebbe).

Reporting Questions
When reporting questions in indirect speech, the structure changes slightly:

Direct: He asked, "Where are you going?" becomes Indirect: He asked where you were going. In Italian: Ha chiesto dove stavi andando ([ah kyehs-toh DOH-veh STAH-vee ahn-DAHN-doh]).

Imperatives in Indirect Speech
Commands or requests in direct speech become infinitive phrases in indirect speech:

Direct: "Please, close the door," he said. becomes Indirect: He asked to close the door. In Italian: Ha chiesto di chiudere la porta ([ah kyehs-toh dee kyoo-DEH-reh lah POR-tah]).

○ Pronominal Verbs

They are a unique feature of the Italian language. They are formed by combining a verb with one or more pronouns. These verbs can often be identified by the pronoun particles attached to them, such as -si, -ne, -ci, and -vi.

The Basics of Pronominal Verbs
A pronominal verb combines a basic verb with one or more pronouns, which modify the meaning of the original verb. These pronouns are usually attached to the end of the infinitive form of the verb, creating a single word. Pronominal verbs can be reflexive, but they also include other types that do not fit the definition of reflexive verbs.

Examples include:

Andarsene (to go away) - [ahn-dahr-SEH-neh]
Fregarsene (to not care) - [fre-GAHR-seh-neh]
Metterci (to take time) - [meh-TEHR-chee]

Volerci (to be necessary) - [voh-LEHR-chee]
Types of Pronominal Verbs

Reflexive Pronominal Verbs:
These verbs indicate that an action is performed by the subject upon itself. For example, "lavarsi" (to wash oneself) - [lah-VAHR-see].

Reciprocal Pronominal Verbs:
They express an action performed mutually between two or more subjects, such as "abbracciarsi" (to hug each other) - [ab-brah-CHAHR-see].

Idiomatic Pronominal Verbs:
These combine with pronouns to create expressions with meanings that cannot be deduced from the individual parts, like "andarsene" (to leave, to go away).

Verbs with "Ci" and "Ne":

"Ci" can mean "about it" or "there," adding a nuance of location or topic to the verb.

"Ne" often means "of it" or "from it," indicating partitive, quantity, or movement away from something.

Conjugation and Usage
Pronominal verbs are conjugated by separating the pronoun from the verb stem in all forms except the infinitive and the imperative. The pronouns are placed before the verb in most tenses or attached to the end of the verb in the imperative form.

For example, the verb "andarsene" in the present tense:

Io me ne vado (I am leaving) - [ee-oh MEH neh VAH-doh]

Tu te ne vai (You are leaving) - [too teh neh vai]

Lui/Lei se ne va (He/She is leaving) - [loo-ee/lay seh neh vah]

Pronominal Particles Explained
Si: Used in reflexive and reciprocal actions. It changes according to the subject (mi, ti, si, ci, vi, si).

Ne: Indicates partitive use (some of it), quantity, or movement from a place.

Ci: Refers to a place (there) or a matter (about it); also used to mean "us" in some contexts.

Vi: Can mean "there" in some dialects or contexts, but is less common in standard Italian.

Special Considerations
Pronunciation: The attachment of pronouns to verbs can sometimes alter the stress of the word. Always pay attention to accentuation.

Idiomatic Expressions: Many pronominal verbs are used in idiomatic expressions with meanings that are not immediately apparent. These should be learned as fixed expressions.

Common Idiomatic Expressions
In Italian, as in English, idioms add color and depth to the language. This section covers some of the most common Italian idiomatic expressions to help you sound more like a native speaker.

1. Essere in gamba (EH-sseh-re in GAM-bah) - To be competent/skilled

Literally meaning "to be in leg," this expression is used to describe someone who is very capable or skilled in a particular area. It's a compliment to someone's ability or competence.

2. Avere la testa tra le nuvole (AH-veh-re lah TEH-stah trah leh NOO-vo-leh) - To have one's head in the clouds

This phrase describes someone who is not paying attention or daydreaming, similar to the English expression "to have one's head in the clouds."

3. Costare un occhio della testa (co-STAH-reh oon OH-kee-oh DEL-lah TEH-stah) - To cost an arm and a leg

This expression is used to indicate that something is very expensive, much like the English idiom "to cost an arm and a leg."

4. Mettere il carro davanti ai buoi (meh-TEH-reh eel KAHR-roh dah-VAN-tee ahee BWAW-ee) - To put the cart before the horse

Used to describe a situation where things are done out of the proper order, similar to the English expression "to put the cart before the horse."

5. Non vedere l'ora (non veh-DEH-reh LOH-rah) - To can't wait/to look forward to

Literally meaning "not to see the hour," it expresses a strong anticipation or eagerness for something to happen.

6. Far ridere i polli (fahr ree-DEH-reh ee POHL-lee) - To make the chickens laugh

An expression used when someone says or does something considered so foolish or unrealistic that even the chickens would laugh.

7. Avere le mani in pasta (AH-veh-reh leh MAH-nee in PAH-stah) - To have one's hands in the dough

This means to be involved in a situation, often with the connotation of having influence or control over it.

8. Tirare acqua al proprio mulino (tee-RAH-reh AH-kwah al proh-PREE-oh moo-LEE-noh) - To draw water to one's own mill

Equivalent to the English "to feather one's own nest," it refers to acting in a way that primarily benefits oneself, often at the expense of others.

9. Essere pan per i suoi denti (EH-sseh-reh pan per ee SOY denti) - To be bread for one's teeth

This idiom means that something is exactly what someone deserves, often with a negative connotation, similar to the English "to meet one's match."

10. Quando il gatto non c'è, i topi ballano (KWAN-doh eel GAHT-toh non cheh, ee TOH-pee bahl-LAH-noh) - When the cat's away, the mice will play

This expression is used to describe how people may take advantage of a situation when an authority figure is absent, identical in meaning to the English version.

11. Rompere il ghiaccio (rom-PEH-reh eel gyah-CHOH) - To break the ice

Used when someone takes an action to overcome initial social awkwardness, just as in English.

12. Buttarsi a capofitto (boot-TAR-see ah kah-poh-FEET-toh) - To dive headfirst

It means to start something with great enthusiasm and energy, without hesitation.

13. Avere un chiodo fisso in testa (AH-veh-reh oon KYOH-doh FEESS-oh in TEH-stah) - To have a fixed nail in one's head

This refers to being obsessed with a single thought or idea, similar to the English "to have a one-track mind."

Training:

Exercise 1

Fill in the Blanks: Direct Speech

Marco ha detto, Sono stanco.
"vado al cinema stasera," ha detto Lucia.
"Non voglio mangiare," ha detto Giovanni.
"Sono felice di vederti," ha detto Marta.
"Domani parto per Parigi," ha detto Anna.
"Vieni con me al concerto?" ha chiesto Carlo.
"Mi piace questa casa," ha detto Laura.
"Dove hai messo le chiavi?" ha chiesto Luca.

Exercise 2

Convert Direct Speech to Indirect Speech

Direct: Luca dice, "Ho fame."
Direct: "Sto arrivando," ha detto Sara.
Direct: "Andiamo al parco domani," ha detto Marco.
Direct: "Ti amo," ha detto Giovanni.
Direct: "Ho vinto la partita," ha detto Paolo.
Direct: "Prendi un ombrello," ha detto Maria.
Direct: "Ho comprato un regalo per te," ha detto Elena.
Direct: "Ti chiamerò più tardi," ha detto Antonio.

Exercise 3

Match the Idiomatic Expressions

Avere la testa tra le nuvole - A. To have one's head in the clouds
Costare un occhio della testa - B. To cost an arm and a leg
Non vedere l'ora - C. To can't wait
Essere in gamba - D. To be competent/skilled
Mettere il carro davanti ai buoi - E. To put the cart before the horse
Rompere il ghiaccio - F. To break the ice
Far ridere i polli - G. To make the chickens laugh
Avere le mani in pasta - H. To have one's hands in the dough

Exercise 4

Choose the Correct Pronominal Verb

Io _____ (andarsene/andare) via domani.
Loro si _____ (lavarsi/lavare) ogni mattina.
Lei _____ (mettersi/mettere) la giacca prima di uscire.
Voi _____ (vestirsi/vestire) bene per la festa.

Noi _____ (arrabbiarsi/arrabbiare) con quella situazione.

Exercise 5

Correct the Mistake: Tense Shift in Indirect Speech

Marco ha detto che è stanco. (Correct tense shift for "said that he was tired")
Lei ha raccontato che va al mercato. (Correct tense shift for "told that she went to the market")
Anna ha detto che arriva presto. (Correct tense shift for "said that she arrives early")
Paolo ha raccontato che vuole mangiare. (Correct tense shift for "told that he wants to eat")
Maria ha detto che esce con gli amici. (Correct tense shift for "said that she goes out with friends")

Exercise 6

Pronominal Particles: Fill in the Blanks

Mi _____ vado domani. (to go away)
Ne abbiamo parlato. (we talked about it)
Non _____ preoccupare, tutto va bene. (to worry)
Vi _____ incontreremo al ristorante. (to meet)
Ci _____ penserò io. (to think)
Si _____ divertono molto insieme. (to have fun)
Vi _____ conosco bene. (to know)
Mi _____ piace questo libro. (to like)

Exercise 7

Identify the Idiomatic Expression

Describes doing things in the wrong order.
Used to express eagerness for something to happen.
Describes someone not paying attention or daydreaming.
Refers to being involved in a situation, often with influence or control.
Means that something is exactly what someone deserves, often with a negative connotation.

Exercise 8

Punctuation Correction: Direct Speech

"andrò al supermercato," ha detto Maria.
"Puoi aiutarmi?" chiese Paolo.
"Sarò in ritardo," disse Giovanni.
"Voglio andare al mare," disse Laura.

"Dov'è il mio telefono?" chiese Luca.
"Mi piace molto questo film," disse Marco.
"Vieni con me al concerto," chiese Elena.
"Stasera c'è una festa," disse Sara.

UNIT 13

Language:

- Advanced Conversational Tools

  ○ Describing Past Events

In Italian, describing past events is primarily done using two tenses: the Passato Prossimo (Perfect Tense) and the Imperfetto (Imperfect Tense).

  ○ Passato Prossimo (Perfect Tense)

Usage: The Passato Prossimo is used for actions that were completed in the past and have no direct connection to the present. It's often used for actions that happened once or for a specific number of times.

Formation: This tense is formed with the auxiliary verbs 'avere' (ah-VEH-reh) or 'essere' (ES-seh-reh) and the past participle of the main verb.

Example: "Ho mangiato" (I have eaten) - [oh man-JAH-toh]

  ○ Imperfetto (Imperfect Tense)

Usage: The Imperfetto is used for past actions that were ongoing or habitual. It's also used for setting the scene in the past, describing people, things, or states of being.

Formation: This tense is formed by removing the '-re' ending from the infinitive form of verbs and adding specific endings.

Example: "Mangiavo" (I was eating/I used to eat) - [man-JAH-voh]

  ○ Describing Future Plans

Discussing future events in Italian primarily involves the Futuro Semplice (Simple Future) and the Futuro Anteriore (Future Perfect).

  ○ Futuro Semplice (Simple Future)

Usage: Used to discuss actions that will happen in the future. It is straightforward and indicates a direct action that will take place.

Formation: Adding specific endings to the infinitive form of the verb.

Example: "Parlerò" (I will speak) - [par-leh-ROH]

○　Futuro Anteriore (Future Perfect)

Usage: Used for actions that will have been completed by a certain future time. It's often used in conjunction with another future action.

Formation: This tense is formed using the futuro semplice of the auxiliary verbs 'avere' or 'essere' and the past participle of the main verb.

Example: "Avrò finito" (I will have finished) - [ah-VROH fee-NEE-toh]

Grammar:

*　Future Tense (Il Futuro)

Regular Formation:
For verbs ending in -are: Replace with -erò, -erai, -erà, -eremo, -erete, -eranno.
For verbs ending in -ere: Replace with -erò, -erai, -erà, -eremo, -erete, -eranno.
For verbs ending in -ire: Replace with -irò, -irai, -irà, -iremo, -irete, -iranno.

Irregular Verbs:
"Essere" (to be) becomes "sar-" (e.g., sarò, sarai, sarà...).
"Avere" (to have) becomes "avr-" (e.g., avrò, avrai, avrà...).
"Fare" (to do/make) becomes "far-" (e.g., farò, farai, farà...).

Example: "Parleremo" (We will speak) - [par-leh-REH-moh]

Irregular Formation: Some verbs have irregular stems in the future tense, but the endings remain consistent.

Example: "Dovrò" (I will have to) from "dovere" - [doh-VROH]

*　Conditional Tense (Il Condizionale)

Usage: Expresses a condition or a wish, similar to the English "would."

Regular Formation:
-are verbs: Replace the infinitive ending with -erei, -eresti, -erebbe, -eremmo, -ereste, -erebbero.
-ere verbs: Replace the infinitive ending with -erei, -eresti, -erebbe, -eremmo, -ereste, -erebbero.
-ire verbs: Replace the infinitive ending with -irei, -iresti, -irebbe, -iremmo, -ireste, -irebbero.

Irregular Verbs:
Similar to the future tense, verbs like "essere", "avere", and "fare" have irregular stems. Examples include "sarei" (I would be), "avrei" (I would have), "farei" (I would do/make).

Example: "Vorrei" (I would like) from "volere" - [vor-REY]

Irregularities: Some verbs have irregular stems in the conditional tense, but the endings remain the same.

Example: "Potrei" (I could) from "potere" - [po-TREY]

- Subjunctive Mood (Il Congiuntivo)

The subjunctive mood is used to express doubt, wishes, hopes, or hypothetical situations. It's more abstract than the indicative and is often used after certain conjunctions, verbs, and expressions.

  ○ Present Subjunctive (Il Congiuntivo Presente)

Usage: To express doubt, hope, or uncertainty in the present or future.

Regular Formation:
For -are verbs: Replace with -i, -i, -i, -iamo, -iate, -ino.
For -ere verbs: Replace with -a, -a, -a, -iamo, -iate, -ano.
For -ire verbs: Replace with -a, -a, -a, -iamo, -iate, -ano.

Irregular Verbs:
"Essere": sia, sia, sia, siamo, siate, siano.
"Avere": abbia, abbia, abbia, abbiamo, abbiate, abbiano.
Example: "Che io parli" (That I speak) - [keh EE-oh PAR-lee]

  ○ Imperfect Subjunctive (Il Congiuntivo Imperfetto)

Usage: Used in hypothetical clauses, often in conjunction with the conditional tense.
Formation: Formed by adding specific endings to the stem of the verbs in the past historic tense.

Regular Formation:
-are verbs: Replace the infinitive ending with -assi, -assi, -asse, -assimo, -aste, -assero.
-ere verbs: Replace the infinitive ending with -essi, -essi, -esse, -essimo, -este, -essero.
-ire verbs: Replace the infinitive ending with -issi, -issi, -isse, -issimo, -iste, -issero.

Irregular Verbs:
"Essere": fossi, fossi, fosse, fossimo, foste, fossero.
"Avere": avessi, avessi, avesse, avessimo, aveste, avessero.

Example: "Se io parlassi" (If I spoke) - [seh EE-oh par-LAH-see]

  ○ Perfect Subjunctive (Il Congiuntivo Passato)

Usage: Used to express a doubt or a possibility about an action that occurred in the past.

Formation:
Formed using the present subjunctive of "avere" or "essere" + past participle of the main verb.
For verbs that normally use "avere":
"Avere" in present subjunctive: abbia, abbia, abbia, abbiamo, abbiate, abbiano + past participle.
For verbs that normally use "essere":
"Essere" in present subjunctive: sia, sia, sia, siamo, siate, siano + past participle.

Example: "Che io abbia parlato" (That I have spoken) - [keh EE-oh AB-bee-ah par-LAH-toh]

  ◦ Pluperfect Subjunctive (Il Congiuntivo Trapassato)

Usage: Used in hypothetical phrases to express something that would have happened in the past.

Formation:
Formed using the imperfect subjunctive of "avere" or "essere" + past participle of the main verb.
For verbs that normally use "avere":
"Avere" in imperfect subjunctive: avessi, avessi, avesse, avessimo, aveste, avessero + past participle.
For verbs that normally use "essere":
"Essere" in imperfect subjunctive: fossi, fossi, fosse, fossimo, foste, fossero + past participle.

Example: "Se io avessi parlato" (If I had spoken) - [seh EE-oh ah-VESS-ee par-LAH-toh]

Training:

Exercise 1:

Complete the following sentences with the appropriate form of the future tense of the verbs provided in parentheses.

Noi _____ (viaggiare) in Spagna l'estate prossima. [viaggeremo]
Lei _____ (aprire) un negozio di fiori in città. [aprirà]
Voi _____ (imparare) a suonare la chitarra. [imparerete]
Io _____ (scrivere) una lettera alla nonna domani. [scriverò]
Loro _____ (comprare) una nuova macchina la settimana prossima. [compreranno]
Tu _____ (finire) il progetto entro domani? [finirai]
Noi _____ (prendere) il treno per Milano domani mattina. [prenderemo]
Lei _____ (cantare) al concerto sabato prossimo. [canterà]

Exercise 2:

Identify and correct the mistakes in the following sentences related to the conditional tense.

Se io avere più tempo, viaggierei in tutto il mondo. [Se io avessi più tempo, viaggierei in tutto il mondo.]

Loro vorrebbe andare al cinema se non è troppo tardi. [Loro vorrebbero andare al cinema se non fosse troppo tardi.]

Se tu sapere la risposta, me lo diresti? [Se tu sapessi la risposta, me lo diresti?]

Io comprerebbe una nuova casa se avrei abbastanza soldi. [Io comprerei una nuova casa se avessi abbastanza soldi.]

Lei farebbe una torta se abbiamo gli ingredienti. [Lei farebbe una torta se avesse gli ingredienti.]

Exercise 3:

Match the verbs in the present subjunctive with their corresponding subjects.

Noi - andiamo
Tu - mangi
Loro - dormano
Io - studi
Lei - abbia
Voi - scriviate
Io - legga
Loro - parlino

Exercise 4:

Connect the two sentences using the present subjunctive form of the verb provided in brackets.

Voglio che tu _____ (essere) felice. (I want you to be happy.)

È importante che noi _____ (imparare) l'italiano. (It's important that we learn Italian.)

È essenziale che lei _____ (fare) esercizio ogni giorno. (It's essential that she exercises every day.)

È necessario che voi _____ (aiutare) i vostri genitori. (It's necessary that you help your parents.)

È fondamentale che loro _____ (rispettare) le regole. (It's fundamental that they respect the rules.)

Io preferirei che tu _____ (venire) con noi. (I would prefer you to come with us.)

È meglio che lui non _____ (mangiare) troppo dolci. (It's better that he doesn't eat too many sweets.)

È importante che voi _____ (prestare) attenzione in classe. (It's important that you pay attention in class.)

Exercise 5:

Choose the correct form of the imperfect tense to complete the sentences.

Io _____ (giocare) a calcio ogni weekend con i miei amici. [giocavo]
Loro sempre _____ (andare) al parco la domenica. [andavano]
Tu _____ (mangiare) la pizza ogni venerdì sera. [mangiavi]
Noi _____ (guardare) i film Disney quando eravamo bambini. [guardavamo]
Lei _____ (leggere) libri ogni sera prima di dormire. [leggeva]
Voi _____ (visitare) i nonni ogni estate. [visitavate]
Io _____ (scrivere) poesie quando ero giovane. [scrivevo]
Loro sempre _____ (fare) gite fuori porta durante le vacanze. [facevano]

Exercise 6:

Identify whether the given sentences are in the perfect tense or the imperfect tense.

Noi _____ (andare) al parco ogni giorno. [imperfect]
Lei _____ (finire) di leggere il libro che le ho prestato. [perfect]
Tu sempre _____ (mangiare) la colazione con la famiglia. [imperfect]
Io _____ (visitare) la Francia l'estate scorsa. [perfect]
Loro _____ (scrivere) una lettera alla nonna ieri sera. [perfect]
Voi _____ (studiare) molto quando eravate studenti. [imperfect]
Lei _____ (guardare) un film ogni venerdì sera. [imperfect]
Io _____ (parlare) con Maria ogni giorno. [imperfect]

Exercise 7:

Translate the given phrases into Italian, using the appropriate tense.

If I had more time, I would learn to play the piano. [Se avessi più tempo, imparerei a suonare il piano.]

He will have finished his homework before dinner. [Lui avrà finito i compiti prima di cena.]

We would go to the beach if the weather were nice. [Andremmo alla spiaggia se il tempo fosse bello.]

She wishes she could speak fluent French. [Lei vorrebbe parlare fluentemente francese.]

They would travel the world if they had enough money. [Viaggerebbero per il mondo se avessero abbastanza soldi.]

Exercise 8:

Create hypothetical statements using the appropriate subjunctive mood.

(Tu / fare) un viaggio in Europa se avessi abbastanza soldi. [Faresti]

(Noi / comprare) una casa in campagna se vincessimo alla lotteria. [Compreremmo]

(Loro / andare) al concerto se avessero trovato i biglietti. [Andrebbero]

(Io / scegliere) quella macchina se avessi il denaro necessario. [Sceglierei]

(Voi / fare) una festa se non ci fosse il maltempo. [Fareste]

(Lei / potere) cucinare una cena speciale se avesse il tempo. [Potrebbe]

(Noi / volere) viaggiare in Asia se avessimo le ferie più lunghe.

UNIT 14

Grammar:

- Cultural Notes: Formal vs. Informal Address
In Italian, the distinction between formal and informal address is often just a matter of etiquette, and it is similar to the old usage of "thou" and "thee" but, unlike those, it is still widely used and is not seen as obsolete or old-fashioned.

Understanding "Tu" and "Lei"
The Italian language has two main ways of saying "you": "tu" (informal) and "Lei" (formal). The choice between these pronouns depends on several factors, including the relationship between the speakers, the setting, and the level of respect or courtesy intended.

Tu (informal) - [too]: Used with family, friends, children, animals, and people of the same age or younger. It signifies closeness and familiarity.

Lei (formal) - [lay]: Used with strangers, older people, professionals, and in formal settings. It conveys respect and a certain social distance.

Pronunciation and Usage Tips
When addressing someone with "Lei," the verb conjugation follows the third person singular, the same as "he" or "she." This may initially confuse learners because you're addressing "you" but conjugating the verb as if talking about someone else. For example, to ask "How are you?" informally, you'd say "Come stai?" ([KO-meh sty?]), but formally, it's "Come sta?" ([KO-meh stah?]).

When to Use "Tu" and "Lei"
In the Workplace: The default in most Italian workplaces is "Lei," especially when interacting with superiors or clients. However, some modern, informal environments may encourage the use of "tu" among colleagues.

In Educational Settings: Students typically address teachers and professors with "Lei," unless the teacher specifies otherwise. Among students, "tu" is the norm.

In Public Spaces and With Strangers: "Lei" is common when engaging with strangers, especially in formal settings like stores, restaurants, or when asking for directions.

With Acquaintances: The transition from "Lei" to "tu" can be a subtle dance. It usually requires a mutual agreement or an invitation to use "tu," often verbalized by the older or higher-ranking person.

Cultural Insights
Asking Permission to Use "Tu": In situations where you're unsure whether to use "tu" or "Lei," it's polite to ask, "Posso darti del tu?" ([POHS-soh DAHR-tee del too?]), meaning "May I address you informally?" This question itself should be posed using "Lei."

Regional Variations: In some regions of Italy, particularly in the south, people may shift to "tu" more quickly than in the north, reflecting a more open and warm local culture.

Signs of Changing Times: The use of "tu" has become more widespread among younger Italians and in digital communication, including social media and emails, reflecting a shift towards informality in certain contexts.

Key Takeaways
Choose "Lei" for formal interactions and "tu" for informal ones.

Pay attention to social cues and be ready to switch between forms of address based on the context and the other person's preference.

Remember that using the correct form of address is not just about following rules; it's about showing respect, building relationships, and navigating Italian social contexts with sensitivity.

- Basic Telephone Etiquette in Italian
Italian telephone etiquette can vary slightly depending on the region and the formality of the situation, but the guidelines provided here will serve you well in most contexts.

Greeting
Answering the phone: When you pick up the phone, it's common to greet the caller with a simple "Pronto" (Hello) - [PRAWN-toh]. This is universally accepted and can be used in both formal and informal settings.

Making a call: When you're the one calling, it's polite to start the conversation with a greeting like "Buongiorno" (Good morning) - [bwon-JOR-no] or "Buonasera" (Good evening) - [bwon-ah-SEH-rah], depending on the time of day. Follow this with "Mi chiamo [Your Name]" (My name is [Your Name]) - [mee KYAH-moh].

Introducing Yourself and Stating the Purpose of the Call
After the initial greeting, if you're calling someone you don't know personally or if it's a formal situation, it's essential to introduce yourself and mention the reason for your call. For instance:

"Sono [Your Name], chiamo per..." (I am [Your Name], I'm calling for...) - [SO-noh, KYAH-moh pehr...].

Asking for Someone
If you need to speak with someone specific and you're not sure if they're available, you can ask:

"Posso parlare con [Name]?" (May I speak with [Name]?) - [POH-soh PAR-lah-reh kohn].

"È disponibile [Name]?" (Is [Name] available?) - [EH dees-poh-NEE-bee-leh].

Leaving a Message
If the person you're calling is not available, you might want to leave a message. You can say:

"Potrei lasciare un messaggio?" (May I leave a message?) - [po-TREY lah-SHA-reh oon meh-SAH-joh].

"Può richiamarmi al numero..." (Can he/she call me back at the number...) - [pwoh ree-kee-AH-mar-mee ahl NOO-meh-roh].

Ending the Call
Concluding a phone call politely is just as important as starting one. Here are some phrases you might use:

"Grazie per l'aiuto, arrivederci!" (Thank you for your help, goodbye!) - [GRAHT-zee-eh pehr l'ah-EEU-toh, ah-ree-veh-DEHR-chee].

"Grazie, ci sentiamo presto!" (Thank you, we'll talk soon!) - [GRAHT-zee-eh, chee sen-TEE-ah-moh PREH-stoh].

Handling Misunderstandings
If there's a misunderstanding or you need something repeated, you can use the following expressions:

"Potrebbe ripetere, per favore?" (Could you repeat, please?) - [po-TREB-beh ree-PEH-teh-reh, pehr fah-VOH-reh].

"Scusa, non ho capito." (Sorry, I didn't understand.) - [SKOO-sah, nohn ho kah-PEE-toh].

Formal vs. Informal
Remember, when speaking to someone you don't know well or in a formal situation, use the polite form "Lei" instead of "tu" for "you". This distinction affects verb conjugations and possessive adjectives and is crucial for showing respect.

- Writing Simple Letters and Emails in Italian
Writing is a crucial aspect of language learning, offering you the opportunity to practice grammar, expand your vocabulary, and understand the nuances of formal and informal communication. Given the context provided by previous units, you are now equipped with the basic grammar, vocabulary, and cultural understanding needed to start writing in Italian.

Formal vs. Informal Tone
Italian differentiates clearly between formal and informal communication. This distinction is crucial when writing letters and emails.

Formal communication is used when writing to someone you don't know well, to professionals, or in official contexts. Formal letters and emails use polite forms of address, such as "Egregio/Egregia" ([EH-greh-joh/EH-greh-jah], "Esteemed") or "Gentile" ([JEN-tee-leh], "Kind"), followed by the surname and use formal verb forms like "Lei" ([lay], "you" formal).

Informal communication is used with friends, family, or people you are familiar with. It uses casual language, personal greetings like "Ciao" ([CHOW], "Hello") or "Caro/Carissimo" ([KAH-roh/kah-REE-see-moh], "Dear/Dearest") for males and "Cara/Carissima" ([KAH-rah/kah-REE-see-mah], "Dear/Dearest") for females, and the informal "tu" ([too], "you") form of verbs.

Structure of Letters and Emails
Greeting

Formal: "Gentile [Name],", "Egregio Signore/Signora,"
Informal: "Ciao [Name],", "Caro/Carissimo [Name],"
Introduction

Begin by stating the purpose of your communication succinctly.

Example: "Le scrivo per..." ([lay SKREE-voh per...], "I am writing to you to...") for formal, "Ti scrivo per..." ([tee SKREE-voh per...], "I am writing to you to...") for informal.
Body

Present your information or request in clear, concise paragraphs.

Use connectors to make your text flow, such as "Inoltre" ([een-OL-treh], "Furthermore"), "Pertanto" ([per-TAN-toh], "Therefore"), "Tuttavia" ([toot-tah-VEE-ah], "However").
Closing

Formal: "In attesa di una Sua risposta, porgo distinti saluti," ([een ah-TEH-sah dee OO-nah SWAH ree-SPO-stah, POR-goh dees-TEEN-tee sah-LOO-tee], "Awaiting your reply, I offer my best regards,")

Informal: "Aspetto tue notizie, un abbraccio," ([ah-SPEHT-toh too-eh noh-TEE-tsyeh, oon ahb-BRAH-choh], "I look forward to hearing from you, a hug,")
Signature

Your name.
Email-Specific Considerations

Subject Line: Be clear and concise, e.g., "Richiesta di Informazioni" ([ree-KEH-stah dee een-for-mah-TSYOH-nee], "Request for Information") for formal, or "Ci vediamo domani?" ([chee veh-DEE-ah-moh doh-MAH-nee?], "Are we seeing each other tomorrow?") for informal.

Email Address: Use a professional-sounding email address for formal communications.

Attachments: Mention any attachments with "In allegato troverà..." ([een ah-LEH-gah-toh troh-veh-RAH...], "Attached you will find...") for formal or "Ti allego..." ([tee ah-LEH-goh...], "I am attaching...") for informal.

Practical Tips
Proofread: Always check your spelling and grammar.

Be Concise: Get to the point without unnecessary detail.

Cultural Sensitivity: Be aware of cultural nuances, especially in formal communication.

Practice: Write regularly to improve your fluency and comfort with written Italian.

Example: Formal Email

Gentile Professoressa Rossi,
Le scrivo per richiedere informazioni riguardanti il programma del corso di italiano avanzato che Lei insegna. Sono molto interessato a partecipare e vorrei sapere quali sono i requisiti per l'iscrizione.

In attesa di una Sua risposta, porgo distinti saluti,
[Mario Bianchi]

Example: Informal Email

Ciao Luca,
Ti scrivo per dirti che ho trovato un nuovo ristorante italiano in centro che sembra fantastico. Che ne dici di provarlo questo weekend? Fammi sapere.

Un abbraccio,
[Maria]

- Tips for Language Learning and Practice
  Learning a new language is an exciting journey, and when it comes to English speakers learning Italian, the process can be both rewarding and challenging. Italian and English share a lot of similarities, thanks to their Latin roots, but there are also significant differences that learners should be aware of. This section aims to provide you with comprehensive tips to effectively learn and practice Italian up to the A2 level, considering the linguistic characteristics and cultural nuances of the Italian language.

  1. Leverage Linguistic Similarities

Cognates: Take advantage of cognates—words that sound similar and have the same meaning in Italian and English. For example, "attore" (ah-TOH-reh) means actor, and "università" (oo-nee-ver-see-TAH) means university. However, be cautious of false friends—words that look similar but have different meanings.

Vocabulary Building: Since many English words are derived from Latin, like Italian, you can often guess the meaning of Italian words. Use this to enrich your vocabulary.

2. Understand Pronunciation Nuances
Italian is a phonetic language, meaning it is largely pronounced as it is written, which is a significant difference from English. Focus on the pronunciation guide provided in Unit 1 to master the sounds of vowels and consonants.

Pay attention to double consonants, as they can change the meaning of a word (e.g., "casa" [KAH-sah] - house vs. "cassa" [KAHS-sah] - cash register).

Stress and accents are crucial in Italian. Unlike English, where stress can fall on any syllable, Italian words are typically stressed on the penultimate (second to last) syllable unless indicated otherwise by an accent mark.

3. Grammar and Sentence Structure
Italian grammar can be complex for English speakers, especially when dealing with gender and number agreement for nouns, adjectives, and articles. Practice this aspect diligently, as it is foundational to fluent Italian use.

Sentence structure in Italian follows a Subject-Verb-Object (SVO) order like English, but it is more flexible. Use this flexibility to experiment with sentence construction, but remember to keep the verb close to the subject to maintain clarity.

4. Practice Regularly and Consistently
Consistency is key. Dedicate time every day to practice, even if it's just 15-20 minutes. Regular exposure to Italian will improve your retention and understanding over time.

Mix your learning materials. Use textbooks, apps, music, movies, and even video games in Italian to keep your learning experience varied and engaging.

5. Engage in Active Use
Speaking: Practice speaking as much as possible. Language exchange meetups or online conversation partners can be incredibly helpful. Don't worry about making mistakes; they are part of the learning process.

Writing: Start writing short texts, such as diary entries, emails, or simple stories. This practice will help you to memorize new vocabulary and understand sentence structure.

6. Listening and Reading

Listening: Italian has a musical quality, so listening to Italian music, podcasts, or watching Italian movies with subtitles can enhance your understanding of pronunciation, intonation, and rhythm.

Reading: Start with children's books or simple articles. This will help you get accustomed to reading in Italian, expanding your vocabulary, and understanding grammatical structures in context.

7. Cultural Immersion

Understanding cultural context is crucial in language learning. Familiarize yourself with Italian customs, traditions, and the way of life to better understand the language's nuances.

If possible, travel to Italy or spend time in Italian-speaking environments. Immersion is one of the most effective ways to learn a language quickly.

8. Use Technology Wisely

Language learning apps and online resources can be highly beneficial. Use them to reinforce what you've learned, practice pronunciation, and test your skills with interactive exercises.

Watch Italian YouTube channels or follow Italian social media accounts to immerse yourself in the language daily.

9. Set Realistic Goals

Set clear, achievable goals for your language learning. Whether it's learning ten new words a day, mastering a particular grammatical structure in a week, or having a 5-minute conversation in Italian by the end of the month, goals will keep you motivated.

10. Be Patient and Persistent

Language learning is a marathon, not a sprint. Progress may seem slow at times, but persistence and patience are key. Celebrate small victories and milestones along your journey.

VERB CONJUGATION TABLES

	Presente Indicativo	Imperfetto Indicativo	Passato Prossimo	Futuro Semplice	Passato Remoto	Trapassato Prossimo
Io	sono	ero	sono stato/a	sarò	fui	ero stato/a
Tu	sei	eri	sei stato/a	sarai	fosti	eri stato/a
Egli	è	era	è stato/a	sarà	fu	era stato/a
Noi	siamo	eravamo	siamo stati/e	saremo	fummo	eravamo stati/e
Voi	siete	eravate	siete stati/e	sarete	foste	eravate stati/e
Essi	sono	erano	sono stati/e	saranno	furono	erano stati/e

VERB **ESSERE**

	Presente Indicativo	Imperfetto Indicativo	Passato Prossimo	Futuro Semplice	Passato Remoto	Trapassato Prossimo
Io	ho	avevo	ho avuto	avrò	ebbi	avevo avuto
Tu	hai	avevi	hai avuto	avrai	avesti	avevi avuto
Egli	ha	aveva	ha avuto	avrà	ebbe	aveva avuto
Noi	abbiamo	avevamo	abbiamo avuto	avremo	avemmo	avevamo avuto
Voi	avete	avevate	avete avuto	avrete	aveste	avevate avuto
Essi	hanno	avevano	hanno avuto	avranno	ebbero	avevano avuto

VERB **AVERE**

	Presente Indicativo	Imperfetto Indicativo	Passato Prossimo	Futuro Semplice	Passato Remoto	Trapassato Prossimo
Io	mangio	mangiavo	ho mangiato	mangerò	mangi	avevo mangiato
Tu	mangi	mangiavi	hai mangiato	mangerai	mangi	avevi mangiato
Egli	mangia	mangiava	ha mangiato	mangerà	mangi	aveva mangiato
Noi	mangiamo	mangiavamo	abbiamo mangiato	mangeremo	mangiammo	avevamo mangiato
Voi	mangiate	mangiavate	avete mangiato	mangerete	mangiaste	avevate mangiato
Essi	mangiano	mangiavano	hanno mangiato	mangeranno	mangiarono	avevano mangiato

VERB MANGI**ARE**

Trapassato Remoto	Futuro Anteriore	Congiuntivo Presente	Congiuntivo Imperfetto	Congiuntivo Passato	Congiuntivo Trapassato
fui stato/a	sarò stato/a	sia	fossi	sia stato/a	fossi stato/a
fosti stato/a	sarai stato/a	sia	fossi	fossi stato/a	fossi stato/a
fu stato/a	sarà stato/a	sia	fosse	fosse stato/a	fosse stato/a
fummo stati/e	saremo stati/e	siamo	fossimo	fossimo stati/e	fossimo stato/e
foste stati/e	sarete stati/e	siate	foste	foste stati/e	foste stato/e
furono stati/e	saranno stati/e	siano	fossero	fossero stati/e	fossero stati/e

Trapassato Remoto	Futuro Anteriore	Congiuntivo Presente	Congiuntivo Imperfetto	Congiuntivo Passato	Congiuntivo Trapassato
ebbi avuto	avrò avuto	abbia	avessi	abbia avuto	avessi avuto
avesti avuto	avrai avuto	abbia	avessi	abbia avuto	avessi avuto
ebbe avuto	avrà avuto	abbia	avesse	abbia avuto	avesse avuto
avemmo avuto	avremo avuto	abbiamo	avessimo	abbiamo avuto	avessimo avuto
aveste avuto	avrete avuto	abbiate	aveste	abbiate avuto	aveste avuto
ebbero avuto	avranno avuto	abbiano	avessero	abbiano avuto	avessero avuto

Trapassato Remoto	Futuro Anteriore	Congiuntivo Presente	Congiuntivo Imperfetto	Congiuntivo Passato	Congiuntivo Trapassato
ebbi mangiato	mangerò mangiato	mangi	avessi mangiato	mangiato avuto	avessi mangiato avuto
avesti mangiato	mangerai mangiato	mangi	avessi mangiato	abbia mangiato	avessi mangiato avuto
ebbe mangiato	mangerà mangiato	mangi	avesse mangiato	abbia mangiato	avessi mangiato avuto
avemmo mangiato	mangeremo mangiato	mangiamo	avessimo mangiato	abbiamo mangiato	avessimo mangiato avuto
aveste mangiato	mangerete mangiato	mangiate	aveste mangiato	abbiate mangiato	aveste mangiato avuto
ebbero mangiato	mangeranno mangiato	mangino	avessero mangiato	abbiano mangiato	avessero mangiato avuto

	Presente Indicativo	Imperfetto Indicativo	Passato Prossimo	Futuro Semplice	Passato Remoto	Trapassato Prossimo
Io	amo	amavo	ho amato	amerò	amai	avevo amato
Tu	ami	amavi	hai amato	amerai	amasti	avevi amato
Egli	ama	amava	ha amato	amerà	amò	aveva amato
Noi	amiamo	amavamo	abbiamo amato	ameremo	amammo	avevamo amato
Voi	amate	amavate	avete amato	amerete	ammaste	avevate amato
Essi	amano	amavano	hanno amato	ameranno	amarono	avevano amato

VERB   AM**ARE**

	Presente Indicativo	Imperfetto Indicativo	Passato Prossimo	Futuro Semplice	Passato Remoto	Trapassato Prossimo
Io	vedo	vedevo	ho visto	vedrò	vidi	avevo visto
Tu	vedi	vedevi	hai visto	vedrai	vedesti	avevi visto
Egli	vede	vedeva	ha visto	vedrà	vide	aveva visto
Noi	vediamo	vedevamo	abbiamo visto	vedremo	vedemmo	avevamo visto
Voi	vedete	vedevate	avete visto	vedrete	vedeste	avevate visto
Essi	vedono	vedevano	hanno visto	vedranno	videro	avevano visto

VERB   VED**ERE**

	Presente Indicativo	Imperfetto Indicativo	Passato Prossimo	Futuro Semplice	Passato Remoto	Trapassato Prossimo
Io	perdo	perdevo	ho perso	perderò	persi	avevo perso
Tu	perdi	perdevi	hai perso	perderai	perdesti	avevi perso
Egli	perde	perdeva	ha perso	perderà	perse	aveva perso
Noi	perdiamo	perdevamo	abbiamo perso	perderemo	perdemmo	avevamo perso
Voi	perdete	perdevate	avete perso	perderete	perdeste	avevate perso
Essi	perdono	perdevano	hanno perso	perderanno	persero	avevano perso

VERB   PERD**ERE**

Trapassato Remoto	Futuro Anteriore	Congiuntivo Presente	Congiuntivo Imperfetto	Congiuntivo Passato	Congiuntivo Trapassato
amai amato	amerò amato	ami	amassi	ami amato	amassi amato
amasti amato	amerai amato	ami	amassi	ami amato	amassi amato
amò amato	amerà amato	ami	amasse	ami amato	amasse amato
amammo amato	ameremo amato	amiamo	amassimo	amiamo amato	amassimo amato
ammaste amato	amerete amato	amiate	amaste	amiate amato	amaste amato
amarono amato	ameranno amato	amino	amassero	amino amato	amassero amato

Trapassato Remoto	Futuro Anteriore	Congiuntivo Presente	Congiuntivo Imperfetto	Congiuntivo Passato	Congiuntivo Trapassato
vidi visto	vedrò visto	veda	vedessi	veda visto	vedessi visto
vedesti visto	vedrai visto	veda	vedessi	veda visto	vedessi visto
vide visto	vedrà visto	veda	vedesse	veda visto	vedesse visto
vedemmo visto	vedremo visto	vediamo	vedessimo	vediamo visto	vedessimo visto
vedeste visto	vedrete visto	vediate	vedeste	vediate visto	vedeste visto
videro visto	vedranno visto	vedano	vedessero	vedano visto	vedessero visto

Trapassato Remoto	Futuro Anteriore	Congiuntivo Presente	Congiuntivo Imperfetto	Congiuntivo Passato	Congiuntivo Trapassato
persi perso	perderò perso	perda	perdessi	perda perso	perdessi perso
perdesti perso	perderai perso	perda	perdessi	perda perso	perdessi perso
perse perso	perderà perso	perda	perdesse	perda perso	perdesse perso
perdemmo perso	perderemo perso	perdiamo	perdessimo	perdiamo perso	perdessimo perso
perdeste perso	perderete perso	perdiate	perdeste	perdiate perso	perdeste perso
persero perso	perderanno perso	perdano	perdessero	perdano perso	perdessero perso

	Presente Indicativo	Imperfetto Indicativo	Passato Prossimo	Futuro Semplice	Passato Remoto	Trapassato Prossimo
Io	dormo	dormivo	ho dormito	dormirò	dormii	avevo dormito
Tu	dormi	dormivi	hai dormito	dormirai	dormisti	avevi dormito
Egli	dorme	dormiva	ha dormito	dormirà	dormì	aveva dormito
Noi	dormiamo	dormivamo	abbiamo dormito	dormiremo	dormimmo	avevamo dormito
Voi	dormite	dormivate	avete dormito	dormirete	dormiste	avevate dormito
Essi	dormono	dormivano	hanno dormito	dormiranno	dormirono	avevano dormito

VERB   DORM**IRE**

	Presente Indicativo	Imperfetto Indicativo	Passato Prossimo	Futuro Semplice	Passato Remoto	Trapassato Prossimo
Io	finisco	finivo	ho finito	finirò	finii	avevo finito
Tu	finisci	finivi	hai finito	finirai	finisti	avevi finito
Egli	finisce	finiva	ha finito	finirà	finì	aveva finito
Noi	finiamo	finivamo	abbiamo finito	finiremo	finimmo	avevamo finito
Voi	finite	finivate	avete finito	finirete	finiste	avevate finito
Essi	finiscono	finivano	hanno finito	finiranno	finirono	avevano finito

VERB FIN**IRE**

Trapassato Remoto	Futuro Anteriore	Congiuntivo Presente	Congiuntivo Imperfetto	Congiuntivo Passato	Congiuntivo Trapassato
dormii dormito	dormirò dormito	dorma	dormissi	dorma dormito	dormissi dormito
dormisti dormito	dormirai dormito	dorma	dormissi	dorma dormito	dormissi dormito
dormì dormito	dormirà dormito	dorma	dormisse	dorma dormito	dormisse dormito
dormimmo dormito	dormiremo dormito	dormiamo	dormissimo	dormiamo dormito	dormissimo dormito
dormiste dormito	dormirete dormito	dormiate	dormiste	dormiate dormito	dormiste dormito
dormirono dormito	dormiranno dormito	dormano	dormissero	dormano dormito	dormissero dormito

Trapassato Remoto	Futuro Anteriore	Congiuntivo Presente	Congiuntivo Imperfetto	Congiuntivo Passato	Congiuntivo Trapassato
finii finito	finirò finito	finisca	finissi	finisca finito	finissi finito
finisti finito	finirai finito	finisca	finissi	finisca finito	finissi finito
finì finito	finirà finito	finisca	finisse	finisca finito	finisse finito
finimmo finito	finiremo finito	finiamo	finissimo	finiamo finito	finissimo finito
finiste finito	finirete finito	finiate	finiste	finiate finito	finiste finito
finirono finito	finiranno finito	finiscano	finissero	finiscano finito	finissero finito

SOLUTIONS

Unit 1:

Exercise 1: Fill in the Vowels
Amore - *Love*
Pesce - *Fish*
Casa – *House, Home*
Cena (or Cane) – *Dinner (or Dog)*
Scuola - *School*

Exercise 2: Word Matching
Ciao - Hello
Amico - Friend
Casa - House
Blu - Blue
Gatto – Cat

Exercise 3: Consonant Recognition
Gatto (H)
Cena (S)
Casa (H)
Giorno (S)

Exercise 4: Accent Identification
Circle: perché, è, sé

Exercise 5: Conjugating "Essere" - Fill in the Blanks
Io sono felice.
Tu sei mio amico.
Loro sono insegnanti.
Noi siamo a casa.
Lei è intelligente.

Exercise 6: True or False – Basic Greetings
False ("Buonasera" means "Good evening.")
True
True
False ("Come ti chiami?" means "What's your name?")

Exercise 7: Link the Regions with Their Capitals
Tuscany - Florence
Lombardy - Milan
Lazio - Rome
Veneto – Venice

Exercise 8: Cultural Etiquette - Choose the Right Option
B) Shake hands
A) Bring a small gift

Unit 2:

Exercise 1: Fill in the Blanks - Numbers 1-10
Due
Cinque
Otto
Dieci
Uno

Exercise 2: Match the Number to its Italian Name
14 - B. Quattordici
19 - C. Diciannove
16 - A. Sedici

Exercise 3: Days of the Week Ordering
Lunedì
Martedì
Mercoledì
Giovedì
Venerdì
Sabato
Domenica

Exercise 4: Translate the Months
Gennaio
Aprile
Luglio
Ottobre

Exercise 5: Complete the Sentence - Basic Vocabulary
"Quanto"
"bagno"
"___" (student fills in their name)

Exercise 6: Verb Conjugation - ARE Verbs
Io gioco
Tu giochi
Loro giocano

Exercise 7: Identify the Meal
Breakfast - La Colazione
Lunch - Il Pranzo
Dinner - La Cena
Exercise 8: Cultural Understanding
Natale - B. Christmas
Carnevale - A. Festivities before Lent
Pasqua - C. Easter

Unit 3:

Exercise 1: Complete with Correct Articles - Solutions
La pizza è deliziosa.
Ho visto un cane in strada.
Dove è lo zucchero?.
Gli uomini mangiano le arance.
L'amica di Maria è molto simpatica.
Vorrei una birra e dell'acqua minerale, per favore.
I bambini giocano nel parco.
Ho comprato un libro interessante ieri.

Exercise 2: Menu Translation - Solutions
Roasted chicken
Mixed salad
Baked lasagna
Vanilla ice cream
Mixed appetizers
Pesto pasta
Fried calamari
Italian espresso

Exercise 3: Identify the Mistake - Solutions
"La ragazza ha un gatto." (The girl has a cat.)
"Ho ordinato la pasta al ristorante." (I ordered the pasta at the restaurant.)
"Vorrei una acqua frizzante." (I would like a sparkling water.)
"L'uva è dolce." (The grape is sweet.)
"Maria ha visitato la Francia l'anno scorso." (Maria visited France last year.)
"Ho visto l'elefante allo zoo." (I saw the elephant at the zoo.)
"Gli studenti studiano italiano." (The students study Italian.)
"Un amico di Paolo è qui." (A friend of Paolo is here.)

Unit 4:

Exercise 1: Fill in the Blanks
Vado alla scuola.
Il libro del ragazzo è interessante.
Ho visto un gatto nel cesto.
Lei viene dalla stazione.

Exercise 2: Translation
Vado al mercato.
Il gatto è sulla sedia.
Ci sono molti alberi nel parco.
Il libro del insegnante.

Exercise 3: True or False
Ci sono un cane nel parco. (False)
C'è molte macchine in strada. (False)
C'è un ristorante buono qui vicino. (True)
Ci sono una penna sul tavolo. (False)

Exercise 4: Matching
Dove si trova la stazione? - d. Where is the station?
Vado alla spiaggia. - b. I go to the beach.
C'è un treno alle 10. - a. There is a train at 10.
Il suono degli uccelli. - c. The sound of the birds.

Exercise 5: Sentence Creation
Example sentences (students' sentences may vary):
Nel libro ci sono molte storie interessanti.
Aspetto l'autobus alla fermata dell'autobus.
Le foto delle vacanze sono sullo schermo.
La festa degli amici è domani.

Exercise 6: Correct the Mistakes
Vado a Roma.
Le chiavi sono sul tavolo.
C'è una bella piazza in città.
Ci sono molte persone qui.

Exercise 7: Articulate Prepositions Practice
Il regalo è dallo zio.
Ho comprato una bici dal negozio.

Lavoro nell' ufficio.
Il cane dorme sul letto.

Exercise 8: Singular vs. Plural
C'è una lettera per te sulla scrivania.
Ci sono molti libri interessanti in biblioteca.
C'è un telefono nella borsa?
Ci sono tre finestre in questa stanza.

Unit 5:

Exercise 1. Translation Practice:
a. "Ciao, come ti chiami?"
b. "Sono di Londra."
c. "Mi piace ascoltare la musica."
d. "Vuoi andare in spiaggia domani?"
e. "Sono sorpreso/a di vederti qui."

Exercise 2. Fill in the Blanks:
a. "Ciao, come ti chiami?"
b. "Sono di [nome della città], ma vivo a Roma."
c. "Ti va di andare a [nome del posto] stasera?"
d. "Ho [fame/sete] di andare in vacanza."
e. "Quanti anni hai?"

Exercise 3. Matching Exercise:
a. (2) "What hobbies do you have?"
b. (4) "I am sad."
c. (3) "I'm sorry."
d. (1) "I am happy."

Exercise 4. Fill in the Blanks:
a. "Quando sono triste, mi piace ascoltare musica."
b. "Se hai freddo, posso prestare il mio cappotto."
c. "In estate, spesso ho sete."
d. "Ogni mattina, mi sveglio alle sette."
e. "Non vedo l'ora di andare al parco domani!"

Exercise 5. Conjugation Exercise:
Io ho (I have)
Tu hai (You have)
Lui/Lei ha (He/She has)
Noi abbiamo (We have)

Voi avete (You all have)
Loro hanno (They have)

Exercise 6. Matching Exercise:
a. (2) "I am from Rome."
b. (1) "I feel so-so."
c. (3) "Do you want to go to the cinema tonight?"
d. (4) "I am twenty years old."
e. (5) "Do we have time for a coffee?"

Exercise 7. Find the Mistake:
a. Correct: "Hai fratelli o sorelle?"
b. Correct: "Noi abbiamo sonno."
c. Correct Response: "Sì, mi piace."
d. Correct: "Loro hanno sete e fame."
e. Correct: "Sono felice perché ho trovato il mio gatto."

Exercise 8. Fill in the Blanks (Grammar Focus):
a. "Io ho una bicicletta nuova."
b. "Tu hai ragione su questo argomento."
c. "Lui ha un appuntamento alle tre."
d. "Noi abbiamo fretta stamattina."
e. "Voi avete i compiti da fare?"
f. "Loro hanno molte idee per la festa."

Unit 6:

Exercise 1
(Io) non parlo francese.
(Tu) non hai il cane.
(Lui) non vede il film.
(Noi) non mangiamo carne.
(Voi) non leggete quel libro.
(Lei) non capisce la domanda.
(Essi) non giocano a calcio.
(Io) non bevo caffè.

Exercise 2
Non vedo nessuno.
Non abbiamo niente da fare.
Non c'è nessuno qui.
Non ho ricevuto nessun messaggio.
Non conosco nessuno in questa città.

Non trovo niente nel cassetto.
Non ho visto niente interessante.
Non ho parlato con nessuno oggi.

Exercise 3
Bambino alto
Scarpe vecchie
Gatto nero
Libri interessanti
Casa grande
Amica simpatica
Studenti gentili
Città bella

Exercise 4
Una scuola grande (Correct: grande)
I gatti bianca (Correct: bianchi)
Le ragazze simpatico (Correct: simpatiche)
Un libro interessanti (Correct: interessante)
Le case piccolo (Correct: piccole)
Un'amica gentile (Correct: gentile)
I ragazzi alto (Correct: alti)
Le penne nuovo (Correct: nuove)

Exercise 5
(Io) lo vedo.
(Tu) lo leggi.
(Lui) la mangia.
(Noi) le abbiamo.
(Voi) le scrivete.
(Lei) li compra.
(Essi) lo vedono.
(Io) la ascolto.

Exercise 6
Mi dai il libro?
Posso chiedere un favore a te?
Ho comprato un regalo per lei.
Vuoi parlare con noi?
Devo inviare una mail a gli.
Racconta la storia a me.
Mandiamo un messaggio a loro.
Chiedo scusa a te.

Exercise 7

Questa è la mia macchina.

Ho perso le mie chiavi.

Il nostro insegnante è molto bravo.

Dove sono i vostri libri?

Mia sorella arriva domani.

Il nostro giardino è bellissimo.

Il tuo amico chiama.

La loro decisione è finale.

Exercise 8

Preferisci questo gelato o quella torta?

Questo libro è interessante, ma quello è noioso.

Guarda quello cane! È così carino.

Non mi piace questo film; preferisco quello abbiamo visto ieri.

Questo maglione è troppo grande per me.

Questi esercizi sono più facili di quelli di ieri.

Hai letto quell' articolo sul giornale?

Queste penne scrivono meglio di quelle.

Unit 7:

Exercise 1

Dove

Come

Quando

Perché

Come

Quanto

Quanto

Cosa

Exercise 2

Come - (3) How

Perché - (4) Why

Quanto - (7) How much/How many

Dove - (5) Where

Chi - (6) Who

Cosa - (1) What

Quando - (2) When

Exercise 3

Quanto tempo abbiamo per completare il progetto? (Quanto)

Quanto zucchero metti nel caffè? (Quanto)

Quanti ragazzi vengono alla festa? (Quanti)

Quante sorelle hai? (Quante)
Quanto costa la maglietta? (Quanto)
Quante pagine deve avere il saggio? (Quante)
Quanta distanza c'è tra Milano e Venezia? (Quanta)
Quante persone hanno confermato la loro presenza? (Quante)

Exercise 4
Chi è andato al cinema? (Corrected: Chi è andato)
Quando fai colazione? (Corrected: Quando)
Dove è il mio telefono? (Corrected as a statement, but it's technically correct as a question)
Perché non ti piace mangiare fuori? (Corrected as a statement, but it's technically correct as a question)
Come si dice "book" in italiano? (Corrected as a statement, but it's technically correct as a question)
Quanto costano queste scarpe? (Corrected: costano queste)
Cosa fai stasera? (Corrected as a statement, but it's technically correct as a question)
Chi è il tuo migliore amico? (Corrected as a statement, but it's technically correct as a question)

Exercise 5
A Maria piace la pasta.
A noi piacciono guardare film d'azione.
A te piacciono i fiori?
A loro piace leggere libri di avventura.
A me non piace il freddo in inverno.
A voi piacciono le vacanze al mare?
A Giorgio piace giocare a calcio.
A me piacciono molto i dolci italiani.

Exercise 6
Lui vuole visitare il museo domani.
Noi dobbiamo studiare per l'esame.
Voi potete andare al concerto stasera?
Lei deve parlare con il professore dopo la lezione.
Io posso prendere in prestito il tuo libro?
Tu devi lavorare fino a tardi oggi?
Elisa e Marco vogliono comprare una nuova casa.
Voi dovete assistere alla riunione domani?

Exercise 7
Quante lingue puoi parlare?
Quando dobbiamo consegnare il rapporto?
Cosa vuoi per il tuo compleanno?
Perché vanno in Italia?
Dove posso comprare i biglietti?
Chi vuole andare in spiaggia?

Come posso imparare l'italiano velocemente?
Perché non ti piace il caffè?

Exercise 8
Non sa cucinare? (Correct format: Sai cucinare?)
Non abbiamo tempo per vedere un film? (Correct format: Abbiamo tempo per vedere un film?)
Non sono felici qui? (Correct format: Sono felici qui?)
Non hai letto questo libro? (Correct format: Hai letto questo libro?)
Non possiamo arrivare presto? (Correct format: Possiamo arrivare presto?)
Non avete un cane? (Correct format: Avete un cane?)
Non capisce l'inglese? (Correct format: Capisce l'inglese?)
Non devo andare ora? (Correct format: Devo andare ora?)

Unit 8:
Exercise 1: Solutions
Io mi alzo alle 6 ogni mattina.
Tu ti lavi le mani prima di mangiare.
Lei si pettina i capelli dopo la doccia.
Noi ci addormentiamo dopo mezzanotte.
Voi vi svegliate presto durante la settimana.
Loro si vestono in fretta per la scuola.
Marco si rilassa nel weekend.
Le ragazze si truccano prima di uscire.

Exercise 2: Solutions
Lavare - D. Lavarsi
Vestire - C. Vestirsi
Svegliare - E. Svegliarsi
Addormentare - A. Addormentarsi
Truccare - F. Truccarsi
Rilassare - G. Rilassarsi
Alzare - B. Alzarsi
Preparare - H. Prepararsi

Exercise 3: Solutions
(Tu) Dormire - A. Dormi!
(Noi) Partire - A. Partiamo!
(Voi) Stare - B. State!
(Tu) Venire - A. Vieni!
(Noi) Fare - C. Facciamo!
(Tu) Dire - A. Dici!
(Voi) Avere - A. Avete!
(Tu) Andare - A. Vai!

Exercise 4: Solutions
Loro si svegliano presto ogni mattina.
Tu ti vesti dopo aver fatto la doccia.
Noi ci laviamo le mani prima di pranzare.
Voi vi rilassate nel fine settimana.
Lei si addormenta leggendo un libro.
Io mi preparo velocemente la mattina.
Lui si trucca prima di uscire.
Noi ci alziamo tardi la domenica.

Exercise 5: Solutions
Vorrei andare al cinema, ma piove.
Mangio la pizza perché mi piace molto.
Lavoro il sabato, ma la domenica riposo.
Studia italiano perché vuole viaggiare in Italia.
Ha freddo, quindi mette un maglione.
Vieni alla festa o no?
Parla sia inglese che spagnolo.
Poiché ha fatto tardi, non usciremo.

Exercise 6: Solutions
Io mi vesto rapidamente ogni mattina.
Tu ti lavi prima di andare a letto.
Lei si trucca per la cena fuori.
Noi ci rilassiamo dopo il lavoro.
Voi vi preparate per l'esame domani.
Loro si svegliano all'alba.
Marco si allena in palestra.
Le ragazze si divertono al concerto.

Exercise 7: Solutions
Io mi lavo → Non mi lavo.
Tu ti vesti → Non ti vesti.
Lei si trucca → Non si trucca.
Noi ci rilassiamo → Non ci rilassiamo.
Voi vi preparate → Non vi preparate.
Loro si svegliano → Non si svegliano.
Marco si allena → Non si allena.
Le ragazze si divertono → Non si divertono.

Exercise 8: Solutions
Parlare (tu, affirmative) + lo = Parlalo!
Non mangiare (tu, negative) + la = Non la mangiare!
Scrivere (noi, affirmative) + le = Scriviamole!

Non prendere (voi, negative) + li = Non li prendete!
Leggere (tu, affirmative) + lo = Leggilo!
Non vendere (tu, negative) + la = Non la vendere!
Aprire (noi, affirmative) + lo = Apriamolo!
Non chiudere (voi, negative) + le = Non le chiudete!

Unit 9:

Exercise 1
sempre
di solito
spesso
mai
a volte
raramente
quasi mai
spesso

Exercise 2
Molto - A. Much/Many
Qualche - C. Some/Few
Poco - D. Little/Few
Tanto - E. So Much/So Many
Troppo - F. Too Much/Too Many
Ogni - B. Every
Alcuni - A. Some/Several (Masculine)
Pochi - D. Few

Exercise 3
troppi -> troppo
qualche -> alcune
molti -> molta
pochi -> poche volte
troppi -> troppo
spesso -> spesso un
qualche -> alcune
molti -> molti

Exercise 4
molti
molta
poco
pochi

molto
poche
poco
molti

Exercise 5
a
a
via
su
fuori
a
di
fuori

Exercise 6
andavo
ho visitato
suonavo
ho avuto
raccontava
ero
ho fatto
giocavo

Exercise 7
faccio fuori
sono andato via
sono tornato indietro
sono andata
abbiamo fatto fuori
sono andato
sono tornato
ho fatto fuori

Exercise 8
molta
pochi
alcuni
Ogni
troppo
molti
poco
tanti

Unit 10:
Exercise 1
Il caffè è più amaro del tè.
Questo film è meno interessante di quello che abbiamo visto ieri.
Luca corre più veloce di Matteo.
Il gatto è meno intelligente del cane.
La bicicletta è meno costosa della moto.
Questo libro è meno noioso di quello.
Lei è tanto bella quanto sua cugina.
L'appartamento è così grande come la casa.

Exercise 2
È la torta più buona che abbia mai mangiato.
Questo è il museo più visitato della città.
Sono le scarpe più comode che ho.
È l'insegnante più apprezzato dagli studenti.
Questa è la strada più corta per arrivare al parco.
Sono i fiori più belli del giardino.
È il lavoro meno stressante che abbia mai avuto.
Questo è il periodo più caldo dell'anno.

Exercise 3
Mangiare - D. Mangiando
Scrivere - C. Scrivendo
Leggere - B. Leggendo
Partire - A. Partendo
Dormire - E. Dormendo
Sentire - F. Sentendo
Capire - G. Capendo (Note: The correct gerund form for "capire" is actually "capendo," but it's rarely used; "capiendo" is not standard Italian.)
Finire - H. Finendo

Exercise 4
La macchina è più veloce della bicicletta.
Sto leggendo il giornale leggendo attentamente. (Corrected to: "Sto leggendo il giornale attentamente.")
Questo è il più piccolo di quella stanza. (Corrected to: "Questo è il più piccolo della stanza.")
Penso spesso a quella vacanza. (Corrected to: "Ci penso spesso a quella vacanza.")
Vorrei dell'uva dal mercato.
Sto ascoltando la musica mentre lavoro. (Corrected to: "Sto ascoltando musica mentre lavoro.")

Exercise 5
Ne
Ci

Ne
Ci
Ci
Ne
Ci
Ne

Exercise 6
Posso avere del latte?
Ho comprato degli occhiali nuovi.
Vorrei dei pomodori per l'insalata.
Hai bisogno di dell' aiuto?
Ci sono dei libri sul tavolo che potrebbero interessarti.
Vorrei delle informazioni sul corso.
Serve ancora della farina per la torta?
Posso offrirti dei biscotti?

Exercise 7
A. Action happening simultaneously
C. To express a cause or reason
A. Action happening simultaneously
C. To express a cause or reason
A. Action happening simultaneously
C. To express a cause or reason
A. Action happening simultaneously
B. As a verbal adverb

Exercise 8
D. e ne vorrei un chilo.
B. quindi ci andiamo domani.
C. e ci esercito ogni giorno.
A. e ne ho visto uno bellissimo.
E. perché ci piace di più.
F. quindi ne ho bisogno di nuovi.
G. quindi ci vestiamo più leggeri.
H. e ne compro sempre qui.

Unit 11:

Exercise 1
prima di
durante
dopo

prima di
dopo
durante
dopo
prima di

Exercise 2
A. I need to drink water.
B. Do you want to come to the cinema with me?
C. We need to wake up early tomorrow.
D. May I use your phone?
E. I need to finish this work by today.
F. I would like some ice cream.
G. It might rain later.
H. We have been studying Italian for three months.

Exercise 3
per
tra/fra
da
per
tra/fra
da
per
per

Exercise 4
Ho bisogno di riposare dopo il lavoro.
Voglio un caffè durante la mattina.
Devo studiare italiano da due anni.
Posso venire da te tra cinque minuti.
Vorrei andare al parco durante il pomeriggio.
Dobbiamo finire il progetto per lunedì.
Può essere freddo in dicembre.
Sono in Italia da tre giorni.

Exercise 5
Studio l'italiano da gennaio.
Ci incontreremo tra tre giorni.
Lei ha bisogno di riposare per un'ora.
Posso entrare?
Devo studiare stasera.
Loro vogliono viaggiare l'anno prossimo.
Bisogna mangiare sano.

So cucinare.

Exercise 6
voglio
puoi
deve
vogliamo
potete
devono
Posso
vuoi

Exercise 7
D. need
B. desire
A. obligation
C. permission or ability
E. ability or knowledge

Exercise 8
Devo andare al supermercato oggi. (devo)
Vuoi venire a pranzo con noi? (vuoi)
Posso chiederti un favore? (posso)
Lei sa parlare tre lingue. (sa)
Vogliamo partire alle nove. (vogliamo)
Devi completare questi documenti. (devi)
Possono giocare fuori dopo i compiti. (possono)
Sapete dove si trova la stazione? (sapete)

Unit 12:

Exercise 1:
Marco ha detto, "Sono stanco."
"Vado al cinema stasera," ha detto Lucia.
"Non voglio mangiare," ha detto Giovanni.
"Sono felice di vederti," ha detto Marta.
"Domani parto per Parigi," ha detto Anna.
"Vieni con me al concerto?" ha chiesto Carlo.
"Mi piace questa casa," ha detto Laura.
"Dove hai messo le chiavi?" ha chiesto Luca.

Exercise 2:
Luca ha detto che aveva fame.

Sara ha detto che stava arrivando.
Marco ha detto che andavano al parco il giorno seguente.
Giovanni ha detto che ti amava.
Paolo ha detto che aveva vinto la partita.
Maria ha detto di prendere un ombrello.
Elena ha detto che aveva comprato un regalo per te.
Antonio ha detto che ti avrebbe chiamato più tardi.

Exercise 3:
Avere la testa tra le nuvole - A. To have one's head in the clouds
Costare un occhio della testa - B. To cost an arm and a leg
Non vedere l'ora - C. To can't wait
Essere in gamba - D. To be competent/skilled
Mettere il carro davanti ai buoi - E. To put the cart before the horse
Rompere il ghiaccio - F. To break the ice
Far ridere i polli - G. To make the chickens laugh
Avere le mani in pasta - H. To have one's hands in the dough

Exercise 4:
Io me ne vado via domani.
Loro si lavano ogni mattina.
Lei si mette la giacca prima di uscire.
Voi vi vestite bene per la festa.
Noi ci arrabbiamo con quella situazione.

Exercise 5:
Marco ha detto che era stanco.
Lei ha detto che andava al mercato.
Anna ha detto che arrivava presto.
Paolo ha detto che voleva mangiare.
Maria ha detto che usciva con gli amici.

Exercise 6:
Mi ci vado domani.
Ne abbiamo parlato.
Non ti preoccupare, tutto va bene.
Vi incontreremo al ristorante.
Ci penserò io.
Si divertono molto insieme.
Vi conosco bene.
Mi piace questo libro.

Exercise 7:
Mettere il carro davanti ai buoi

Non vedere l'ora
Avere la testa tra le nuvole
Avere le mani in pasta
Essere pan per i suoi denti

Exercise 8:
"Andrò al supermercato," ha detto Maria.
"Puoi aiutarmi?" chiese Paolo.
"Sarò in ritardo," disse Giovanni.
"Voglio andare al mare," disse Laura.
"Dov'è il mio telefono?" chiese Luca.
"Mi piace molto questo film," disse Marco.
"Vieni con me al concerto," chiese Elena.
"Stasera c'è una festa," disse Sara.

Unit 13:

Exercise 1:
Viaggeremo
Aprirà
Imparerete
Scriverò
Compreranno
Finirai
Prenderemo
Canterà

Exercise 2:
Se io avessi più tempo, viaggerei in tutto il mondo.
Loro vorrebbero andare al cinema se non fosse troppo tardi.
Se tu sapessi la risposta, me lo diresti?
Io comprerei una nuova casa se avessi abbastanza soldi.
Lei farebbe una torta se avesse gli ingredienti.

Exercise 3:
Noi - studi
Tu - mangi
Loro - dormano
Io - legga
Lei - abbia
Voi - scriviate
Io - parli
Loro – parlino

Exercise 4:
Voglio che tu sia felice.
È importante che noi impariamo l'italiano.
È essenziale che lei faccia esercizio ogni giorno.
È necessario che voi aiutiate i vostri genitori.
È fondamentale che loro rispettino le regole.
Io preferirei che tu venissi con noi.
È meglio che lui non mangi troppo dolci.
È importante che voi prestiate attenzione in classe.

Exercise 5:
giocavo
andavano
mangiavi
guardavamo
leggeva
visitavate
scrivevo
facevano

Exercise 6:
Imperfect: 1, 3, 5, 6, 8
Perfect: 2, 4, 7

Exercise 7:
Se avessi più tempo, imparerei a suonare il piano.
Lui avrà finito i compiti prima di cena.
Andremmo alla spiaggia se il tempo fosse bello.
Lei vorrebbe parlare fluentemente francese.
Viaggerebbero per il mondo se avessero abbastanza soldi.

Exercise 8:
Faresti
Compreremmo
Andrebbero
Sceglierei
Fareste
Potrebbe
Vorremmo

Italian Phrasebook For
Beginners

Learn Common Phrases In Context With
Explanations For Everyday Use and Travel

Worldwide Nomad

UNIT 1
Getting Started

Vocabulary:

- Basic Greetings and Introductions:

Ciao	Hello/Goodbye
Buongiorno	Good morning
Buonasera	Good evening
Mi chiamo...	My name is...
Come ti chiami?	What's your name?
Piacere	Nice to meet you

Culture:

- Overview of Italy: Regions and Major Cities

Italy, a European country with a long Mediterranean coastline, has left a powerful mark on Western culture and cuisine. The country is divided into 20 regions, each boasting its own unique identity, culture, and traditions. This rich diversity makes Italy a fascinating place to explore, both geographically and culturally.

- Piedmont (Turin): Piedmont, located in the northwest corner of Italy, is a region surrounded on three sides by the Alps, including the Monviso (where the Po River originates) and the Monte Rosa. It borders France, Switzerland, and the Italian regions of Lombardy, Liguria, Aosta Valley, and Emilia-Romagna. Turin, former and first Italian capital, is now the capital of Piedmont, is known for its refined architecture and cuisine. The Alps form a majestic backdrop to this elegant city, which is characterized by grand boulevards and palaces, old-world cafés, and art nouveau architecture.

- Lombardy (Milan): Lombardy, in northern Italy, is a powerhouse of the country's economy and home to its financial capital, Milan. Milan is not just a global fashion hub; it's also known for its high-end dining and shopping scenes, historical and modern architecture, and significant artworks like Leonardo da Vinci's "The Last Supper."

- Lazio (Rome): Lazio, with Rome as its crown jewel, is steeped in history. Rome, the capital city, is often referred to as the "Eternal City." It's a sprawling, cosmopolitan city with nearly 3,000 years of globally influential art, architecture, and culture on display. Ancient ruins such as the Forum and the Colosseum evoke the power of the former Roman Empire.

- Tuscany (Florence): Tuscany is world-renowned for its landscapes, artistic heritage, and influence on high culture. Florence, its capital, is home to many masterpieces of Renaissance art and architecture. One of its most iconic sights is the Duomo, a cathedral with a terracotta-tiled dome engineered by Brunelleschi and a bell tower designed by Giotto.

- ◦ Veneto (Venice): Veneto is famous for Venice, the "City of Canals." This region combines beautiful landscapes with rich historic and cultural heritage. Venice is known for its canals, Gothic and Renaissance architecture, and notable artworks. It's also famous for its Venetian glass and lace, and the Venice Film Festival.

Other notable regions include Sicily, with its rich history and unique cultural blend; and Emilia-Romagna, home to culinary treasures like Parmesan cheese and balsamic vinegar.

- • Italian Etiquette and Manners: Greetings

Italians are renowned for their expressive communication and warm greetings. In Italy, greetings are considered an important part of social etiquette.

- ◦ Handshakes: Upon meeting someone, it's common to exchange a firm handshake with direct eye contact. Handshakes signify respect and are typical in professional contexts or when meeting someone for the first time.

- ◦ Hugs and Kisses: Friends and family often greet each other with a warm embrace or a light kiss on each cheek, starting from the right. This gesture, while common, varies depending on the region and personal preferences.

- ◦ Using "Lei" and "Tu": In Italian, there are formal ("Lei") and informal ("tu") forms of address. "Lei" is used in formal situations, with strangers, or with elders as a sign of respect. "Tu" is used among friends, family, and peers. It's crucial for learners of Italian to understand this distinction to navigate social interactions appropriately.

- ◦ Additional Tips: Italians appreciate punctuality but are also understanding of slight delays. When invited to someone's home, it's customary to bring a small gift, such as a dessert or wine. Table manners are important – keep your hands visible (not on your lap) and try to finish everything on your plate.

UNIT 2
Daily Life

Vocabulary:

- ◦ Greetings Part II and Common Expressions

Come stai?	How are you?
Bene, grazie!	Fine, thank you!
Scusa!	Excuse me - informal
Scusi!	Excuse me - formal
Per favore	Please
Grazie!	Thank you
Di nulla/Prego	You're welcome
Mi chiamo...	My name is...
Piacere!	Nice to meet you!
Dove è il bagno?	Where is the bathroom?
Quanto costa?	How much does it cost?

- ◦ Shopping and Dining

Vorrei...	I would like...
Il conto, per favore.	The bill, please.
Acqua	Water
Vino	Wine
Birra	Beer
Caffè	Espresso

Culture:

- • Italian Daily Routine

The rhythm of daily life in Italy is a fascinating blend of tradition, culture, and modernity. Understanding the typical Italian daily routine provides insight into the Italian way of life.

- ◦ La Colazione (Breakfast)

The day in Italy usually begins with 'la colazione' (lah coh-lah-TZEE-oh-neh), a typically light breakfast. This meal often consists of a cappuccino or espresso accompanied by a cornetto (kohr-NET-toh) or other pastries. Italians prefer to start their day with something simple and sweet.

- ◦ La Mattina (Morning Activities)

Mornings, 'la mattina' (lah mah-TEEN-ah), are generally dedicated to work or school. In smaller towns and rural areas, the pace can be more leisurely, with a strong emphasis on community and social interaction.

- ○ Il Pranzo (Lunch)

Lunch, 'il pranzo' (eel PRAHN-zoh), is a significant meal in Italy and is typically enjoyed from 1 PM to 2:30 PM. This meal may consist of several courses, including antipasti (ahn-tee-PAH-stee), primo (PREE-moh), secondo (seh-KOHN-doh), contorni (kohn-TOHR-nee), and dolci (DOHL-chee).

- ○ La Pausa (The Midday Break)

'La pausa' (lah POW-sah), the midday break, is a cherished tradition in Italy. This break allows people to relax after lunch, spend time with family, or take a short nap ('pisolino' [pee-zoh-LEE-noh]).

- ○ Il Pomeriggio (Afternoon)

After the pause, the afternoon, or 'il pomeriggio' (eel poh-meh-REE-joh), is a time for work or leisure activities. This time is also popular for a leisurely walk or 'passeggiata' (pahs-seh-JAH-tah).

- ○ La Cena (Dinner)

Dinner, 'la cena' (lah CHEH-nah), is typically a lighter meal than lunch and is served later, often between 8 PM and 10 PM. It is a social event, an opportunity to gather with family or friends.

- Italian Holidays and Festivals

- ○ Natale (Christmas)

'Natale' (nah-TAH-leh), Christmas, is celebrated with family gatherings, special meals, and religious observances. Traditional foods include 'panettone' (pah-neht-TOH-neh) and 'pandoro' (pahn-DOH-roh).

- ○ Pasqua (Easter)

Easter, 'Pasqua' (PAHS-kwah), is marked with various traditions, such as the consumption of 'colomba' (kohl-OHM-bah), and special masses.

- ○ Carnevale (Carnival)

'Carnevale' (kahr-neh-VAH-leh), celebrated before Lent, is a time of festivities and parades. The Venice Carnival is particularly renowned.

◦ Other Festivals

Italy is home to numerous local festivals and celebrations, each with its own unique traditions and customs, like the Palio di Siena horse race and various food festivals.

Understanding these aspects of Italian culture enhances not only the language learning experience but also provides a deeper appreciation of the rich cultural tapestry of Italy.

UNIT 3
Food and Dining

Vocabulary:

- Basic Food Vocabulary:

In this section, we start by introducing basic Italian food items. We'll cover fruits ('frutta'), vegetables ('verdura'), meats ('carne'), and beverages ('bevande'). Alongside each item, you'll find a pronunciation guide to help you master the correct Italian pronunciation.

- ○ **Fruits (Frutta):**
  In Italy, fruits are cherished for their freshness and natural sweetness. You'll find a variety of 'frutta' in Italian markets, from the common 'mela' (apple) with its crisp texture, to the succulent 'pesca' (peach) that symbolizes summer in Italy. Other popular fruits include 'arancia' (orange), known for its juicy zest, and 'limone' (lemon), essential in many Italian recipes

Mela	Apple	MEH-lah
Pera	Pear	PEH-rah
Banana	Banana	bah-NAH-nah
Arancia	Orange	ah-RAN-chah
Limone	Lemon	LEE-moh-neh
Pesca	Peach	PEHS-kah
Fico	Fig	FEE-ko

- ○ **Vegetables (Verdura):**
  Vegetables, or 'verdura', are the heart of many Italian dishes. The 'pomodoro' (tomato), with its bright red color and versatile use, is a staple. 'Carota' (carrot) and 'lattuga' (lettuce) are common in salads, while 'melanzana' (eggplant) is a key ingredient in dishes like 'parmigiana.'

Carota	Carrot	kah-ROH-tah
Lattuga	Lettuce	LAT-too-gah
Pomodoro	Tomato	poh-moh-DOH-ro
Cipolla	Onion	chee-POHL-lah
Patata	Potato	pah-TAH-tah
Melanzana	Eggplant	meh-lahn-ZAH-nah

- ○ **Meats (Carne):**
  Meat plays a significant role in Italian cuisine, with each region having its specialties. 'Pollo' (chicken) and 'manzo' (beef) are widely used, while 'maiale' (pork) is often seen in cured forms like 'prosciutto.' Coastal areas favor 'pesce' (fish), fresh and often simply prepared.

Pollo	Chicken	POHL-lo
Manzo	Beef	MAHN-zoh
Maiale	Pork	mah-YAH-leh
Agnello	Lamb	ah-NYEH-lo
Pesce	Fish	PEH-sheh

Italy's beverages, 'bevande', are as integral as its food. 'Vino' (wine) is a cultural icon, varying from robust reds to crisp whites. 'Caffè' (coffee), particularly espresso, is a daily ritual, while 'acqua' (water), often sparkling, complements every meal.

Acqua	Water	AHK-kwah
Vino	Wine	VEE-no
Birra	Beer	BEER-rah
Caffè	Coffee	kah-FEH
Succo	Juice	SOOK-koh

- Ordering in a Restaurant and Expressing Preferences and Allergies.

  ◦ **Basic Phrases:**

Un tavolo per due, per favore	A table for two, please	oon TAH-voh-loh per DOO-eh per fah-VOH-reh
Vorrei il menù, per favore	I would like the menu, please	vor-RAY eel meh-NOO per fah-VOH-reh
Vorrei ordinare, per favore	I would like to order, please	vor-RAY or-dee-NAH-reh per fah-VOH-reh
Il conto, per favore	The bill, please	eel KOHN-toh per fah-VOH-reh

  ◦ **Expressing Preferences and Allergies:**

Mi piace la pizza	I like pizza	mee PYAH-cheh lah PEE-tzah
Non mi piace il pesce	I don't like fish	non mee PYAH-cheh eel PEH-sheh
Sono allergico a...	I am allergic to...	SOH-noh al-ler-JEE-koh ah...
Non posso mangiare...	I cannot eat...	non POHS-soh man-JAH-reh...

Culture:

Italian cuisine is not just a display of recipes; it's a narrative of flavors, local ingredients, and age-old traditions. At the heart of this culinary philosophy is the emphasis on fresh, locally sourced ingredients. Italians take great pride in using produce that is in season and sourced from local suppliers, believing that the quality and authenticity of each ingredient play a crucial role in the final taste of the dish.

- Fresh Local Ingredients: The Soul of Italian Cooking

In every region, you'll find markets bustling with vendors selling fresh fruits, vegetables, meats, and cheeses, each item boasting a history and a connection to the land. The use of these fresh, local ingredients isn't just a preference; it's a deeply ingrained cultural practice that respects the natural cycle of the seasons. This approach ensures that every dish is a reflection of the region's unique environment and cultural heritage.

- Regional Culinary Variations

Each Italian region has its own specialties, shaped by its geography and history. From the risottos and polentas of the North, rich in dairy and grains, to the olive oil-drenched dishes of Central Italy, and the sun-kissed fruits and seafood of the South, Italian cuisine is a mosaic of flavors.

  - The North: A Symphony of Creamy Risottos and Hearty Polentas
    In the cooler climes of the North, cuisine is characterized by hearty ingredients such as corn, rice, and dairy products. Lombardy is renowned for its risotto, a creamy rice dish often infused with saffron, as in the famous Risotto alla Milanese. Moving to the mountains, polenta, a cornmeal porridge, becomes a staple, served with rich stews and cheeses.

  - Central Italy: The Heartland of Olive Oils and Rustic Flavors
    Tuscany and Umbria, the heartlands of Italy, boast a cuisine that is simple yet rich in flavors. Olive oil is the star, drizzled over crusty breads in a traditional bruschetta or used to cook classic dishes like Florentine steak. The region's love for legumes and vegetables is evident in soups like Ribollita and pasta dishes like Pici al cacio e pepe.

  - The South: A Celebration of Sun-Kissed Produce and Seafood
    As we travel further south, the warmth of the Mediterranean sun blesses the cuisine with an abundance of fresh vegetables, citrus fruits, and seafood. Naples, the birthplace of pizza, offers the authentic Pizza Margherita, with its simple yet perfect combination of tomatoes, mozzarella, and basil. Sicily adds to the culinary mosaic with its Arab-influenced dishes like the sweet-and-sour Caponata.

Dining Etiquette

Understanding Italian dining etiquette is crucial to fully appreciate the country's food culture. Meals in Italy are not just about food; they're a social affair, a time to enjoy the company of family and friends.

- The Structure of an Italian Meal

  A typical Italian meal is an art form, structured in several courses. It starts with 'antipasti' (appetizers), followed by 'primo' (first course, usually pasta or rice), 'secondo' (main course, meat or fish), 'contorni' (side dishes), and ends with 'dolci' (desserts). Each course is meant to be savored, and there's an unspoken rhythm to the progression of dishes.

  ○ The Timing of Meals: Influenced by Latitude

    Italian meal times can vary significantly from region to region, often influenced by geographical location. In the North, dinner might be served earlier, aligning with cooler climates and earlier sunsets. As one moves south, dinner times become progressively later, especially in the summer months where eating late in the evening is a respite from the day's heat.

- Table Manners and Practices

  Table manners in Italy are formal yet relaxed. Always use utensils, and remember that bread is typically not served with butter. It's common to use bread to 'fare la scarpetta', or mop up sauce from your plate. During a meal, conversation is lively, and it's customary to wait for everyone to be served before starting to eat. Wine plays a crucial role, often specifically paired with dishes, enhancing the dining experience.

- The Italian Approach to Eating Out

  Eating out in Italy is a leisurely experience. Italians value the quality of food and the ambiance of the restaurant over speed. It's common for meals to last a couple of hours, especially dinner. When dining out, remember to ask for the bill; it's considered rude for the waiter to bring it without being requested.

UNIT 4
Travel and Transportation

Vocabulary:

Asking for and Giving Directions, Booking a Hotel Room

- ○ Key Phrases and Vocabulary:

Dove si trova...?	Where is...?	Doh-veh see troh-vah
Vai dritto	Go straight	Vai dree-toh
Gira a sinistra/destra	Turn left/right	Jee-rah ah seen-ees-trah/deh-strah
È vicino/lontano	It's near/far	Eh vee-chee-no/lon-tah-no
Vorrei prenotare una camera singola/doppia	I would like to book a single/double room	Vor-ray preh-noh-tah-reh oo-nah cah-meh-rah seen-go-lah/dohp-pyah
Per quante notti?	For how many nights?	Per quahn-teh noh-tee
A che ora è il check-out?	What time is check-out?	Ah keh oh-rah eh eel chek-owt

- ○ Grammar Focus: Remember, the gender and number of nouns affect the prepositions. For example, "Il ristorante è vicino alla piazza" (The restaurant is near the square) – here, 'alla' changes due to 'la piazza' being feminine.

Transportation Vocabulary

- ○ Essential Terms:

L'autobus	bus	Lau-toh-boos
Il treno	train	Eel treh-no
La macchina	car	Lah mack-kee-nah
La bicicletta	bicycle	Lah bee-chee-klet-tah
A piedi	on foot	Ah pee-eh-dee

- ○ Useful Phrases:

A che ora parte l'autobus?	What time does the bus leave?	Ah keh oh-rah par-teh lau-toh-boos
Dove si trova la stazione?	Where is the station?	Doh-veh see troh-vah lah stah-tzee-oh-neh

Culture:

- Popular Tourist Attractions in Italy

  ○ Rome: The Eternal City

    ○ The Colosseum: A Monument of Might
    The Colosseum, an enduring symbol of Rome's imperial might, stands as a testament to ancient engineering prowess. Its elliptical structure, capable of seating up to 50,000 spectators, once hosted gladiatorial combats and public spectacles that mesmerized ancient Rome. Imagine the roar of the crowd and the spectacle of combat that once filled this arena.

    ○ Vatican City: A Sovereign Splendor
    Vatican City, a sovereign enclave within Rome, is a treasure trove of religious and artistic heritage. The Vatican Museums boast an astonishing collection of artworks, including the Sistine Chapel with Michelangelo's frescoes. St. Peter's Basilica, with its imposing dome, is a masterpiece of Renaissance architecture.

  ○ Venice: The City on Water

    ○ Gondolas and Canals: Navigating the Venetian Labyrinth
    Venice, a city built on a lagoon, is an architectural wonder, a city where streets are canals, and cars are boats. The Grand Canal, a sweeping waterway lined with palatial buildings, reflects the city's history as a wealthy maritime republic. A gondola ride through these canals is not just a tourist activity; it's a plunge into the heart of Venetian culture and history.

    ○ St. Mark's Basilica: A Mosaic of History
    St. Mark's Basilica, a gem of Italo-Byzantine architecture, stands proudly in the famous St. Mark's Square. The basilica's opulent design, adorned with golden mosaics and intricate marble inlays, tells stories of Venice's rich past.

  ○ Florence: The Renaissance Jewel

    ○ The Uffizi Gallery: A Treasury of Art
    In the heart of Florence, the Uffizi Gallery holds a collection of art that is unrivaled in its breadth and quality, showcasing the genius of the Italian Renaissance. This gallery, once the offices of Florentine magistrates, now houses masterpieces such as Botticelli's "The Birth of Venus" and Leonardo da Vinci's "Annunciation." Each room unveils a different chapter in the history of art, from medieval works to the High Renaissance.

- The Duomo: Florence's Crown
  Florence's skyline is dominated by the magnificent Duomo, officially known as the Cathedral of Santa Maria del Fiore. Its massive dome, engineered by Filippo Brunelleschi, was a marvel of its time and remains one of the most significant architectural achievements of the Renaissance.

- The Amalfi Coast: Mediterranean Paradise

  - Scenic Drives and Seaside Towns
    The Amalfi Coast, a stretch of coastline on the southern edge of Italy's Sorrentine Peninsula, is famed for its rugged terrain, scenic beauty, and picturesque towns. This UNESCO World Heritage Site enchants visitors with its dramatic cliffs, azure waters, and colorful villages clinging to the mountainside.

- Sicily: The Island of Diversity

  Agrigento's Valley of the Temples
  In Sicily, the Valley of the Temples near Agrigento stands as a magnificent reminder of the island's Greek heritage. This archaeological park, one of the most significant in the Mediterranean, consists of well-preserved ancient Greek temples, each with its own history and architectural style. The Temple of Concordia, one of the best-preserved Greek temples in the world, offers a glimpse into the ancient world's architectural prowess.

- Tips for Traveling Within Italy

  The Italian Train Experience
  High-Speed vs Regional Trains
  Traveling by train in Italy offers a window into the country's varied landscapes and cultural nuances. The high-speed trains, like Frecciarossa and Italo, connect major cities quickly, while regional trains allow for a more leisurely exploration of the picturesque countryside. Utilizing the train network is an efficient way to journey across the diverse regions of Italy.

- Car Rental: Exploring Beyond the Beaten Path
  Understanding ZTLs and Parking
  Renting a car in Italy opens up a world of possibilities for exploring beyond the typical tourist paths. However, it's essential to be aware of ZTLs (Zona Traffico Limitato, Limited Traffic Zone), areas in city centers with traffic restrictions, and the unique challenges of parking in urban areas. This allows travelers to venture into rural areas like Tuscany's rolling hills or the dramatic landscapes of Sicily, discovering hidden gems and experiencing a more authentic Italy.

- ◦ Venice's Unique Transportation
  The Vaporetto: Venice's Water Bus
  In Venice, the vaporetto acts as the city's aquatic bus service, connecting various parts of the city and its surrounding islands. These water buses are an efficient and cost-effective way to navigate Venice's canals and visit iconic locations like Murano and Burano.

- ◦ Gondola Etiquette: Tips for a Memorable Ride
  A gondola ride in Venice, while a quintessential experience, comes with its own set of etiquettes. It's advisable to discuss the route and price before embarking. Evening rides tend to be more expensive but offer a serene and intimate experience as the city lights reflect on the water.

- ◦ Walking and Cycling: The Eco-Friendly Choice

  - ◦ Discovering Italy's Hidden Gems on Foot
    Walking through Italian cities offers an intimate experience of their rich history and vibrant culture. This slower pace of exploration allows travelers to appreciate the intricate details of the architecture and enjoy authentic culinary delights.

  - ◦ Cycling Culture in Italy
    Cycling in Italy provides a unique way to explore both urban and rural landscapes. Many cities have developed extensive bike lanes and rental services. In rural regions, it provides a way to experience Italy's natural beauty, like the rolling hills of Tuscany and the vineyards of Piedmont.

UNIT 5
Social Situations

Vocabulary:

○   Making Friends and Small Talk

Engaging in small talk is an essential part of making friends in Italian culture. This section helps you to start conversations, ask basic questions, and respond appropriately.

○   Key Phrases

Ciao, come ti chiami?	Hello, what's your name?	CHAH-oh KOH-meh tee KYAH-mee?
Mi chiamo [Your Name]. E tu?	My name is [Your Name]. And you?	Mee KYAH-moh... EH too?
Di dove sei?	Where are you from?	Dee DOH-veh say?
Sono di [Your City/Country].	I am from [Your City/Country].	SOH-no dee...
Qual è il tuo lavoro?	What is your job?	Kwah-LEH eel TOO-oh lah-VOH-roh?
Quanti anni hai?	How old are you?	KWAN-tee AHN-nee eye?
Ti piace la musica?	Do you like music?	Tee PYAH-cheh lah MOO-see-kah?
Che hobby hai?	What hobbies do you have?	Keh OHB-bee eye?
Hai fratelli o sorelle?	Do you have brothers or sisters?	Eye frah-TEHL-lee oh soh-REHL-leh?

○   Cultural Insight

Italians value personal relationships and often engage in friendly conversations even with strangers. Understanding how to initiate and maintain a light conversation is key to integrating into Italian social life.

○   Planning Social Events

Discussing plans and organizing social events are common aspects of Italian social life. This section covers how to make invitations, suggest activities, and confirm details.

○   Key Phrases

Vuoi andare al cinema stasera?	Do you want to go to the cinema tonight?	VWOH-ee AHN-dah-reh ahl CHEE-neh-mah stah-SEH-rah?
Che film vuoi vedere?	Which movie do you want to see?	Keh FEELM vwoh-ee veh-DEH-reh?

A che ora ci incontriamo?	What time shall we meet?	Ah keh OH-rah chee een-kohn-TRAH-ee-moh?
Dove ci incontriamo?	Where shall we meet?	DOH-veh chee een-kohn-TRAH-ee-moh?
Ti va di andare a cena fuori?	Do you feel like going out for dinner?	Tee vah dee ahn-DAH-reh ah CHEH-nah FWOH-ree?
Possiamo andare al parco domani?	Can we go to the park tomorrow?	Pohs-SYAH-moh ahn-DAH-reh ahl PAR-koh doh-MAH-nee?
Che ne dici di un caffè?	How about a coffee?	Keh neh DEE-chee dee oon kahf-FEH?
Ti andrebbe di vedere una mostra?	Would you like to see an exhibition?	Tee ahn-DEHR-reh-bee dee veh-DEH-reh OO-nah MOH-stah?

- ◦ Cultural Insight

Italians often make plans spontaneously and are known for their flexibility. Understanding how to navigate these social arrangements can help in forming deeper connections with native speakers.

- ◦ Expressing Emotions and Feelings

Expressing emotions and feelings is a fundamental aspect of Italian communication. This section provides vocabulary and phrases to articulate a wide range of emotions.

- ◦ Key Phrases

Sono felice.	I am happy.	SOH-noh feh-LEE-cheh
Sono triste.	I am sad.	SOH-noh TREE-steh
Mi dispiace.	I'm sorry.	Mee dees-PYAH-cheh
Sto benissimo.	I am very well.	Stoh beh-NEES-see-moh
Mi sento così così.	I feel so-so.	Mee SEHN-toh koh-SEE koh-SEE
Ho paura.	I am afraid.	Oh POW-rah
Sono sorpreso/a.	I am surprised.	SOH-noh sohr-PREH-soh/ah
Mi sento stanco/a.	I feel tired.	Mee SEHN-toh STAHN-koh/ah

- ◦ Cultural Insight

Emotional expression in Italy is often more direct and expressive compared to many other cultures. Being able to express your feelings authentically can greatly enhance your social interactions.

Culture:

- Italian Social Norms and Values

  - Embracing La Dolce Vita
    Italy, a nation steeped in history and culture, is synonymous with the art of enjoying life, encapsulated in the phrase "La Dolce Vita." This concept is more than just a saying; it's a lifestyle that prioritizes pleasure, relaxation, and the appreciation of life's finer things. Italians tend to focus on the quality of life, finding joy in everyday moments, whether it's a leisurely coffee break at a local café or an impromptu gathering with friends. This philosophy reflects a broader cultural attitude towards life, emphasizing the importance of slowing down and savoring the moment.

  - The Importance of Family
    In Italian culture, the family is the cornerstone of social structure. This extends beyond the nuclear family to include a wide network of relatives. Family gatherings are not just occasional events; they are vital social rituals, often marked by elaborate meals that can last for hours. Such occasions are replete with animated discussions and are an essential part of maintaining family bonds. Respect for elders is paramount, and their advice is often sought in family matters. This deep-rooted family-centric culture shapes many aspects of Italian life, from business to daily social interactions.

  - Gestures and Communication
    Italians are known for their passionate and expressive communication style, often punctuated with a range of gestures that can be considered an art form in itself. These gestures are an integral part of the Italian language, adding emphasis and emotion to conversations. Understanding these gestures can be as crucial as learning the language itself, providing insights into the unspoken nuances of Italian communication. For example, a flick of the chin might indicate indifference, while tapping one's temple can suggest cleverness or a good idea. This vivid style of communication is a window into the Italian spirit, reflecting a culture that values expressiveness and emotion.

  - Fashion and Appearance
    Italians place great importance on appearance and fashion, viewing it as a form of self-respect and respect for others. This doesn't necessarily mean following the latest trends or wearing expensive brands. Rather, it's about presenting oneself with elegance and propriety. The Italian fashion sensibility is about finding a personal style that is both classic and tasteful. This emphasis on appearance is evident in the immaculate street styles seen in Italian cities, where everyday fashion often looks like it's straight out of a magazine shoot. For Italians, dressing well is a way of life, reflecting a culture that values aesthetics and quality.

- Italy's Art and Entertainment Scene

  ○ A Legacy of Artistic Brilliance
  Italy's contribution to the world of art is immeasurable, stretching from ancient Roman times through the Renaissance to contemporary art. This rich history is visible in every corner of the country, from the Vatican's Sistine Chapel to the Uffizi Gallery in Florence. These masterpieces are not just relics of the past; they are living testimonies of Italy's enduring artistic spirit. Italian art is characterized by a passion for beauty and an unwavering commitment to craftsmanship and detail. Modern Italian artists continue this legacy, blending traditional techniques with contemporary themes, ensuring that Italy remains at the forefront of the global art scene.

  ○ The Pulse of Italian Cinema
  Italian cinema has a storied history, deeply interwoven with the nation's cultural fabric. The post-World War II era of neorealism brought global attention to Italian filmmakers, with directors like Federico Fellini and Roberto Rossellini revolutionizing cinematic storytelling. Their films, characterized by a focus on everyday life and social issues, left a lasting impact on the film industry. Today, Italian cinema is a vibrant and dynamic field, continuing to produce films that are celebrated for their artistic innovation and narrative depth. Film festivals like the Venice Film Festival are key events, showcasing the best of Italian and international cinema, and maintaining Italy's position as a significant force in the global film industry.

  ○ Music: From Opera to Contemporary Beats
  Italy's music scene is a rich tapestry that intertwines the traditional with the modern. It is the birthplace of opera, a genre that continues to captivate audiences worldwide with its dramatic storytelling and powerful vocal performances. Composers like Giuseppe Verdi and Gioachino Rossini have left an indelible mark on the world of classical music. However, Italy's musical landscape extends far beyond opera. The country has a vibrant contemporary music scene, with genres ranging from pop to rock, and electronic music gaining popularity. Music festivals and live performances are an integral part of Italian culture, reflecting the nation's love for music and its role in everyday life.

  ○ Festivals: A Celebration of Life and Culture
  Festivals in Italy are not just events; they are vibrant celebrations of life, culture, and history. Each region has its own unique festivals, many of which have roots in historical events or religious traditions. The Venice Carnival, with its iconic masks and costumes, is a world-famous event that epitomizes the Italian flair for combining artistry with celebration. The Palio di Siena, a historic horse race, is another example of Italy's rich festival culture, steeped in tradition and local pride. These festivals are more than just entertainment; they are a vital part of Italy's cultural identity, offering a glimpse into the nation's soul and an opportunity for communal joy and celebration.

○ Culinary Arts: More Than Just Pizza and Pasta
Italian cuisine is celebrated globally for its delicious flavors and regional diversity. While pizza and pasta are beloved staples, Italian culinary arts offer a vast array of regional specialties, each reflecting local ingredients and culinary traditions. From the seafood-rich dishes of the coastal regions to the hearty, rustic fare of the countryside, Italian cuisine is a journey through the country's diverse landscapes and history. Food in Italy is much more than sustenance; it's a cultural expression, a form of art, and a central part of social life. Cooking and eating in Italy are activities that involve passion, creativity, and a deep appreciation for the finest ingredients and time-honored techniques.

UNIT 6
Shopping and Services

Vocabulary:

- ○ Clothing and Shopping Vocabulary

Shopping in Italy is not just a transaction; it's an experience. Italy is renowned for its fashion and style, and understanding the vocabulary of clothing and shopping is your key to enjoying this aspect of Italian culture.

- ○ Basic Clothing Items:

Shirt	camicia	cah-MEE-chah
Pants	pantaloni	pahn-tah-LOH-nee
Dress	vestito	veh-STEE-toh
Shoes	scarpe	SKAHR-peh

- ○ Clothing Accessories:

Belt	cintura	cheen-TOO-rah
Hat	cappello	kah-PEHL-loh
Scarf	sciarpa	SHYAR-pah

- ○ Asking About Prices and Bargaining

In Italy, asking about prices and occasionally bargaining, especially in markets and small shops, is a part of the shopping experience.

- ○ Inquiring About Price:

| How much does it cost? | Quanto costa? | KWAHN-toh KOH-stah |
| Is there a discount? | C'è uno sconto? | cheh OO-noh SKON-toh |

- ○ Bargaining Phrases:

| Can we make it less? | Possiamo fare di meno? | poh-SYAH-moh FAH-reh dee MEH-noh |
| I can only pay [amount] | Posso pagare solo [amount] | POH-soh pah-GAH-reh SOH-loh |

- ○ Services Vocabulary

Knowing how to navigate various services like the post office, banks, and supermarkets is crucial for daily life in Italy. Cultural Insight: Services in Italy are often personalized. Building a rapport with your local service providers, like your hairdresser or tailor, is a quintessential part of Italian culture.

- ◦ Daily Services:

Supermarket	supermercato	soo-pehr-mehr-KAH-toh
Hairdresser	parrucchiere	pah-roo-KYEH-reh
Tailor	sarto	SAHR-toh

- ◦ Financial and Postal Services:

ATM	bancomat	BAHN-koh-maht
To send a letter	spedire una lettera	speh-DEE-reh OO-nah let-TEH-rah

Cultural Insight: Even in the age of digital communication, visiting a local post office in Italy is a unique experience, often involving friendly chats and a slower pace of service, "slower" being the keyword, as the post office is an often considered the place of long queues and boring wait.

Culture:

- Shopping Culture in Italy
  When you step into the vibrant world of Italian shopping, you're not just entering a marketplace; you're immersing yourself in a cultural experience that reflects centuries of tradition and innovation. In Italy, shopping is not just a transaction; it's an art form, a social activity, and a testament to the country's rich history and contemporary flair.

- The Italian Market Scene
  Italian markets are bustling hubs where the community gathers, not only to shop but also to socialize and share news. From the open-air mercati in small towns to the grandiose mercati coperti in cities like Rome and Milan, these markets offer a feast for the senses. Fresh, local produce, artisanal crafts, and a kaleidoscope of colors and aromas create an enchanting atmosphere that is quintessentially Italian.

  - ◦ Local Markets: In towns and villages, local markets are often the heartbeat of the community. Here, you'll find fresh fruits, vegetables, cheeses, and meats, often sourced from surrounding farms. These markets are not just about food; they are a celebration of regional specialties and a testament to Italy's commitment to quality and freshness.

  - ◦ Street Markets: Italy's street markets are a treasure trove for bargain hunters and fashionistas alike. You can find everything from vintage clothing and accessories to home goods and antiques. The famous Via Sannio market in Rome or the Fiera di Sinigaglia in Milan are perfect examples, offering a unique blend of history, culture, and retail therapy.

- Shopping Tips and Etiquette
  Shopping in Italy can be a delightful experience, but it's important to understand some local customs and tips to make the most of it.

- Understanding Italian Opening Hours
  Shops in Italy often close for a midday break, particularly in smaller towns. It's common for businesses to shut down between 1 pm and 3:30 pm. Planning your shopping trips around these hours is crucial to avoid inconvenience.

- Tax-Free Shopping
  For non-EU residents, tax-free shopping can offer significant savings. Look for shops displaying the 'Tax-Free Shopping' sign and be sure to keep your receipts for a VAT (Value Added Tax) refund when you leave the country.

UNIT 7
At Work and School

Vocabulary:

- ○ Occupations and Workplaces Vocabulary

Understanding the vocabulary related to occupations and workplaces is essential for any student of Italian, especially for those interested in professional contexts.

- ○ Occupations

Insegnante	Teacher	in-seh-GNAN-teh
Dottore/Dottoressa	Doctor	dot-TO-re/dot-to-RESS-a
Ingegnere	Engineer	in-geg-NE-re
Impiegato/Impiegata	Employee	im-pie-GAH-to/im-pie-GAH-ta
Direttore/Direttrice	Director	di-RET-tore/di-RET-trice
Studente/Studentessa	Student	stu-DEN-te/stu-DEN-tes-sa

One unique aspect of Italian is how professions are often gender-specific in their declension. This means that the word itself changes depending on whether the subject is male or female. Let's explore this with our list of occupations.

Masculine to Feminine Conversion:
Words ending in -o in the masculine often change to -a in the feminine (e.g., impiegato' to 'impiegata').
For professions, a masculine term ending in -tore often becomes -trice in feminine (e.g., 'direttore' to 'direttrice').

Exceptions:
Some words remain the same for both genders, especially those ending in -e (e.g., 'insegnante', 'ingegnere').
Newer professions or those borrowed from other languages often retain the same form (e.g., 'manager', 'designer').

Pluralization:
Masculine words ending in -o change to -i for plural (e.g., 'impiegatii').
Feminine words ending in -a change to -e for plural (e.g., 'impiegate').
For words ending in -e, the plural form ends in -i regardless of gender (e.g., 'insegnanti').

- ○ Workplaces

Scuola	School	SKWO-la
Università	University	oo-nee-ver-SEE-ta
Ufficio	Office	oof-FI-cho
Azienda	Company	a-TSYEN-da

These terms are foundational for navigating conversations in academic and professional settings. Practice using them in sentences to describe where you work or study, your role, and your daily tasks.

In Italian, several terms can be used to refer to a "company," each with its own subtle connotations and specific uses. Understanding these differences is crucial for accurately describing various business entities.

Ditta [DEE-tah]
Meaning: Often refers to a small or medium-sized business, typically family-owned or a sole proprietorship.
Usage: "La ditta di mio zio produce vino artigianale." (My uncle's company produces artisanal wine.)

Azienda [a-TSYEN-dah]
Meaning: A generic term for "company," used broadly for businesses of various sizes and industries.
Usage: "Lavoro in un'azienda che fa software." (I work at a company that makes software.)

Compagnia [com-pa-NYA]
Meaning: Often used for larger businesses and can also imply a partnership. Sometimes used for "company" in the sense of a troupe, like a dance or theater company.
Usage: "La Compagnia del Teatro Nazionale è famosa in Italia." (The National Theatre Company is famous in Italy.)

Società [so-chee-e-TA]
Meaning: Refers to a company or corporation, often used in formal and legal contexts. It implies a structured organization with shareholders or members.
Usage: "La società è quotata in borsa." (The corporation is listed on the stock market.)

Impresa [im-PRE-sa]
Meaning: Often used for businesses focusing on ventures, projects, or construction. It carries a connotation of entrepreneurial effort.
Usage: "L'impresa edile sta costruendo un nuovo palazzo." (The construction company is building a new building.)

Ente [EN-te]
Meaning: Used for organizations or bodies, often in public or semi-public sectors.

Usage: "L'ente turistico promuove la regione." (The tourist board promotes the region.)

○ Describing Study and Work Routines

Understanding how to describe daily routines in work and study is crucial. Here are some key verbs, along with their pronunciation:

Studiare	To study	stu-DYA-re
Lavorare	To work	la-vo-RA-re
Iniziare	To start	i-ni-TSYA-re
Finire	To finish	fi-NE-re
Prendere una pausa	To take a break	PREN-de-re OO-na POW-sa

Use these verbs to construct sentences about your daily activities. For example, "Inizio a lavorare alle otto" (I start working at eight) or "Studio all'università nel pomeriggio" (I study at the university in the afternoon).

Culture:

- Italian Education System
  A Journey Through Italian Academia
  Italy, a country celebrated for its rich history and cultural heritage, also boasts a unique and structured education system. This journey begins in the early years of childhood and extends well into the realms of higher education and beyond.

- Early Education: The First Steps
  In Italy, education commences with 'Scuola dell'infanzia', also known as kindergarten, welcoming children aged three to six. This stage is not compulsory but is highly encouraged as it lays the foundation for social and cognitive development. Here, children are introduced to the basics of Italian language, mathematics, and the arts, fostering an environment of creativity and curiosity.

- Primary Education: Building the Blocks
  Following kindergarten, children step into 'Scuola primaria' or primary school, which spans five years. This compulsory phase emphasizes the Italian language, English, mathematics, natural sciences, history, geography, technology, music, and physical education. It's a period marked by a multidisciplinary approach, aimed at providing a well-rounded educational foundation.

- Secondary Education: Diverging Paths
  Secondary education in Italy is divided into two main stages: 'Scuola secondaria di primo grado' (middle school) and 'Scuola secondaria di secondo grado' (high school). Middle school, lasting three years, builds upon the knowledge gained in primary school, with a greater focus

on languages and sciences. High school, lasting five years, is where educational paths diverge. Students choose between various types of high schools, including classical, scientific, linguistic, and vocational, each tailored to different future academic or career paths.

- Higher Education: Pursuing Excellence

The Italian university system, steeped in history yet dynamically modern, is a cornerstone of global academia. Originating in the Middle Ages, epitomized by the founding of the University of Bologna, the oldest university in existence, this system has profoundly influenced the European educational model. Its structure, conforming to the Bologna Process, comprises a three-tier degree system: the three-year 'Laurea' (Bachelor's), two-year 'Laurea Magistrale' (Master's), and the 'Dottorato di Ricerca' (Doctorate) focusing on advanced research.

Beyond conventional universities, Italy prides itself on specialized institutes like 'Politecnici' and 'Accademie di Belle Arti', emphasizing engineering, architecture, arts, and music. These institutions blend traditional learning with innovation, actively engaging in research and fostering entrepreneurship. Internationalization is a key focus, with numerous English-taught programs and participation in global exchange programs like Erasmus+, creating a diverse, multicultural learning environment. University life in Italy transcends academic learning, integrating rich social and cultural experiences. Campuses, often nestled in historic locales, offer a vibrant cultural life, encouraging a holistic educational journey. Emphasis on self-directed learning ('autoformazione') and financial accessibility through various scholarships, makes Italian higher education both inclusive and empowering. Despite facing challenges like funding and the need for modernization, Italian universities continue to evolve, balancing their rich heritage with the demands of contemporary academia. This blend of tradition and innovation not only shapes academically proficient individuals but also culturally enriched, globally aware citizens, maintaining Italy's legacy in the realm of higher education..

UNIT 8
Beyond Basics

Culture:

The Dance of Time - Tenses in Italian and English
Embarking on this chapter is like stepping into a time machine, where the gears and cogs are the tenses of Italian and English. This isn't just a grammar lesson; it's a voyage across centuries, a dive into the collective psyche of nations.

The Roots of Italian Verb Tenses
Imagine standing in the ruins of ancient Rome, the birthplace of Italian. Latin, the forefather of Italian, was a language of complexity and precision, a reflection of the Roman Empire's grandeur. Italian inherited this legacy, a language where time is painted with a palette of tenses, each shade telling its own story. Fast forward to the Renaissance, an era where Italy redefined art, philosophy, and, subtly, its language. Italian tenses became canvases for expression, with each verb form offering a different stroke of meaning, a different color of emotion.

The English Tapestry
Now, cross the English Channel to the misty isles of Britain. Here, the English language, a tapestry woven from diverse threads – Germanic, Norse, and Norman French. Each wave of invaders and settlers left their mark, simplifying the language, streamlining the tenses.

1066 AD - The Normans arrive. Contrary to expectations, their influence led to a simplification of English verb tenses. Why? To ease communication in a land of diverse tongues. English became a language of practicality, where time is a straight line, unencumbered by the complexities of the past or the uncertainties of the future.

The Cultural Mirror
Languages are mirrors of their cultures. Dive into the Italian way of life, where history breathes in every alley, where every moment is a link to the past and a step towards the future. The Italian verb tenses are a dance of continuity, an embrace of life's complexities. In contrast, the English language, with its straightforward tenses, reflects a culture of pragmatism. Here, time is a resource, not a story. The future is a challenge to be met head-on, not a mystery to be pondered.

What do these linguistic paths tell us? That the way we use tenses is more than habit; it's a reflection of our worldview. In the nuances of Italian verbs, there's a celebration of life's intricacies. In the simplicity of English tenses, a call to action, a focus on the immediate.

Italian is a language where the past isn't just gone; it's a foundation for the present, a whisper in today's conversations. The Italian mindset doesn't just acknowledge complexity; it revels in it, finds comfort in the layered tapestry of existence.

English, with its linear approach to time, encourages a culture of directness. Here, clarity is king, and efficiency is the queen. The English-speaking world looks forward, often with an eye on innovation and progress, where time is a path to the future, not a labyrinth of the past.

As this chapter closes, remember, language learning is a journey into the heart of a culture. The Italian and English tenses are more than grammatical forms; they're keys to unlocking different perceptions of time, life, and our place in history.

Italian Short Stories For

Language Learners

Learn and Improve Your Italian Comprehension and Vocabulary Through 30 Short Stories Based Off Captivating Italian History

Worldwide Nomad

I PRINCIPI ABBANDONATI

Nell'antica città di Alba Longa, c'era un uomo che pianificò contro suo fratello, il re, e si fece re con la forza. In seguito, dalla figlia del vecchio re nacquero due giovani principi, Romolo e Remo. Poiché il loro prozio, il falso re, temeva che crescessero e diventassero più forti di lui, ordinò ai suoi servi di prendere i piccoli principi e di lasciarli sulla riva di un fiume.

I principi furono salvati da persone gentili e furono portati in una terra sconosciuta al di là del fiume, dove furono accuditi. Divennero ragazzi molto forti, intelligenti e gentili e tutte le persone intorno a loro li amavano. Un giorno divennero così popolari che Amulio, il falso re, venne a sapere di loro.

Si spaventò di nuovo e mandò i suoi servi a prendere i giovani principi e a metterli in prigione. I servi riuscirono ad arrestare solo Remo e successivamente Romolo si recò nella città di Alba Longa per salvare il fratello. Durante la permanenza in città, il popolo amava così tanto i principi che chiese loro di diventare re al posto del crudele prozio. I principi rifiutarono, ma fecero tornare re il loro nonno, Numitore.

I fratelli tornarono nel villaggio sconosciuto in cui erano cresciuti e decisero di creare la loro città. Romolo voleva che la loro città fosse a est, mentre Remo voleva che fosse a ovest. Non potendo concordare con il fratello, Remo se ne andò e Romolo diede alla città il nome di Roma.

Questa storia si ispira alla leggenda popolare di Romolo e Remo, che si dice siano stati abbandonati sulla riva del fiume, salvati dal dio del fiume e allevati dai lupi.

THE ABANDONED PRINCES

In the Ancient city of Alba Longa, there was a man who planned against his brother, the King and made himself king by force. Later, two young princes, Romulus and Remus, were born to the daughter of the old king. Because their great uncle, the false King, was afraid that they would grow up and become stronger than him, he ordered his servants to take the little princes and leave them at the bank of a river.

The princes were saved by kind people and were taken to an unknown land across the river where they were taken care of. They grew up to be very strong, smart and kind boys and all the people around loved them. One day, they became so popular that Amulius, the false king, heard about them.

He became afraid once again and sent his servants to take the young princes and put them in jail. The servants were only able to arrest Remus and later Romulus went into the city of Alba Longa to save his brother. While in the city, the people loved the princes so much that they asked them to be their king instead of their cruel great uncle. The princes refused but made their grandfather, Numitor, king again.

The brothers returned to the unknown village where they grew up and decided to create their own city. Romulus wanted their city to be in the east while Remus wanted it to be in the west. Unable to agree with his brother, Remus departed and Romulus named the city Rome, after himself.

This story is inspired by the popular legend of Romulus and Remus who are said to have been abandoned on the river bank, saved by the river god and brought up by wolves.

Vocabulary

Banca - Bank
Benevolo - Kind
Figlia - Daughter
Fratello - Brother
Crudele - Cruel
Servi - Servants
Principe - Prince
Falso - False
Sconosciuto - Unknown
Villaggio - Village
Popolare - Popular
Arresto - Arrest
Creare - Create

Comprehension Questions

Dove sono nati i principi? Where were the princes born?

Perché il falso re ordinò ai suoi servi di mettere in prigione i principi? Why did the false king order his servants to put the princes in jail?

Come fece il falso re a sapere dei principi? How did the false king hear about the princes?

Historical Note

The ancient Latin City of Alba Longa was near the site that later became known as Rome. There the princes were said to have been born to Rhea Silva, daughter of the deposed king. It is popularly said in the legend that Romulus and Remus were suckled by a she-wolf as babies and the image of a she-wolf suckling twins has been a symbol of Rome since the 3rd Century BCE up until recent times. Romulus and Remus did indeed found Rome together but after a disagreement on the name and site of the city, Romulus killed his brother and became the first King of Rome, also naming the city after himself.

IL RE STOLTO E SUPERBO

Dopo il regno di sei re, Tarquinio il Superbo divenne il settimo re di Roma. Il popolo ebbe paura perché si sapeva che era un uomo molto malvagio. Non si curava dei membri della sua famiglia e danneggiava i poveri. Inoltre, non ascoltava i consigli dei suoi senatori, ma prendeva tutte le decisioni da solo.

Un giorno, il re malvagio fu avvicinato dalla sacerdotessa dell'Oracolo di Apollo, la Sibilla Cumea. Gli offrì nove libri di profezie e gli chiese di pagare una somma per ottenerli. Sebbene il re Tarquinio desiderasse i libri per poter conoscere i pericoli in arrivo, non volle pagare così tanto per i libri e si rifiutò di comprarli.

La sacerdotessa prese tre dei libri e li gettò nel fuoco. I tre libri si ridussero in cenere e lei portò gli altri sei al re. Gli chiese di comprarli al prezzo dei nove libri. Anche in questo caso, il re rifiutò perché non voleva separarsi dal suo denaro.

La sacerdotessa prese altri tre libri e li gettò nel fuoco. Tornò dal re con i tre libri rimanenti e chiese lo stesso prezzo dei nove libri. Temendo di non sapere cosa stessero progettando i suoi nemici, il re Tarquinio comprò subito i libri.

THE FOOLISH PROUD KING

After the reign of six kings, Tarquinius the proud became the seventh King of Rome. The people became afraid because he was known to be a very wicked man. He did not care for the members of his family and hurt people who were poor. He also did not listen to advice from his senators but made all the decisions by himself.

One day, the wicked king was approached by the priestess of Apollo's Oracle, Cumean Sibyl. She offered him nine books of prophecy and asked him to pay an amount to get them. Although King Tarquinius wanted the book so he could know whatever dangers were coming, he did not want to pay so much money for the book and refused to buy them.

The priestess took three of the books and threw them into a fire. The three books burnt to ashes and she took the other six to the King. She asked him to buy them at the price of the nine books. Again, the King refused because he did not want to part with his money.

The priestess took another three of the books and threw them into the fire. She returned to the King with the remaining three books and asked for the same price of the nine books. Afraid that he would never know what his enemies were planning, King Tarquinius bought the books at once.

Vocabulary

Superbo - Proud
Profezia - Prophecy
Sacerdotessa - Priestess
Malvagia - Wicked
Offerto - Offered
Pericolo - Danger
Denaro - Money
Nemici - Enemies
Membri - Members

Comprehension Questions

Il re fu saggio a non comprare i nove libri? Was the king wise to not buy the nine books?

Qual era l'importanza dei libri di profezia per il re Tarquinio? What was the importance of the books of prophecy to King Tarquinius?

Cosa fece la sacerdotessa ai libri quando il re si rifiutò di comprarli? What did the priestess do to the books when the King refused to buy them?

Historical Facts

Tarquinius Superbus (the Proud) was the seventh and last king of Rome. He ascended to the throne by tricky means, turning the senators away from his father-in-law, the old king, and murdering him by throwing him down the stairs of the senate house and out into the streets. His wife was equally as wicked, driving her chariot over the body of her dead father in the street. King Tarquinius Superbus started his reign by refusing to bury the old king and his reign was marked with prosecutions and executions of people who did not support him. He also waged wars against neighboring Latin cities who refused to ally with him. In the end, he was overthrown by the people after his son ravished the wife of a kinsman. From then on, the people of Rome vowed never to be ruled by a king again.

L'UOMO AMMANTATO

Quando il re malvagio fu rovesciato, il popolo si chiese come sarebbe stato governato. I patrizi elessero due capi, chiamati pretori o consoli. I pretori emettevano leggi e governavano il popolo in base a queste leggi. I pretori venivano cambiati ogni anno dai senatori, in modo che non avessero un potere totale.

Il popolo entrò in un periodo di pace e tutti erano felici del nuovo sistema. Finché un giorno un pretore si rifiutò di essere rimosso dall'incarico. Arrestò il secondo pretore e tutti i senatori che erano contro di lui. Tutti tornarono ad avere paura.

Ma un uomo usciva ogni sera e camminava di strada in strada. Parlava del pretore al popolo e lo chiamava tiranno. Nessuno sapeva chi fosse quell'uomo, perché era apparso dal nulla. Indossava un lungo mantello nero e aveva capelli scuri e macilenti. Anche il suo volto era sconosciuto e nessuno ricordava di averlo mai visto.

Ogni notte l'uomo ammantato predicava e il pretore si inquietava. Mandò i suoi soldati ad arrestare l'uomo ammantato, ma non lo trovarono mai. La gente amava l'uomo ammantato e lasciava del cibo per lui, ma lui disse loro di dare il cibo agli affamati.

Un giorno, i soldati del pretore trovarono l'uomo ammantato e lo inseguirono. Quando lo presero, si scoprì che era lo stalliere del pretore. Arrabbiato, il pretore ordinò di giustiziarlo, ma il popolo uscì in gran numero, salvò l'uomo ammantato e cacciò il pretore dalla città.

THE CLOAKED MAN

When the wicked King was overthrown, the people wondered how they would be ruled. Two leaders were elected by the patricians and they were called Praetors or Consuls. The praetors made laws and ruled the people by these laws. The praetors were changed every year by the senators so that they would not have total power.

The people came into a time of peace and everyone was happy with the new system. Until one day, a praetor refused to be removed from office. He arrested the second praetor and all the senators who were against him. Everyone became afraid again.

But one man came out every night and walked from street to street. He talked about the praetor to the people and called him a tyrant. No one knew who the man was because he appeared out of nowhere. He wore a long, black cloak and had dark, grisly hair. His face was also unknown, and no one could remember ever seeing him.

Every night, the cloaked man preached and the praetor grew restless. He sent his soldiers to arrest the cloaked man but they never found him. The people loved the cloaked man so they left food out for him but he told them to give the food to the hungry people instead.

One day, the praetor's soldiers found the cloaked man and chased after him. When they caught him, he turned out to be the praetor's stablehand. Angry, the praetor ordered him to be executed but the people went out in large numbers, saved the cloaked man and chased the praetor out of the city.

Vocabulary

Tiranno - Tyrant
Mantello - Cloak
Macabro - Grisly
Soldati - Soldiers
Irrequieto - Restless
Stalliere - Stablehand
Numeri - Numbers
Rovesciare - Overthrow
Richiamo - Remember

Comprehension Questions

Come venivano chiamati i capi eletti? What were the elected leaders called?

Cosa disse l'uomo ammantato al popolo? What did the cloaked man say to the people?

Chi conosceva il volto dell'uomo ammantato? Who knew the cloaked man's face?

Historical Notes

Following the removal of Tarquinius Superbus, a fairer system of government was introduced to ancient Rome. Plebeian members called conscripti were introduced into the senate and the people, both patricians and plebs elected two leaders called praetors annually to handle the governance. The plebs were however not legally eligible to be praetors so the praetors had to be from the patrician populace. This eventually led to discontent and struggle between the two factions and preceded the socio-political changes that would be instituted in the Roman Republic till this day.

LA FANCIULLA E L'AVIDO TIRANNO

Il popolo romano guardò le sue leggi e pensò che non fossero giuste. Così, scelse dieci uomini, chiamati Decemviri, per fare nuove leggi per loro.

Le cose andavano bene, ma uno di quei dieci, Appio Claudio, convinse gli altri a fare ciò che voleva e prese il controllo del governo. La gente temeva di tornare a un'epoca di duro dominio, ma nessuno osava opporsi a lui.

Un giorno, Appio Claudio vide Virginia, che era molto bella, ed era la figlia di un suo amico. Cercò di conquistarla con denaro e regali, ma lei disse di no perché era già fidanzata con un altro uomo.

Per ottenere ciò che voleva, Appio Claudio mandò il padre di Virginia in guerra e fece mentire uno dei suoi amici, dicendo che Virginia era la sua schiava. L'amico arrestò Virginia e la portò al gruppo dei dieci capi.

Il padre di Virginia si precipitò in città per salvare la figlia, ma Appio Claudio non lo ascoltò e disse che Virginia era davvero una schiava.

Per evitare di essere disonorata, Virginia si gettò da un edificio e morì. Questo fece arrabbiare così tanto il padre che iniziò una ribellione e si liberò del cattivo sovrano, Appio Claudio.

THE MAIDEN AND THE GREEDY TYRANT

The Roman people looked at their laws and thought they were not fair. So, they chose ten men, called Decemviri, to make new laws for them.

Things were going fine, but one of those ten, Appius Claudius, convinced the others to do what he wanted and took control of the government. People were scared that they were going back to a time of harsh rule, but nobody dared to speak up against him.

One day, Appius Claudius saw Verginia, who was very pretty, and she was the daughter of his friend. He tried to win her over with money and presents, but she said no because she was already engaged to another man.

To get what he wanted, Appius Claudius sent Verginia's father off to war and had one of his friends lie, saying that Verginia was his slave. The friend arrested Verginia and brought her to the group of ten leaders.

Verginia's father rushed back to the city to save his daughter, but Appius Claudius wouldn't listen to him and said Verginia was truly a slave.

To avoid being dishonored, Verginia jumped from a building and died. This made her father so angry that he started a rebellion and got rid of the bad ruler, Appius Claudius.

Vocabulary

Fiera - Fair
Controllo - Control
Governo - Government
Schiavo - Slave
Disonorato - Dishonoured
Costruire - Building
Ribellione - Rebellion
Duro - Harsh

Comprehension Questions

Qual era il rapporto tra il padre di Virginia e Appio Claudio? What was the relationship between Virginia's father and Appius Claudius?

Perché l'amico di Appio Claudio mentì sul fatto che Virginia fosse una schiava? Why did Appius Claudius' friend lie that Virginia was a slave?

Come fece Appio Claudio a prendere il controllo del governo? How did Appius Claudius take control of the government?

Historical Facts:

To further protect their rights, the plebeians tried to institute a five man council that could check the powers of the Consuls but they were met with opposition from the patricians. They decided to employ a different method and asked for a council of ten men with equal patrician and plebeian representation. This council would revise the laws and make new laws. It took a long time but this proposition was eventually accepted and the Decemvirate was appointed in 451 BCE. Two of their most important laws were the legalization of marriage between plebs and patricians and the provision for a plebeian consul in later years.

This story of Verginia and Appius Claudius was said by Levi to have happened during the tenure of the second Decemvirate. However, modern historians disagree.

LA FOLLIA DEL GUERRIERO UBRIACO

Una volta, quando Roma stava diventando più grande e più forte, combatté molte battaglie contro altre città e le vinse tutte. Questo rendeva Roma molto potente e le città vicine avevano paura.

Un giorno, un condottiero romano navigò vicino a una città greca chiamata Tarentum. Gli abitanti di Tarentum avevano fatto festa ed erano molto ubriachi, così ordinarono ai loro soldati di affondare le navi romane.

Quando il condottiero romano vide quello che era successo, tornò a Roma e Roma decise di entrare in guerra con Tarentum. Tarentum aveva paura di combattere contro Roma da sola, così chiese a Pirro, il re dell'Epiro, di aiutarli.

Pirro era un buon generale, ma non capiva bene i Romani e non aveva abbastanza risorse per combatterli. Vinse alcune battaglie, ma perse molti soldati e denaro.

Alla fine Pirro perse la guerra e dovette tornare nella sua città. Non molto tempo dopo, Roma sconfisse Tarentum in una guerra e la rese parte del suo Paese.

THE FOLLY OF THE DRUNK WARRIOR

Once upon a time, when Rome was getting bigger and stronger, they fought many battles against other cities and won them all. This made Rome very powerful, and nearby cities were afraid.

One day, a Roman leader sailed near a Greek city called Tarentum. The people of Tarentum had been partying and were very drunk, so they ordered their soldiers to sink the Roman ships.

When the Roman leader saw what had happened, he went back to Rome, and Rome decided to go to war with Tarentum. Tarentum was afraid to fight Rome alone, so they asked Phyrrus, the King of Epirus, to help them.

Pyrrhus was a good general, but he didn't understand the Romans well, and he didn't have enough resources to fight them. He won some battles, but he lost a lot of his soldiers and money in the process.

In the end, Pyrrhus lost the war and had to go back to his city. Not long after, Rome defeated Tarentum in a war and made it part of their country.

Vocabulary

Generale - General
La guerra - War
Vela - Sail
Affondare - Sink
Battaglie - Battles
Potente - Powerful
Risorse - Resources
La nave - Ship

Comprehension Questions

Perché i soldati di Tarentum affondarono le navi romane? Why did the Tarentum soldiers sink the Roman ships?

Cosa accadde quando Pirro perse la guerra? What happened when Pyrrhus lost the war?

Perché Tarentum chiese a Pirro di aiutarli? Why did Tarentum ask Pyrrhus to help them?

Historical Note

A series of wars were waged by Rome to ensure its expansion and hegemony over the Italian peninsula. They fought wars against the Estrucans that culminated in the defeat of Veii. Following this, other estrucan cities surrendered to Rome. Although Rome was sacked and burned by the Gauls in 390 BCE, this did not deter their pursuit of expansion. They fought against the Samnites of Southern Italy who felt threatened by their expansion, a powerful coalition of Estrucans, Guals, and Umbrians in the north and of Lucanians, Bruttii, and Samnites in this south. A revolt of Latins and Volscians was dealt with and they fought the last war against Tarentum and their ally Pyrrhus. The following the year witnessed Rome's subjugation of all of southern Italy.

L'UMILE FORNAIO E IL MALVAGIO SOVRANO

Molto tempo fa, nell'antica Roma, c'era un potente sovrano di nome Cesare. Durante un periodo di problemi e disordini, governò con grande forza e fu molto crudele. Fece molte cose brutte e fece del male a molte persone.

A Cesare piaceva assistere a spettacoli brutali in un grande luogo chiamato Colosseo. Le persone dovevano combattere per rimanere in vita e a lui piacevano la violenza e la sofferenza. Il pubblico applaudiva, senza sapere che la crudeltà di Cesare faceva accadere questi eventi terribili.

Un giorno, un semplice fornaio di nome Lucio commise un errore e non cucinò correttamente il pane di Cesare. Cesare si arrabbiò molto perché pensava di meritare solo il meglio. In un impeto di rabbia, Cesare ordinò che Lucio fosse gettato nel Colosseo, senza armi né protezione, per affrontare un leone.

Quando i grandi cancelli si aprirono, Lucio si spaventò. Il leone gli saltò addosso, cercando di fargli del male. Ma prima che il leone potesse fare del male, una persona coraggiosa tra la folla gettò una corda per aiutare Lucio. Lucio si arrampicò per mettersi in salvo, sfuggendo al leone.

Per la prima volta, la folla applaudì la persona che non ci si aspettava vincesse. Anche i senatori più importanti cominciarono a mettere in dubbio la crudeltà di Cesare. Sebbene Lucio sia scampato alla morte, ha dimostrato che anche quando viene trattato molto male, lo spirito delle persone può trionfare.

Le azioni di Cesare dimostrarono la sua crudeltà, ma accesero anche una scintilla di resistenza tra il popolo. Forse un giorno si sarebbero sollevati contro il sovrano ingiusto e avrebbero voluto un mondo più gentile.

THE HUMBLE BAKER AND THE WICKED RULER

A long time ago in ancient Rome, there was a powerful ruler named Caesar. During a time of trouble and unrest, he ruled with great strength and was very cruel. He did many bad things and hurt a lot of people.

Caesar liked to watch brutal shows in a big place called the Colosseum. People had to fight there to stay alive, and he enjoyed the violence and suffering. The audience cheered, not knowing that Caesar's cruelty made these terrible events happen.

One day, a simple baker named Lucius made a mistake and didn't bake Caesar's bread properly. Caesar got very angry because he thought he deserved only the best. In a fit of rage, Caesar ordered that Lucius be thrown into the Colosseum, without any weapons or protection, to face a lion.

When the big gates opened, Lucius was scared. The lion jumped at him, trying to hurt him. But just before the lion could do any harm, a brave person in the crowd threw down a rope to help Lucius. Lucius climbed to safety, escaping from the lion.

For the first time, the crowd cheered for the person who was not expected to win. Even the important senators began to question Caesar's cruelty. Although Lucius escaped from death, he showed that even when treated very badly, people's spirit can triumph.

Caesar's actions showed how cruel he was, but they also lit a spark of resistance among the people. Maybe one day, they would rise up against the unfair ruler and want a kinder world.

Vocabulary

Problemi - Trouble
Disordini - Unrest
Brutale - Brutal
Violenza - Violence
Allegria - Cheer
Errore - Mistake
Pane - Bread
Armi - Weapons
Leone - Lion
Trionfo - Triumph

Comprehension Questions

Perché Cesare era un sovrano crudele? Why was Caesar a cruel ruler?

Come fece Lucio a sfuggire al leone? How did Lucius escape from the lion?

Cosa accadde dopo questo evento? What happened after this event?

Historical Notes

Julius Caesar was a powerful general of the Roman Republic. Along with two of his allies he formed a group, the first Triumvirate, that would dominate Roman politics for many years. He became so powerful through his military exploits that the senate felt threatened and ordered him to step down from his command. He chose to disobey this order and started a civil war which he won. He declared himself a dictator for life and made reforms to the state . Eventually, he was assassinated to curtail his increasing power.

IL DIPINTO DI UN BEL CUORE

In una zona trafficata di Firenze, molto tempo fa, c'era un artista di grande talento di nome Alessio. Visse in un'epoca in cui i Romani, guidati da Ottaviano Augusto, godettero di molti anni di pace e di prosperità e la gente si dilettava con l'arte e i libri.

Alessio non proveniva da una famiglia ricca. È cresciuto in una piccola casa soleggiata fuori città. Suo padre lavorava con rocce colorate e questo ha fatto sì che Alessio amasse i colori e le texture. Un giorno, nella chiesa di Santa Croce, vide i bellissimi dipinti di un famoso artista di nome Giotto e decise di diventare un artista.

Man mano che Alessio cresceva, diventava più bravo a dipingere. Utilizzava colori e pennelli diversi per realizzare quadri pieni di vita e di sentimenti. A Firenze, persone molto ricche e importanti videro il suo talento. Volevano che dipingesse la storia della loro famiglia in immagini.

Un giorno arrivò una lettera speciale. Aveva il marchio della famiglia Medici, che governava Firenze. Volevano che Alessio dipingesse un quadro di Lorenzo de Medici, il giovane leader della città. Alessio era emozionato ma anche un po' spaventato. Accettò di farlo e si impegnò a fondo.

Per molto tempo, Alessio dipinse il volto di Lorenzo, il suo corpo e ciò che pensava. Voleva mostrare chi era veramente Lorenzo con la sua arte. Ogni pennellata era piena d'amore e ogni colore scelto aveva un significato.

Quando mostrarono il dipinto a Palazzo Medici, tutti rimasero stupiti. Non era solo un quadro; mostrava il vero Lorenzo e il suo amore per l'arte, i libri e Firenze. Il dipinto di Alessio era un simbolo di quanto fosse grande l'arte in quel periodo, mescolando libri, politica e dipinti.

La notizia dell'incredibile dipinto si diffuse rapidamente e Alessio divenne famoso. Continuò a fare arte bellissima che portava con sé lo spirito di quel periodo speciale.

THE PAINTING OF A BEAUTIFUL HEART

In the busy part of Florence, a long time ago, there was a very talented artist named Alessio. He lived in a time when the Romans, led by Octavian Augustus, enjoyed many years of peace and prosperity so people enjoyed art and books.

Alessio didn't come from a rich family. He grew up in a small, sunny house outside the city. His father worked with colorful rocks, and this made Alessio love colors and textures. One day, in the Santa Croce church, he saw beautiful paintings by a famous artist named Giotto and decided to be an artist.

As Alessio got older, he got better at painting. He used different paints and brushes to make pictures full of life and feelings. People in Florence who were very rich and important saw his talent. They wanted him to paint their family history in pictures.

One day, a special letter arrived. It had the mark of the Medici family, who ruled Florence. They wanted Alessio to paint a picture of Lorenzo de Medici, the young leader of the city. Alessio was excited but also a bit scared. He agreed to do it and worked really hard.

For a long time, Alessio painted Lorenzo's face, his body, and what he thought about. He wanted to show who Lorenzo really was with his art. Every stroke of the brush was filled with love, and every color he picked had a meaning.

When they showed the painting at the Medici Palace, everyone was amazed. It wasn't just a picture; it showed Lorenzo's true self and his love for art, books, and Florence. Alessio's painting was a symbol of how great art was during that time, mixing books, politics, and paintings.

News about the amazing painting spread quickly, and Alessio became famous. He kept making beautiful art that carried the spirit of that special time.

Vocabulary

Simbolo - Symbol
Speciale - Special
Artista - Artist
Pennello - Brush
Talento - Talent
Immagine - Picture
Amore - Love
Tratto - Stroke

Comprehension Questions

Qual era il talento di Alessio? What was Alessio's talent?

Perché il dipinto era così bello? Why was the painting so beautiful?

Come è diventato famoso Alessio? How did Alessio become famous?

Historical Note

The reign of Emperor Octavian Augustus who succeeded the Republic was a rare era of peace in Rome. He carried out many societal and political reforms, combating corruption and all the other vices that characterized the republic. It was also dubbed the Golden Age of Literature as it was during this time that Rome had its surge in literary activities. It was also during this time that Jesus of the Christian faith was born although his birth went unnoticed.

L'ESILARANTE COMBATTENTE

Molto tempo fa, i Romani si recarono in Britannia per combattere una guerra comandata dall'imperatore Claudio. Tra i combattenti c'era un gruppo di soldati guidati da un buffo condottiero di nome Maximus Comedius. Egli credeva che far ridere la gente fosse il modo migliore per vincere.

I soldati romani camminavano nei campi fangosi e incontravano forti tribù celtiche. Invece delle armi normali, Massimo disse ai suoi soldati di indossare grandi elmi colorati con piume e di portare con sé degli spaventapasseri. Dipinsero facce buffe sui loro scudi. Quando i Celti lo videro, iniziarono a ridere. Massimo faceva anche scherzi e trucchi durante i combattimenti.

Un giorno, Massimo fece una gara divertente con il capo dei Celti, Grufus. Usarono tutti i tipi di tattiche divertenti, come scherzi e trucchi. Grufus, che era un duro, non riusciva a smettere di ridere. Alla fine Grufus si arrese, non perché avesse perso un combattimento, ma perché rideva così tanto.

Così, i soldati romani continuarono ad attraversare la Britannia, facendo ridere la gente con i loro strani modi. Maximus Comedius conquistò la terra e il cuore della gente con il suo senso dell'umorismo. La sua storia fu ricordata a lungo.

THE HILARIOUS FIGHTING MAN

Long ago, the Romans went to Britain to fight a war commanded by emperor Claudius. Among the fighters there was a group of soldiers led by a funny leader named Maximus Comedius. He believed that making people laugh was the best way to win.

The Roman soldiers walked in the muddy fields and met strong Celtic tribes. Instead of regular weapons, Maximus told his soldiers to wear big, colorful helmets with feathers and carried scarecrows. They painted funny faces on their shields. When the Celtic people saw this, they started laughing. Maximus even did jokes and tricks during the fight.

One day, Maximus had a funny contest with the Celtic leader, Gruffus. They used all kinds of funny tactics like jokes and tricks. Gruffus, who was tough, couldn't stop laughing. In the end, Gruffus gave up, not because he lost a fight, but because he laughed so much.

So, the Roman soldiers kept going through Britain, making people laugh with their strange ways. Maximus Comedius won the land and the hearts of the people with his sense of humor. His story was remembered for a long time.

Vocabulary

Tribù - Tribes
Divertente - Funny
Leader - Leader
Spaventapasseri - Scarecrows
Scherzi - Jokes
Trucchi - Tricks
Concorso - Contest
Strano - Strange

Comprehension Questions

Cosa indossavano i soldati romani in Britannia? What did the Roman soldiers wear to Britain?

Come si chiamava il capo celtico? What was the name of the Celtic leader?

Come vinsero la guerra i Romani? How did the Romans win the war?

Historical Note

Emperor Claudius ruled after the famously insane and tyrannical Caligula. His reign was temperate and he borrowed from the rule of Caesar and Augustus, continuing their public works and administrative reforms. The single distinguishing act of his reign was the conquest of Britain.

NERO ANCORA

Quando Nerone era appena stato nominato imperatore, il fratellastro Britannico veniva ogni sera a parlare con lui delle questioni dell'impero. Insieme alla madre di Nerone, Agrippina, Nerone e Britannico passeggiavano per il suo palazzo mentre discutevano delle politiche e lavoravano alla loro attuazione.

Un giorno, Agrippina suggerì di continuare questo modo di prendere decisioni per il resto del governo di Nerone. Nerone, però, si arrabbiò perché la considerava una mancanza di libertà e smise di passeggiare con loro per il palazzo. Sua madre e il fratellastro continuarono a seguire la routine e ogni giorno cercavano di parlare con lui. In preda alla rabbia, Nerone si scagliò contro di loro pubblicamente e si rifiutò di prendere in considerazione le loro opinioni su questioni riguardanti lo Stato.

Un giorno, Agrippina invitò a palazzo la figlia della sua amica Augusta. Nerone la trovò bellissima e si preparò immediatamente a sposarla. Tuttavia, Agrippina si oppose al matrimonio perché Augusta era già fidanzata con un altro uomo. Nerone si rifiutò di ascoltare la madre, ma il giorno del matrimonio Augusta scomparve. Mandò i suoi uomini a cercarla, ma non si trovava da nessuna parte. In preda all'ira, ordinò a uno dei suoi uomini di fiducia di uccidere Agrippina e di dare poi una grande festa.

ANGRY NERO

When Nero had just been made Emperor, his stepbrother Britannicus came every evening to speak with him about the matters of the empire. Together with Nero's mother, Agrippina Nero and Britannicus would walk through his palace as they discussed policies and worked on their implementations.

One day, Agrippina suggested that they continue this manner of decision-making for the rest of Nero's rule. However, Nero was angry as he saw this as a lack of freedom and he stopped walking with them through the palace. His mother and his stepbrother kept up with the routine and each day, they would try to speak with him. In anger, he spoke against them publicly and refused to consider their opinions in matters relating to the state.

One day, Agrippina invited the daughter of her friend, Augusta to the palace. Nero found her beautiful and immediately made preparations to marry her. However, Agrippina spoke against the marriage because Augusta was already engaged to another man. Nero refused to listen to his mother but on the day of their marriage, Augusta went missing. He sent his men to look for her but she was nowhere to be found. In anger, he ordered one of his trusted men to kill Agrippina and threw a big party afterward.

Vocabulary

Questioni - Matters
Passeggiata - Walk
Discusso - Discussed
Mancanza - Lack
Routine - Routine
Attraverso - Through
Sposarsi - Marry
Preparativi - Preparations
Considerare - Consider
Fidanzati - Engaged
Il matrimonio - Marriage

Comprehension Questions

Cosa fece Nerone con la madre e il fratellastro? What did Nero do with his mother and his stepbrother?

Cosa rese Nerone scontento? What made Nero displeased?

Cosa fece Nerone dopo la morte della madre? What did Nero do after his mother's death?

Historical Note

Emperor Nero, who reigned over the Roman Empire from 54 to 68 AD, is infamous for his tyrannical rule and extravagant lifestyle. Initially, he showed promise, but his reign descended into corruption and cruelty. Nero is best known for the Great Fire of Rome in 64 AD, which he allegedly fiddled during, and then blamed on Christians. His brutal persecution of Christians began here. Nero's extravagance strained the empire's finances, and his political purges led to the deaths of many prominent figures, including his mother, Agrippina. Ultimately, his rule ended in revolt and his suicide in 68 AD, marking a tumultuous chapter in Roman history.

IL MIRACOLO DI UN BAMBINO

Nella città di Napoli viveva una giovane coppia, Mario e Agata, molto amata dalle persone che li circondavano. Erano sposati da anni senza figli e sia il marito che la moglie erano sempre più tristi e cominciavano a non sopportarsi. Agata desiderava disperatamente un bambino e fece offerte agli dei della terra, ma per diversi anni non accadde nulla.

Un giorno, Mario andò in città e incontrò un uomo, Johan Christian Dahl, un pittore appena arrivato in città. Questo sconosciuto, Johan, gli chiese indicazioni per il Vesuvio e Mario condusse Johan sulla montagna per garantire la sua sicurezza. Mentre Johan dipingeva, Mario lo osservava e lo intratteneva. Quando Johan finì di dipingere, Mario lo portò a casa con sé e Agata preparò una grande zuppa e invitò i vicini ad accogliere Johan.

Quando tutto fu finito e tutti andarono a letto, Agata si diresse verso la stanza di Johan e lo pregò di fare un quadro di lei incinta. Johan la dipinse per il resto della notte e la mattina dopo, di buon'ora, il ventre di Agata era gonfio di un bambino. Agata partorì un maschio l'anno successivo e gli diedero il nome di Johan, lo strano pittore

THE MIRACLE OF A CHILD

In the city of Naples, there lived a young couple, Mario and Agata who were well loved by people around them. They had been married for years with no children and both husband and wife were increasingly sad and began to dislike each other. Agata became desperate for a baby and she made offerings to the gods of the land, but nothing happened for several years.

One day, Mario went to town and met a man, Johan Christian Dahl, a painter who had just arrived in town. This stranger, Johan, asked him for directions to Mount Vesuvius and Mario led Johan to the mountain to ensure his safety. As Johan painted, Mario watched and entertained him. When Johan finished painting, Mario took him home with him and Agata made a big pot of soup and invited her neighbors to welcome Johan.

After everything was done and everyone had gone to bed, Agata made her way to Johan's room and begged him to make a painting of her as a pregnant woman. Johan painted her for the rest of the night and early the next morning, Agata's belly was swollen with a baby. Agata gave birth to a boy the next year and they named him after Johan, the strange painter.

Vocabulary

Pittore - Painter
Strano - Strange
Diversi - Several
Indicazioni - Directions
Incinta - Pregnant
Invitato - Invited
Vicini di casa - Neighbors
Gonfio - Swollen
Disperata - Desperate
Nascita - Birth
Assicurarsi - Ensure

Comprehension Questions

Mario e Agata erano felici? Were Mario and Agata happy?

Cosa fece Mario per Johan? What did Mario do for Johan?

Come è rimasta incinta Mario? How did Mario become pregnant?

Historical Note

In 79 AD, the eruption of Mount Vesuvius near Pompeii, Italy, was a catastrophic event. It began with a massive cloud of ash and pumice, which darkened the sky and rained down on the city. The eruption's explosive force sent deadly pyroclastic surges, superheated gasses, and volcanic debris racing down the mountainside, engulfing Pompeii and nearby Herculaneum. The cities were buried under layers of ash, preserving them for centuries. Thousands perished, and the disaster froze daily life in time, providing a remarkable archaeological window into ancient Roman society when the cities were rediscovered in the 18th century.

ERBA A GRAZIA

Fin da piccolo, Diocle si era sempre interessato all'esercito. Era uno dei ragazzi più forti tra i suoi coetanei ed era un bambino ambizioso. Si arruolò nell'esercito romano in giovane età, lasciandosi alle spalle la famiglia e gli amici per dedicarsi alla difesa dell'impero.

Sebbene i suoi amici credessero nella sua forza, il suo status di famiglia umile era un grosso problema, poiché nessuno credeva che potesse avere una buona posizione nell'esercito. Tuttavia, si allenava ogni giorno e non aveva paura di accettare incarichi, anche se difficili. Si offrì volontario per andare a combattere in regioni difficili e ben presto divenne popolare tra i soldati. L'imperatore Carus conobbe subito questo giovane soldato coraggioso e presto divenne il soldato preferito dell'imperatore. Col tempo, salì di grado fino a diventare comandante di cavalleria dell'esercito dell'imperatore.

In seguito, l'imperatore si recò in Persia per una campagna e fu ucciso insieme al figlio Numeriano. Le truppe nominarono allora Diocle imperatore ed egli prese il nome di Diocleziano. Regnò come imperatore dell'Impero Romano fino alla sua abdicazione e istituì il governo più burocratico della storia dell'impero.

GRASS TO GRACE

From an early age, Diocles had always been interested in the military. He was one of the strongest boys amongst his peers and he was an ambitious young child. He joined the Roman military at a young age, leaving his family and friends behind to focus on defending the empire.

Although his friends believed in his strength, his lowly family status was a big problem as no one believed he could have a good position in the military. However, he trained every day and was not afraid to take on assignments no matter how hard. He volunteered to go to difficult regions to fight and soon enough, he became popular amongst the soldiers. The emperor, Carus was quick to know this young courageous soldier and he soon became the emperor's favorite soldier. Over time, he rose in rank to become a Cavalry commander of the Emperor's army.

Later, the Emperor went on a campaign to Persia and he was killed alongside his son, Numerian. The troops then made Diocles Emperor and he took the name Diocletian. He ruled as emperor of the Roman Empire up until his abdication and established the most bureaucratic government in the history of the empire.

Vocabulary

Interessato - Interested
Militare - Military
Focus - Focus
Storia - History
Rango - Rank
Coraggioso - Courageous
Preferito - Favorite
Campagna - Campaign
Regioni - Regions
Abbastanza - Enough
Stabilito - Established
Burocratico - Bureaucratic

Comprehension Questions

Quando Diocle si è arruolato nell'esercito? When did Diocles join the military?

Aveva una famiglia ricca? Did he have a rich family?

Come è diventato popolare? How did he become popular?

Historical Note

Diocletian was a Roman emperor who ruled from 284 to 305 AD. He's known for helping the Roman Empire during a tough time. Diocletian split the empire into two parts, the Eastern and Western Roman Empires, to make it easier to govern. He also brought stability by enforcing strict laws and trying to control inflation. Diocletian is famous for his persecution of Christians, but he's also remembered for stepping down from power voluntarily, which was unusual for emperors. He retired to a peaceful life, showing a desire for stability and a prosperous future for the Roman Empire.

FEDE SENZA PAURA

Molto tempo fa, nella vecchia città di Roma, quando il cristianesimo era un crimine e i cristiani erano diventati un culto segreto, c'era un giovane commerciante, Felix, che amava adorare con i cristiani. Ogni sera si riuniva con le persone che pregavano in segreto e insieme cantavano lodi e pregavano. Tuttavia, non poteva dichiararsi cristiano perché aveva paura della morte. Era sposato da poco e non voleva che la sua giovane moglie rimanesse vedova, così uscì di nascosto per unirsi a loro.

Sua moglie Felicia cominciò a chiedersi dove andasse ogni sera e pensò che avesse un'altra donna. Così, iniziò a seguirlo finché non scoprì la verità. Felicia era una donna coraggiosa, non aveva paura di andare contro la cattiva legge, così iniziò a partecipare alle riunioni che si tenevano di giorno. Felix fu turbato dalle sue azioni e la scoraggiò dal frequentare gli altri cristiani per evitare di essere uccisa. Tuttavia, la sua fede era diventata forte e alla fine fu arrestata.

Felix era preoccupato e triste, mentre pregava con gli altri cristiani per giorni. Non prese alcun pasto e, qualche giorno dopo, l'imperatore Costantino concesse al cristianesimo lo status legale, dopodiché la donna fu rilasciata.

L'UOMO MALATO

Molto tempo fa, nell'antica città di Roma, quando i poteri degli imperatori erano diventati così deboli da essere in balia dei militari che erano per lo più di origine tedesca, viveva un uomo tedesco con la moglie e due figli. Quest'uomo era molto fragile di salute e si ammalava quasi ogni settimana, tanto che la moglie spendeva tutto quello che aveva per la sua salute. Tuttavia, non stava migliorando.

Ben presto i vicini cominciarono a prendersi gioco di lui e lo chiamavano l'uomo debole. Cominciò a stare più spesso in casa per evitare gli insulti, mentre sua moglie commerciava al mercato. All'insaputa di tutti, il comandante dell'esercito romano, Odoacre, era suo grande amico e l'uomo aveva ospitato Odoecer quando erano più giovani.

Col tempo, l'uomo era diventato così debole da non poter più uscire e la moglie era ricorsa all'accattonaggio, dato che avevano venduto tutto ciò che avevano. Un giorno, la moglie andò al mercato e sentì le donne parlare di come Odoecer avesse rovesciato l'imperatore e fosse il nuovo sovrano. Corse a casa, con il cuore che le scoppiava di gioia, mentre informava il marito. Organizzarono un viaggio a palazzo e incontrarono Odoacre dopo molte difficoltà. Odoacre riconobbe subito il suo vecchio amico e decise di lasciare che i medici reali si prendessero cura di lui. Diede loro anche una casa ed essi entrarono a far parte del suo gabinetto.

L'AMORE GIOVANE

Ai tempi in cui l'Impero Romano aveva iniziato a rivendicare le terre che lo circondavano, l'imperatore inviò una truppa di soldati in una delle città della penisola italiana per rivendicare la città. Tra questi soldati c'era Giulio, uno dei più giovani della truppa. Aveva appena compiuto 14 anni quando si arruolò ufficialmente nell'esercito e, tre anni dopo, fece parte della truppa inviata a sconfiggere una grande città italiana.

Come la maggior parte dei giovani soldati dell'epoca, Marco era entusiasta della prospettiva di conquistare la città. Era determinato a far sì che il comandante della truppa notasse le sue capacità, per cui era sempre sul fronte di guerra.

La truppa si fermò in un piccolo villaggio accanto alla città appena conquistata e decise di riposare per la notte prima di proseguire il viaggio. Mentre si riposavano e discutevano, Marcus si incamminò verso la periferia della città. Mentre camminava, incontrò una giovane ragazza, Liv, di cui si innamorò immediatamente e decise di portarla con sé quando la guerra fosse finita. La convinse ad aspettare e a tornare con lui a Roma quando la guerra fosse finita. Lei accettò, ma Marcus fu ucciso in guerra. Liv continuò ad aspettarlo senza sapere che anche lei si era innamorata di lui. Invecchiò e morì, credendo che un giorno lui sarebbe tornato a cercarla.

YOUNG LOVE

In the times when the Roman Empire had begun to claim the lands around them, the emperor sent a troop of soldiers to one of the Italian peninsula cities to claim the city. Amongst these soldiers was Julius who was one of the youngest in the troop. He had just turned 14 when he joined the army officially and 3 years later, he was part of the troops sent to defeat a major town in Italy.

Like most young soldiers at the time, Marcus was excited at the prospect of conquering the town. He was determined for the commander of the troop to notice his skills, so he was always at the war front.

The troop stopped at a small village beside the town which they had just conquered and decided to rest for the night before moving on in the journey. While they rested and discussed, Marcus walked off towards the outskirts of the town. While walking, he met a young girl, Liv and immediately fell for her and he decided to take her back with him when the war was over. He convinced her to wait and go back with him to Rome when the war was over. She agreed to this but Marcus was killed in the war. Liv continued to wait for him not knowing this as she had also fallen in love with him. She grew old and died, believing he would one day come back to find her.

Vocabulary

Rivendicazione - Claim
Truppa - Troop
Ufficialmente - Officially
Sconfitta - Defeat
Comandante - Commander
Abilità - Skill
Conquistato - Conquered
Periferia - Outskirts
Prospettiva - Prospect
Determinato - Determined

Comprehension Questions

Dove Marcus ha conosciuto Liv? Where did Marcus meet Liv?

Marcus era orgoglioso del suo lavoro di soldato? Was Marcus proud of his job as a soldier?

Per quanto tempo Liv ha aspettato Marcus? For how long did Liv wait for Marcus?

Historical Notes

The conquest of Italy began around the 4th century BCE and lasted for several centuries. It involved Rome gradually subjugating various city-states, tribes, and kingdoms in the Italian Peninsula, ultimately leading to the formation of the Roman Republic. This expansion played a crucial role in shaping the Roman Empire's foundation and influencing its subsequent territorial growth and governance

FEDE

Paolo era un governante cristiano in una delle principali città d'Italia. Il declino dell'impero bizantino aveva giocato a suo favore, perché era riuscito a rendere sicura la sua città e a tenere al sicuro il suo popolo. Ogni mese teneva una riunione con gli altri governanti cristiani e insieme contribuivano alla costruzione di altre chiese, in modo da incoraggiare il cristianesimo in tutta la terra.

Tuttavia, Paolo era molto preoccupato per i suoi figli, Marco e Giovanni. Sebbene fosse un fervente cristiano, i suoi figli non credevano nel suo Dio e si presentavano pubblicamente a eventi pagani. Parlò spesso con loro e con i suoi consiglieri, ma essi rimasero irremovibili. Cominciò a farli pregare perché cambiassero. Ogni volta che pregava, lo sosteneva donando un terreno alla chiesa. Credeva che in questo modo le sue preghiere sarebbero arrivate più velocemente a Dio.

Un giorno Mark decise che non sarebbe più andato agli eventi pagani e iniziò a seguire la sua famiglia in chiesa. Insieme a Paolo, convinse anche Giovanni. Ancora una volta, Paolo donò altre terre alla Chiesa e sostenne l'istituzione dello Stato Pontificio. In segno di riconoscenza, concesse al Papa il potere sovrano sulla sua città. A sua insaputa, i suoi figli si erano uniti alla Chiesa a causa delle belle ragazze presenti. Paolo continuò a ringraziare Dio per la transizione dei suoi figli fino alla sua morte.

FAITH

Paul was a Christian ruler in one of the major cities in Italy. The decline of the Byzantine empire had worked in his favor as he was able to secure his city and keep his people safe. Every month, he held a meeting with the other Christian rulers and together, they contributed to the building of more churches so Christianity would be encouraged throughout the land.

However, Paul worried a lot about his sons, Mark and John. Although he was a fervent Christian, his sons didn't believe in his God and publicly showed up at pagan events. He spoke to them often and his advisers as well, but they remained adamant. He began to put them in prayers so they could change. Each time he prayed, he backed it up by donating land to the church. He believed his prayers would transcend to God faster that way.

Mark decided one day that he was no longer going to pagan events and began following his family to church. Together with Paul, he convinced John as well. Again, Paul donated more land to the church and supported the establishment of the papal states. In appreciation, he gave the pope sovereign power over his city. Unknown to him, his sons had joined the church because of the beautiful girls in the church. Paul continued to thank God over the transition of his sons until his death.

Vocabulary

Declino - Decline
Chiesa - Church
Sicuro - Secure
Mese - Month
Contribuito - Contributed
Papa - Pope
Transizione - Transition
Pagano - Pagan
Donati - Donated
Fervente - Fervent
Adamante - Adamant
Trascendere - Transcend

Comprehension Questions

In che modo i figli di Paolo lo hanno ingannato? How did Paul's sons deceive him?

Quali furono i contributi di Paolo al cristianesimo? What were Paul's contributions to christianity?

Perché Paolo era preoccupato per i suoi figli? Why was Paul worried about his sons?

Historical Note

The Papal States, established in ancient Italy, emerged as a result of the growing influence of the Roman Catholic Church in late antiquity. In the 8th century, Pope Stephen II sought protection from the Lombard threat, leading to the creation of the Papal States. Charlemagne, the Frankish king, responded by granting the Pope territorial holdings, including significant parts of central Italy. This marked the birth of the Papal States, a theocratic entity ruled by the Pope and central to medieval European politics. These states endured for over a thousand years, until Italian unification in the 19th century, when they were gradually absorbed into the Kingdom of Italy.

AMORE VERO

Quando Paolo morì, Marco divenne il capo della città e, come suo padre, continuò a seguire le vie della Chiesa. Permise al papa di dirigere gli affari della città. Giovanni era contrario a questa decisione e cominciarono a litigare finché non fu bandito dalla città. Si trasferì in Europa con la famiglia e fondò un proprio regno sotto il Sacro Romano Imperatore.

Lì incontrò una donna, Claudia, che nel suo modo di fare gli ricordava la sua defunta madre. Incarnava la testardaggine del fratello e la bellezza della madre. Iniziò a corteggiarla segretamente. Ogni sera la invitava a palazzo per cantare per lui. Ma la moglie si accorse della strana predilezione di Giovanni per Claudia e scatenò un putiferio quando Giovanni ammise di amarla. Andò da Claudia e minacciò di ucciderla se non avesse lasciato John.

Claudia decise di lasciare il regno senza dirlo a John. Quando non si presentò a palazzo per giorni, John si preoccupò e non riuscì a dormire. Smise di mangiare e sua moglie si preoccupò e confessò la minaccia. Alla fine Giovanni mandò le sue guardie a cercarla attraverso il Sacro Romano Impero. La sposò la notte stessa in cui la riportarono a casa e vissero felicemente.

TRUE LOVE

When Paul died, Mark became the ruler of the city and like his father, he continued in the ways of the church. He allowed the pope to direct the affairs of the city. John was against this decision and they began to fight until he was banished from the city. He moved to Europe with his family and founded his own Kingdom under the Holy Roman Emperor.

There, he met a woman, Claudia who reminded him of his late mother in her mannerism. She embodied the stubbornness of his brother and the beauty of his mother. He began to court her secretly. Every evening, he invited her to the palace to sing for him. But, his wife noticed the strange fondness John had for Claudia and caused a ruckus when John admitted to loving her. She went to Claudia and threatened to kill her if she didn't leave John.

Claudia decided to leave the kingdom without telling John. When she didn't come to the palace for days, John

became worried and couldn't sleep. He stopped eating and his wife became worried and confessed the threat. John eventually sent his guards to look for her through the Holy Roman Empire. He wedded her the night they brought her back and lived happily after.

Vocabulary

Diretto - Direct
Tribunale - Court
Manierismo - Mannerism
Incarnato - Embodied
Regno - Kingdom
Sposato - Wedded
Bandito - Banished
Affari - Affairs
Confessati - Confessed
Affetto - Fondness

Comprehension Questions

Perché Giovanni fu bandito dalla città? Why was John banished from the city?

Perché a Giovanni piaceva Claudia? Why did John like Claudia?

Cosa accadde a Giovanni quando Claudia se ne andò? What happened to John when Claudia left?

Historical Note

The Holy Roman Empire, established in 800 AD, was a complex political entity that endured until its dissolution in 1806. Despite its name, it was neither truly Roman nor consistently holy. Spanning Western and Central Europe, it included regions of present-day Germany, Austria, Italy, and more. Characterized by a decentralized structure, it had emperors who were crowned and legitimized by the Pope. Over its history, the empire faced internal conflicts, territorial disputes, and power struggles, resulting in both periods of stability and fragmentation. It finally succumbed to the pressures of Napoleon Bonaparte in 1806, leading to its dissolution and reshaping of Europe.

LA CONTROVERSIA SULLE INVESTITURE

Enrico IV fu uno dei più giovani imperatori d'Europa, poiché divenne imperatore all'età di cinque anni. Fu nominato imperatore dal papa Gregorio VII e i due divennero presto amici. Tuttavia, cominciarono a sorgere tensioni da entrambe le parti, poiché Gregorio VII, il papa, e l'imperatore avevano in mente persone diverse per il prossimo papa.

Enrico IV crebbe con il suo amico Matteo al suo fianco e Matteo era uno dei migliori cristiani dell'impero. Faceva spesso donazioni alla chiesa e aiutava i poveri, tanto che il popolo lo aveva etichettato come il gentile Matteo. Enrico IV decise di incontrarsi con Gregorio VII per discutere della persona in grado di essere il prossimo vescovo della città. Egli riteneva che il suo amico Matteo fosse la persona migliore per questo incarico. Voleva usarlo come forma di gratitudine.

Tuttavia, anche Gregorio VII aveva il suo candidato e stava preparando un giovane per il ruolo. Alla fine dell'incontro, il re e l'imperatore non riuscirono a trovare un accordo, il che portò Gregorio VII a scrivere una lettera pubblica per discutere il suo punto di vista sull'intera questione. Egli credeva nella completa autonomia della Chiesa, del Papa e dei suoi vescovi. La lettera irritò a tal punto Enrico IV che rimosse Gregorio dalla sua posizione di papa. Gregorio, a sua volta, lo rimosse dalla carica di Sacro Romano Imperatore e per anni i due litigarono senza trovare una vera soluzione.

Questa storia è un adattamento fittizio della controversia sulle investiture nel Medioevo.

FOLLIA DI JAMES

Un tempo la Sicilia era sotto un dominio islamico autonomo e i cristiani non potevano servire facilmente il loro Dio. Tra questi cristiani c'erano Giacomo e la sua vecchia moglie. A 70 anni, Giacomo era cristiano dall'età di 20 anni e aveva conosciuto sua moglie Marta nell'ovile. Lavorava nel tempio e aiutava a tradurre le lettere che venivano inviate da altri luoghi.

Con il passare del tempo, divenne sempre più difficile mantenere la sua fede nello Stato islamico e cominciò a pensare di trasferirsi in un nuovo Stato al di fuori dell'Emirato di Sicilia, dove avrebbe potuto trovare un gran numero di cristiani. Una mattina d'autunno, prese la sua borsa e uscì di casa, lasciando la moglie in Sicilia. Si trasferì nel sud e trovò subito un tempio da servire, ma la sua mente non era in pace. Non riusciva a concentrarsi e le nuove persone che incontrava gli ricordavano la moglie. Si ammalò gravemente e cercò di tornare in Sicilia, ma era troppo vecchio e il senso di colpa lo indebolì ulteriormente.

Mesi dopo, giunse la notizia che Roberto il Guiscardo e suo fratello Ruggero avevano ottenuto il controllo dell'isola, che non faceva più parte dell'Emirato. La notizia lo rallegrò a tal punto che gli tornarono le forze e si mise in viaggio per incontrare la sua vecchia moglie. Trascorse il resto della sua vita scrivendo e traducendo lettere nel tempio.

JAMES' FOLLY

Once, Sicily was under an autonomous Islamic rule and the Christians there couldn't serve their God easily. Amongst these Christians were James and his old wife. At 70 years, James had been a Christian since he was 20 and met his wife, Martha in the fold. He worked in the temple and helped translate letters that were sent from other places.

As time went by, it became harder to maintain his faith in the Islamic state and he began to think of moving to a new state outside the Emirate of Sicily where he could find a vast number of Christians. One morning in the fall, he picked up his bag and left home, leaving his wife in Sicily. He moved to the south and soon found a temple to serve, but his mind was not at peace. He couldn't focus because the new people he met reminded him of his wife. He became very sick and tried to travel back to Sicily but he was too old and his guilt weakened him further.

Months later, news came that Robert Guiscard and his brother, Roger had gained control of the island and it was no longer part of the Emirate. The news gladdened him so much that his strength came back and he traveled back to meet his old wife. He spent the rest of his life writing and translating letters in the temple.

Vocabulary

Piegare - Fold
Tempio - Temple
Tradurre - Translate
Mantenere - Maintain
Colpa - Guilt
Adulata - Gladdened
Isola - Island
Luoghi - Places
Vasto - Vast
Ulteriore - Further

Comprehension Questions

Perché James è andato via di casa? Why did James leave home?

Che lavoro faceva James? What work did James do?

A James piacque il periodo trascorso nel Sud? Did James enjoy his time in the south?

Historical Note

Sicily, a vital part of the Roman Empire, experienced a complex history. It was conquered by Rome in the 3rd century BC and served as a crucial grain source. In 476 AD, the Roman Empire fell, but Sicily continued under various rulers, including the Byzantines and Arabs. Norman conquest in the 11th century brought a new chapter. Eventually, the Kingdom of Sicily was established, becoming a center of culture and trade. It later merged with the Kingdom of Naples. The island's history includes periods of Norman, Spanish, and Bourbon rule. It wasn't until Italian unification in 1861 that Sicily became part of modern Italy.

LA MORTE NERA

Il 1347 fu un anno molto brutto per Lucas. Viveva in un piccolo villaggio del Nord Africa con la sua famiglia, ma la vita non andava più bene per lui. La peste aveva ucciso suo fratello all'inizio dell'anno e ora anche sua madre era malata. La gente gli disse che la sua famiglia aveva offeso gli dei della terra e che doveva offrire dei sacrifici. Gli chiesero di andare dai sacerdoti per pregare. Lucas lasciò la madre malata da sola a casa e si recò nella capitale per visitare il tempio.

Il sacerdote gli chiese di offrire cinque capre agli dei e di portare sua madre al tempio per le preghiere. Ma lui non aveva soldi. L'uomo si sentì sconvolto e insistette per non andarsene finché il sacerdote non avesse pregato per sua madre. Il sacerdote divenne comprensivo e decise di aiutare Lucus. Chiese invece a Lucas di portare 3 capre e anche in questo caso Luças non poteva permetterselo. Il sacerdote rimase perplesso e chiese a Lucas di portare ciò che poteva permettersi. Lucas gli diede il suo vecchio flauto e il sacerdote mandò a chiamare sua madre. Ma quando arrivò a casa, la madre di Lucas era morta, insieme a tutti gli altri abitanti della città. Lucas tornò al tempio e suonò il flauto fino alla morte.

THE BLACK DEATH

The year 1347 was a very bad year for Lucas. He lived in a small village in North Africa with his family but life was no longer going well for him. There was a plague spreading around and it had claimed his brother earlier in the year and now, his mother was ill as well. People around told him that his family had offended the gods of the land and he needed to offer sacrifices. They asked him to go to the priests for prayers. Lucas left his ailing mother alone at home and went to the capital to visit the temple.

The priest asked him to offer five goats to the gods and bring his mother to the temple for prayers. But he had no money. He became devastated and insisted on not leaving until the priest prayed for his mother. The priest became sympathetic and decided to help Lucus. He asked Lucas to bring 3 goats instead and again, Luças couldn't afford it. The priest was concerned and asked Lucas to bring what he could afford. Lucas gave him his old flute and the priest sent for his mother. But on getting home, Lucas's mother had died, alongside the rest of the people in town. Lucas went back to the temple and played the flute until his death.

Vocabulary

Peste - Plague
Malato - ill
Devastato - Devastated
Sacrifici - Sacrifices
Accordarsi - Afford
Flauto - Flute
Preoccupato - Concerned
Malato - Ailing
Simpatico - Sympathetic

Comprehension Questions

Perché il sacerdote chiese delle capre? Why did the priest request goats?

Cosa accadde agli abitanti della città? What happened to the people in the town?

Cosa fece Lucas quando scoprì la cattiva notizia? What did Lucas do when he found out the bad news?

Historical Note

The Black Death, a devastating pandemic of bubonic and pneumonic plague, struck Italy in the mid-14th century. Originating in Asia, it reached Italy by 1347, spreading rapidly through trade routes and ports. The consequences were catastrophic. Italy's population dwindled, with some regions losing up to 60% of their inhabitants. The economy crumbled as labor shortages spiked wages. Society was profoundly disrupted, with widespread fear, social upheaval, and religious fervor. Artists, like Boccaccio, chronicled the despair in works like the Decameron. Italy's Renaissance, emerging decades later, was marked by the stark contrast of revival and renewal after the devastation of the Black Death.

IL BAMBINO CON DUE PADRI

In una piccola città d'Europa, una giovane donna, Ruth, aveva appena partorito dopo 5 anni di sterilità. La gente del paese accorreva a casa sua con doni per dare il benvenuto ai nuovi figli, ma c'era qualcosa di strano. Suo marito non si trovava da nessuna parte. Secondo Ruth, era uscito la mattina della nascita dei bambini e da allora non era più tornato a casa. La gente organizzò delle squadre di ricerca per cercarlo, ma non si trovava da nessuna parte. Ruth pianse per tre anni prima di prendere un altro marito, ma non ebbe alcun figlio da questo nuovo uomo.

Il bambino, Adrian, crebbe come il padre e divenne presto un mercante che commerciava con il Medio Oriente nel 1499. Questo commercio aprì il loro villaggio al mondo e presto iniziarono a comunicare di più con persone provenienti da altre parti del mondo e a far crescere la loro economia. Un giorno, mentre commerciava in mare, incontrò un uomo che gli somigliava. Confuso, corse a casa e raccontò a sua madre di quell'uomo. Il giorno dopo, andò in mare con sua madre e cercò tra i marinai.

Incontrarono l'uomo che si rivelò essere suo padre. Ruth era troppo scioccata di vedere il suo vecchio marito e chiese di sapere cosa fosse successo. Ahimè, era annegato in mare e i marinai lo avevano salvato e curato finché non era guarito. Si riunirono e Adrian divenne il ragazzo con due padri.

L'AMORE IN LUOGHI SCONOSCIUTI

Stranamente, Aldina incontrò Diana durante l'invasione dell'Italia da parte del re francese Carlo VIII, quando c'era un conflitto tra il Sacro Romano Impero, la Francia, la Spagna e diverse città italiane. Diana era originaria della Siba, una delle cittadine invase, e Aldina era uno dei medici che seguivano i soldati in battaglia per curare le loro ferite. Aldina si trovava nella foresta per procurarsi erbe medicinali da usare per curare le ferite quando incontrò Diana, che si trovava lì per lo stesso motivo. Suo padre era malato e lei non poteva permettersi le medicine, così era venuta a prenderle da sola.

Tuttavia, era incerta su quale erba scegliere e, nella sua confusione, iniziò a piangere. Questo suono incuriosì Aldina, che si inoltrò nella foresta per trovarne la fonte. Lì vide Diana che piangeva. Si informò sul problema e la aiutò a procurarsi le erbe necessarie, dopodiché le promise di tenersi in contatto.

Tornato al nascondiglio con i soldati, si rese conto di aver dimenticato le erbe con Diana e di doverle recuperare per iniziare il viaggio. Si mise a cercarla di casa in casa finché non la trovò. Quando la trovò era con il padre malato. Decise di curare l'uomo prima di partire. Dopo la cura, si apprestò a partire con le erbe quando Diana gli trattenne il cappotto. Si rifiutò di lasciarlo finché lui non promise di portarla con sé. La sposò subito e vissero insieme anche dopo la guerra.

LOVE IN STRANGE PLACES

Strangely, Aldina met Diana during the time the French king, Charles VIII invaded Italy, when there was conflict between the Holy Roman Empire, France, Spain and various Italian cities. Diana was a native of the Siba, one of the small towns that were invaded and Aldina was one of the medical practitioners who followed the soldiers in battle to treat their injuries. Aldina was in the forest to get medicinal herbs that could be used to treat wounds when he met Diana who was there for the same reason. Her father was ill and she could not afford the medicine so she came to get them herself.

However, she was unsure about which herb to pick and in her confusion, she began to cry. This sound intrigued Aldina and he walked further into the forest to find the source. There, he saw Diana weeping. He enquired about the problem and helped her get the needed herbs after which he promised to keep in touch.

On getting back to the hideout with the soldiers, he realized that he had forgotten his herbs with Diana, and he needed to get them for the journey to start. He set out to look for her from house to house until he found her. She was with her ailing father when he found her. He decided to treat the man before leaving. After the treatment, he set out to leave with the herbs when Diana held his coat. She refused to leave him until he promised to take her with him. He married her right away and they lived together after the war.

Vocabulary

Durante - During
Invaso - Invaded
Incerto - Unsure
Conflitto - Conflict
Fonte - Source
Nativo - Native
Medico - Medical
Ferite - Wounds
Nascondiglio - Hideout
Ferite - Injuries
Erbe - Herbs

Comprehension Questions

Che cosa cercava Diane nella foresta? What did Diane search for in the forest?

In che modo Aldina aiutò gli altri soldati? How did Aldina help the other soldiers?

Perché Aldina tornò a casa di Diane? Why did Aldina return to Diane's house?

Historical Note

The War of Northern Italy, occurring from 1494 to 1559, was a series of conflicts involving major European powers, primarily France and Spain, fighting for control of the Italian peninsula. It began when Charles VIII of France invaded Italy in 1494, sparking a decades-long struggle. The conflict included battles at places like Fornovo, Marignano, and Pavia. The Peace of Cateau-Cambrésis in 1559 ended the war, leaving Italy divided between the Spanish Habsburgs and the French Valois dynasty. This war marked a crucial phase in the Italian Wars, shaping the political landscape and culture of the region during the Renaissance.

L'UCCELLO CHE CANTA

Durante le guerre d'Italia, poco prima della firma del trattato di Cateau-Cambrésis, Albina viveva con lo zio Carlo in Italia. Avendo perso i genitori a causa della guerra, era diventata una bambina venditrice. Non rideva più come gli altri bambini, né parlava. Di giorno era sempre imbronciata e di notte aveva difficoltà a dormire. Era talmente dimagrita che Charles cominciò a temere per la sua vita.

Un giorno, Albina incontrò un uccello mentre piangeva nella fattoria. Questo uccello era blu e ricordava facilmente ad Albina sua madre. L'uccello cantò a lungo per Albina e le asciugò le lacrime con il becco. Albina portò l'uccello a casa con sé e costruì una gabbia. Gli diede da mangiare ogni giorno e poi l'uccello cantò per lei fino a farla sorridere. Lentamente, parlò all'uccello e gli raccontò i suoi dolori e i suoi incubi. L'uccello intrecciò questi racconti in canzoni che fecero ridere Albina e dormire sonni tranquilli.

Charles notò il cambiamento di Albina e la convinse a presentarle l'uccello. Quando arrivarono alla gabbia, l'uccello cantò anche per Carlo, lodandolo per la sua gentilezza. Charles costruì una gabbia più grande per l'uccello e insieme vissero come una grande famiglia felice.

THE SINGING BIRD

During the Italian wars, just before the treaty of Cateau-Cambrésis was signed, Albina lived with her uncle, Charles in Italy. Having lost her parents to the war, she had become a sad child. She no longer laughed like the other children, or even spoke. She was always sullen during the day and at night, she found it difficult to sleep. She lost so much weight that Charles began to fear for her life.

One day, Albina met a bird while crying on the farm. This bird was blue and easily reminded Albina of her mother. The bird sang for Albina for a long time and wiped her tears with his beak. Albina took the bird home with her and made a cage. She fed the bird daily and after, the bird sang for her until she smiled. Slowly, she spoke to the bird and told of her sorrows and nightmares. The bird weaved these tales into songs that made Albina laugh and sleep soundly.

Charles noticed the change in Albina and convinced her to introduce her to the bird. When they got to the cage, the bird sang for Charles as well, praising him for his kindness. Charles made a bigger cage for the bird and together, they all lived as one big happy family.

Vocabulary

Blu - Blue
Con forza - Soundly
Introdurre - Introduce
Dolori - Sorrows
Racconti - Tales
Gentilezza - Kindness
Incubo - Nightmare
Gabbia - Cage
Trattato - Treaty
Raggiungere - Spoke
Intrecciato - Weaved

Comprehension Questions

Perché Albina era triste? Why was Albina sad?

L'uccello ha reso Albina felice? Did the bird make Albina happy?

Quanti nuovi amici si è fatta Albina? How many new friends did Albina make?

Historical Note

The Italian Wars were a broader series of conflicts that spanned from the late 15th century to the mid-16th century and included a wider geographical scope. These wars were characterized by power struggles and alliances involving major European states, such as France, Spain, and the Holy Roman Empire, in addition to Italian city-states. The Italian Wars encompassed both northern and central Italy and had a significant impact on the entire Italian peninsula.

In summary, while the War of Northern Italy was a subset of the Italian Wars, the latter term refers to a more extensive and prolonged series of conflicts with broader geopolitical implications involving Italy and major European powers

IL RAGAZZO CHE AMAVA MARTIN

Giacomo era uno dei numerosi cugini di Martin Lutero, il monaco e teologo tedesco. Non era solo un membro della famiglia, ma anche uno dei suoi più stretti collaboratori. Lo considerava con così tanto rispetto che le persone intorno a lui si chiedevano se stesse venerando suo zio.

Parlava di Martin, parlava con un tale bagliore negli occhi e sua madre temeva che sarebbe diventato un monaco proprio come Martin. La madre escogitò allora un piano per impedirgli di andare di nuovo a casa di Martin. Mandò degli uomini a dirgli che la casa di Martin era stata rasa al suolo e che non accettava più visite. Gli uomini dissero inoltre a Giacomo che Martin stava pregando da solo con Dio e che voleva la solitudine.

Ma Giacomo non era convinto, conosceva Martin meglio delle bugie e aveva sentito parlare dell'inchiodatura delle 95 Tesi alla porta della chiesa di Wittenberg. Sapeva che Martin non avrebbe potuto farlo in solitudine e quindi si rattristò per le buffonate della madre. Fece i bagagli e partì per Wittenberg, dove incontrò Martin e Giovanni Calvino. Si unì alla loro missione e li aiutò a margine mentre protestavano contro alcune pratiche della Chiesa cattolica.

In seguito Giacomo si sposò contro i dubbi della madre ed educò i suoi figli a seguire le idee di Martin.

THE BOY WHO LOVED MARTIN

James was one of the numerous cousins of Martin Luther, the German monk and theologian. He wasn't just a family member, he was also one of the close associates of the man. He regarded him with so much respect that people around him wondered if he was worshiping his uncle.

He spoke of Martin, he spoke with such glow in his eyes and his mother became afraid that he would become a monk just like Martin. His mother then devised a plan to stop him from going to Martin's place again. She sent men to tell him that Martin's place had been razed down and he no longer accepted visitors. They further told James that Martin was currently praying alone to God and he wanted solitude.

But, James wasn't convinced, he knew Martin better than the lies and he had heard of the nailing of 95 Theses to a church door in Wittenberg. He knew Martin couldn't have done that from solitude so he became sad at his mother's antics. He packed his bags and left for Wittenberg where he met up with Martin and John Calvin. He joined their mission and helped them on the side as they protested against several practices of the catholic church.

James later got married against his mother's doubt and raised his children to follow Martin's ideas.

Vocabulary

Numerose - Numerous
Bugie - Lies
escogitate - Devised
Inchiodare - Nailing
Solitudine - Solitude
Buffonate - Antics
Missione - Mission
Pratiche - Practices
Dubbio - Doubt
Bagliore - Glow

Comprehension Questions

Perché la madre di James era preoccupata? Why was James's mother worried?

Cosa fece la madre per impedirgli di andare da Martin? What did his mother do to stop him from going to Martin?

James rimase celibe? Did James remain unmarried?

Historical Note

The Reformation, spanning the 16th century, was a pivotal religious and social movement in Europe. Triggered by Martin Luther's 95 Theses in 1517, it sought to reform the Roman Catholic Church, challenging its practices and doctrines. Luther's ideas, emphasizing faith and scripture over papal authority, sparked a religious schism. This movement paved the way for other reformers like John Calvin and Henry VIII to break with the Catholic Church, leading to the establishment of Protestant denominations. The Reformation transformed Europe, leading to religious wars, new forms of Christianity, and profound changes in politics and society, leaving an enduring legacy in the Western world.

PETER LO STUPIDO

Peter aveva sempre odiato John Churchill fin da piccolo. Erano cresciuti insieme come coetanei, ma fin da piccoli John era il più forte dei due. Correva più veloce, si muoveva con rapidità ed era anche il più fine. Questo fece arrabbiare Peter a tal punto che si rifiutò di giocare ancora con John fino a quando John non fu arruolato nell'esercito e Peter no, a causa della sua salute cagionevole.

Peter si rifiutò di considerare la sua salute cagionevole come una scusa, poiché credeva fermamente che John avesse preso il suo posto nell'esercito. Così, ogni giorno, saliva sulla collina e malediceva Giovanni. Gli augurava la morte e sperava che gli uccelli si cibassero delle sue carcasse. Dopo un po' di tempo, Peter sposò una brava ragazza, ma l'odio era ancora evidente, visto che il giorno delle nozze fece un brindisi alla morte di John.

Col passare del tempo, John salì di grado nell'esercito fino a diventare un leader militare e si fece chiamare Duca di Marlborough. Ogni volta che l'esercito di John vinceva in battaglia, Peter piangeva per giorni. Quando Peter seppe che John Churchill aveva portato il suo esercito alla vittoria nella battaglia di Blenheim, divenne così geloso che smise di mangiare e morì di fame.

IL GRANDE

Marco era un ragazzo all'Isola d'Elba quando Napoleone Bonaparte fondò l'impero francese. Ammirava lo zelo del condottiero e spesso citava le sue parole parlando con gli amici. Voleva cambiare le cose come Napoleone Bonaparte e iniziò a dare ai poveri intorno a lui. Era determinato ad avere un impatto intorno a sé, tanto che i suoi amici si stancarono delle sue parole. Credevano che non potesse fare molto.

Cominciarono a prenderlo in giro e smisero di parlare con lui. Vergognandosi, Mark iniziò a rubare i soldi del padre per darli ai poveri. Ogni sera entrava nella stanza dell'uomo, prendeva un po' di denaro e lo metteva in una zona dell'isola designata dove i poveri erano soliti recarsi. Col tempo, queste persone si abituarono alla strana vista del denaro e chiamarono questo salvatore sconosciuto che lasciava i soldi per loro, il grande. I suoi amici continuarono a prenderlo in giro, senza sapere che era la leggenda dell'isola.

Alla fine smise di dare soldi alla gente quando Napoleone Bonaparte fu esiliato all'Elba. Non poteva sopportare il fallimento della persona che aveva ammirato per tutta la vita. Lasciò l'Elba e non fu mai più visto.

THE GREAT

Mark was a young boy on the Island of Elba when Napoleon Bonaparte established the French empire. He admired the zeal of the leader and would often quote his words while speaking with his friends. He wanted to bring about change like Napoleon Bonaparte and he began to give to the poor around him. He was determined to make an impact around him, so much so that his friends became tired of his words. They believed he couldn't do much.

They began to make fun of him and stopped speaking with him. Ashamed, Mark began to steal his father's money to give to the poor. Every night, he would walk into the man's room, take some money and put it in a designated part of the island where the poor frequented. Over time, these people became used to the strange sight of money and called this unknown savior who left money for them, the great. His friends continued to tease him, without knowing he was the legend on the island.

He eventually stopped giving people money when Napoleon Bonaparte was exiled to Elba. He couldn't stand the failure of the person he had admired all through his life. He left Elba and was never seen again.

Vocabulary

Zelo - Zeal
Ammirato - Admired
Stuzzicare - Tease
Citazione - Quote
Vergognati - Ashamed
Impatto - Impact
Vista - Sight
Esiliato - Exiled
Salvatore - Savior
Leggenda - Legend

Comprehension Questions

Cosa ha spinto Mark a volere un cambiamento? What inspired Mark to want change?

In che modo ha ottenuto questo risultato? In what way did he achieve this?

Pensate che Mark abbia avuto successo? Do you think Mark was successful?

Historical Notes

Napoleon's presence in Italy was transformative. He created the Kingdom of Italy in 1805, fostering a sense of unity and promoting legal reforms. However, his 1812 Russian campaign weakened his control, allowing anti-Napoleonic sentiments to grow. As the European coalition pushed against him, Napoleon retreated to France in 1814, briefly abdicating. The fall of Napoleon had a significant impact on Italy. The Congress of Vienna redrew boundaries, returning Italy to a patchwork of states. Yet, Napoleon's legacy lingered, influencing the Italian unification movement that would lead to the Risorgimento. Ultimately, his invasion and fall left an enduring mark on the Italian peninsula's path toward unity and independence.

SFIDARE LE PROBABILITÀ

Alberta era una donna di mezza età che viveva in Italia nel XIX secolo. Era una commerciante e contadina che scambiava i suoi raccolti con altre parti della penisola italiana. Era amata da tutti ed era una delle persone più popolari e gentili del suo Stato.

Tuttavia, Alberta aveva un problema: non aveva figli né marito. Non si era mai sposata e sembrava piuttosto disinteressata alla prospettiva. Nonostante ciò, ogni giorno gli uomini e le donne della sua zona andavano a casa sua per consigliarle di sposarsi, ma Alberta li derideva.

Un giorno, un giovane commerciante di fuori dello Stato la visitò e cercò alloggio a casa di Alberta. Questo commerciante, Luca, si innamorò di Alberta e del suo modo di fare. Decise di corteggiarla, ma la gente mise in giro la voce che Alberta era troppo vecchia per lui. Lo convinsero a corteggiare qualcun altro. Alberta ne fu delusa e decise di trasferirsi in un altro Stato. Sulla sua strada incontrò i soldati di Giuseppe Garibaldi che le parlarono dei vantaggi dell'unità d'Italia. Si unì al suo esercito nella lotta per l'unità d'Italia. Dopo l'unificazione, incontrò il re Vittorio Emanuele II, si innamorò di uno dei suoi cugini e infine si sposò.

DEFYING ODDS

Alberta was a middle-aged woman who lived in Italy in the 19th century. She was a trader and farmer who traded her crops with other parts of the Italian peninsula. She was loved by everyone and was one of the most popular and kind people in her state

However, Alberta had one problem: she had no child nor husband. She had never gotten married and she seemed quite uninterested at the prospect. Regardless, each day, the men and women of her place would go to her place every night and advise her to marry but Alberta would laugh them off.

One day, a young trader outside the state visited and sought accommodation at Alberta's home. This trader, Luca fell in love with Alberta and her mannerism. He decided to court her but the people spread rumors that Alberta was too old for him. They convinced him to court someone else. On hearing this, Alberta was disappointed and decided to move away to another state. She met Giuseppe Garibaldi's soldiers on her way and they told her about the benefit of the unification of Italy. She joined his army in the fight for the unification of Italy. After the unification, she met with King Victor Emmanuel II, fell in love with one of his cousins, and finally got married.

Vocabulary

Problema - Problem
Nonostante - Regardless
Deciso - Decided
Bambino - Child
Unificazione - Unification
Sistemazione - Accommodation
Beneficio - Benefit
Disinteressato - Uninterested

Comprehension Questions

Perché Alberta ha lavorato? Why did Alberta do for work?

Perché Luca non ha sposato Alberta? Why did Luca not marry Alberta?

Qual era l'unico problema di Alberta? What was Alberta's single problem?

The unification of Italy in the 19th century was a complex and tumultuous process. Prior to unification, the Italian peninsula was divided into numerous independent states and territories, controlled by foreign powers like Austria and the Papal States. Visionaries like Giuseppe Garibaldi, Count Camillo di Cavour, and Giuseppe Mazzini played pivotal roles in the movement for unification. Wars, uprisings, and diplomatic maneuvering ultimately led to the formation of the Kingdom of Italy in 1861 under King Victor Emmanuel II. This unification, known as the Risorgimento, symbolized a significant step towards Italy's emergence as a modern nation-state, marked by cultural diversity, regional differences, and political challenges.

LA CAPRA

Emily era una bambina testarda, non stava mai ferma e si trovava sempre in un guaio o nell'altro. Per quanto le persone intorno si sforzassero, Emily non ascoltava mai né si preoccupava delle regole. Considerava tutti insensati e sceglieva di fare sempre a modo suo.

Ora, questo era un periodo molto delicato in Prussia, quando Otto von Bismarck aveva appena sconfitto i francesi e tutti si muovevano con cautela. Tuttavia, per Emily era il momento di festeggiare la vittoria di un Ministro-Presidente che conosceva appena.

Un giorno la madre di Emily uscì, con l'ordine tassativo di non lasciare la casa se non per motivi importanti. Tuttavia, Emily uscì subito dopo che la madre se ne fu andata. Entrò nel mercato e usò tutti i suoi soldi per comprare dei dolci. Dopo averli comprati, si sedette in un angolo e li mangiò tutti, senza alcuna cautela. I denti cominciarono a dolerle e il suo corpo divenne troppo pesante. Spaventata da ciò che stava accadendo al suo corpo, Emily urlò, ma nessuno la sentì. La sua voce era sparita. Aveva mangiato dolci avvelenati. Arrivò la notizia che Bismarck aveva ufficialmente costituito l'impero tedesco e il popolo cominciò a esultare. Emily cercò di strisciare verso casa, ma fu calpestata e uccisa dalla folla che si precipitava a festeggiare.

THE GOAT

Emily was a stubborn child, she never sat still and was always in one trouble or the other. No matter how much people around tried, Emily never listened or cared about the rules. She regarded everyone as senseless and chose to do things her way every time.

Now, this was a very sensitive period in Prussia when Otto von Bismarck had just defeated the French and everyone walked about carefully. Yet for Emily, this was a time to celebrate the victory of a Minister-President whom she barely knew.

Emily's mother went out one day, with strict instructions that Emily shouldn't leave the house unless it was important. However, Emily left immediately after her mother went away. She walked into the market and used all of her money to buy sweets. After buying the sweets, she sat in a corner and ate it all without caution. Her teeth began to ache and her body became too heavy. Afraid of what was happening to her body, Emily screamed but no one heard her. Her voice was gone. She had eaten poisoned sweets. News came that Bismarck had officially formed the German empire and the people began to jubilate. Emily tried to crawl home but she was stepped on to death in a stampede as the people rushed to celebrate.

Vocabulary

Curato - Cared
Svelto - Stampede
Sensitivo - Sensitive
Avvelenato - Poisoned
Strisciare - Crawl
Insensibile - Senseless
Acciaccato - Ache
Attenzione - Caution
Dolci - Sweets
Giubilare - Jubilate

Comprehension Questions

Perché Emily non ha ascoltato gli altri? Why did Emily not listen to others?

Perché Emily ha ricevuto i dolci? Why did Emily get the sweets?

Cosa le è successo dopo aver mangiato i dolci? What happened to her after eating the sweets?

Historical Note

The establishment of the Italian nation-state was a complex and lengthy process. Italy was fragmented into various city-states and regions for centuries. In the 19th century, the Italian unification movement, known as the Risorgimento, gained momentum. Key figures like Giuseppe Garibaldi and Count Camillo di Cavour played pivotal roles. In 1861, the Kingdom of Italy was proclaimed under King Victor Emmanuel II, encompassing much of the Italian peninsula. However, it took further efforts, including the capture of Rome in 1870, to fully unify Italy. The nation-state solidified, and Italy became a single political entity, laying the foundation for the modern Italian state.

LA BATTAGLIA DI CUSTOVA

Gareth era uno dei soldati delle forze italiane nel 1866. Era sotto la squadra guidata dal re Vittorio Emanuele II e dal suo generale La Marmora. Ma, a differenza degli altri soldati, era un uomo malato. Quando fu reclutato, era sano, ma negli ultimi mesi era diventato fragile e combatteva solo quando era necessario. Di solito non sarebbe stato arruolato per combattere nella battaglia di Custova, ma lui nascose a tutti la sua malattia.

Tuttavia, ciò che gli mancava in forza, lo aveva in magia. Poteva trasformarsi facilmente in qualsiasi animale, anche se la sua mancanza di forza si trasferiva all'animale stesso. Così, sul campo di battaglia, si trasformava in un ratto per evitare di essere ucciso. Ogni giorno lo faceva ed era uno dei fortunati a sopravvivere.

Ciò di cui non si rendeva conto era che alcuni soldati avevano notato che era sempre assente quando combattevano. Iniziarono a osservarlo, ma non riuscivano a capire come facesse a sparire ogni volta. Così lo denunciarono al generale. Non aveva altra scelta che dire la verità e si aspettava la morte come punizione. Ma al generale piacque la sua arguzia e decise che si sarebbe trasformato in un leone che avrebbe attaccato i loro nemici, visto che stavano perdendo la battaglia.

Durante la trasformazione, Gareth esaurì la sua energia e crollò subito dopo essersi trasformato in leone. Inutile, il generale lo uccise e la battaglia fu persa.

Questa è una storia di fantasia ispirata alla battaglia di Custova.

THE BATTLE OF CUSTOVA

Gareth was one of the soldiers of the Italy forces in 1866. He was under the team led by King Victor Emmanuel II and his general, La Marmora. But unlike other soldiers, he was a sick man. When he was recruited, he was healthy but over the last months, he had soon become frail and only fought when necessary. Usually, he wouldn't be enlisted to fight in the battle of Custova but he hid his illness away from everyone.

However, what he lacked in strength, he had in magic. He could transform himself into any animal easily although his lack of strength would also transfer to the animal. So, on the battlefield, he would transform into a rat and avoid being killed. Every day, he did that and was one of the lucky ones who survived.

What he didn't realize was that some of the soldiers had noticed that he was always absent whenever they battled. They began to watch him but couldn't understand how he disappeared every time. So, they reported him to the general. He had no choice but to tell the truth and he expected death as punishment. But, the general liked his wit and decided that he would turn into a lion that would attack their enemies since they were losing the battle.

While transforming, Gareth expended his energy and collapsed immediately after he turned into the lion. Useless, the general killed him and the battle was lost.

This is a fictional story inspired by the battle of Custova.

Vocabulary

Assente - Absent
Con - Wit
Crollato - Collapsed
Trasferimento - Transfer
Sopravvissuto - Survived
Segnalato - Reported
Magia - Magic
Attacco - Attack
Perdita - Losing
Fragile - Frail

Comprehension Questions

Perché Gareth cercava sempre di evitare le battaglie? Why did Gareth always try to avoid battles?

Come è riuscito a sopravvivere? How did he manage to survive them?

Era in grado di aiutare il generale? Was he able to help the general?

Historical Notes

The Third Italian War of Independence occurred in 1866, a pivotal moment in Italy's unification. Italy, under the leadership of Victor Emmanuel II and Prime Minister Bettino Ricasoli, aimed to liberate Venetia from Austrian control. The conflict unfolded as a part of larger European power dynamics. Italy formed an alliance with Prussia, which was engaged in the Austro-Prussian War. Italian forces clashed with the Austrians in battles such as Custoza and Lissa. Despite initial setbacks, Prussian victories elsewhere forced Austria to cede Venetia to France, who then handed it over to Italy. This significant territorial gain marked another step towards a unified Italy under a constitutional monarchy.

LUCAS LO SCIENZIATO

Lucas può essere considerato uno di quelli che hanno trovato fortuna nei posti più strani. Era un tedesco che viveva nel cuore della Germania. Era uno scienziato che coltivava germi nel suo piccolo laboratorio e ne testava le reazioni sugli animali. Questo lo rendeva facilmente odiato dai suoi coetanei perché rubava gli animali per allevare i germi.

Quando scoppiò la Prima Guerra Mondiale, impacchettò gli animali e alcuni dei germi che aveva coltivato e scappò, lasciando morire la sua famiglia. Rilasciava alcuni di questi germi non appena lasciava un luogo, in modo che la gente non sopravvivesse abbastanza a lungo da esporlo. Disinteressato a combattere, si rifugiò sulle colline e osservò ogni giorno lo svolgersi della guerra. Credeva davvero che la guerra non lo avrebbe raggiunto e scappò di nuovo, ogni volta che gli eserciti si avvicinavano a lui.

Alcuni soldati tedeschi lo sorpresero mentre correva e decisero di ucciderlo per la sua fuga. In cambio della sua vita, offrì loro alcuni dei suoi microrganismi, uno dei quali era l'antrace. Si offrì anche di coltivarne altri e di aiutarli a sconfiggere i loro nemici. Lo tennero comunque in ostaggio e quando l'uso dei virus non ebbe il successo da lui vantato, lo uccisero.

Questa storia è fittizia e si basa sull'uso dell'antrace come arma biologica nella Prima guerra mondiale.

LUCAS THE SCIENTIST

Lucas could be regarded as one of those who found luck in the strangest places. He was a German living in the heart of Germany. He was a scientist who cultivated germs in his small laboratory and tested their reactions on animals. This easily made him hated by his peers as he stole animals to breed germs.

When the First World War broke out, he packed up the animals and some of the germs he had grown and ran away, leaving his family to die. He released some of these germs as soon as he left a place, so people there wouldn't survive long enough to expose him. Uninterested in fighting, he fled to the hills and watched the war unfold every day. He truly believed the war wouldn't reach him and he ran again, each time the armies drew closer to him.

Some of the German soldiers caught him while he ran and decided to kill him for fleeing. In exchange for his life, he offered them some of his microorganisms, one of which was anthrax. He even offered to grow more and help them defeat their enemies. They held him hostage regardless and when the use of the viruses was not as successful as he boasted, they killed him off.

This story is fictional and based on the use of anthrax as a biological weapon in the First World War.

Vocabulary

La fortuna - Luck
Germi - Germs
Reazioni - Reactions
Coltivato - Cultivated
Colline - Hills
Ostaggio - Hostage
Vantato - Boasted
Laboratorio - Laboratory
Scienziato - Scientist
Esporre - Expose

Comprehension Questions

Perché Lucas ha allevato germi? Why did Lucas breed germs?

Meritava di essere odiato dagli altri? Did he deserve to be hated by others?

Pensate che il suo comportamento fosse onesto e giusto? Do you think his behavior was honest and right?

Historical Note

Italy's involvement in World War I was marked by shifting alliances. Initially, Italy was part of the Triple Alliance with Germany and Austria-Hungary. However, in 1915, driven by territorial ambitions and dissatisfaction with the alliance, Italy switched sides and joined the Triple Entente, which included France, Britain, and Russia. Italian forces then engaged in battles along the Italian Front, primarily against Austro-Hungarian forces in the rugged Alpine region. The war's toll on Italy was immense, with significant casualties and economic strain. Ultimately, Italy gained some territories but paid a high price, setting the stage for political and social changes that led to fascism in the 1920s.

L'AMICO DEL PAPA

Il papato e il governo italiano erano ai ferri corti quando Ruth nacque. Così sua madre, Marta, una lontana amica del papa, decise di non festeggiare la sua nascita fino a quando non fosse accaduto qualcosa di degno di essere celebrato nel papato. Si rifiutò di permettere a Ruth di giocare con i suoi coetanei o di andare a scuola. La trascurò, in solidarietà con il papa. La gente intorno implorava Marta di addestrare Ruth, ma lei si rifiutava e, col tempo, la gente smise di parlare.

Ruth crebbe fino a diventare una delinquente priva di cure parentali e odiava la madre. Ogni giorno rubava le cose di Martha e faceva in modo che ci fosse disordine in casa. Tutti cominciarono a incolpare Martha per la minaccia che aveva causato, a causa della sua mancanza di empatia nei confronti della figlia. Ben presto, Martha si stancò di tutta questa tiritera e portò Ruth con sé dal vescovo per farla partorire.

Mentre si trovava lì, Martha venne a sapere della firma del Trattato Lateranense e cambiò immediatamente atteggiamento nei confronti di Ruth, ma ormai era troppo tardi. Organizzò una festa per Ruth, ma a Ruth non importava più. Quando finalmente Ruth incontrò il Papa da adulta, questi non si ricordò nemmeno di Martha.

THE FRIEND OF THE POPE

The papacy and the Italian government had a disagreement when Ruth was born. So, her mother, Martha, a distant friend of the pope, decided not to celebrate her birth until something worthy of celebration happened in the papacy. She refused to allow Ruth to play with her peers or go to school. She neglected her, in solidarity with the pope. People around begged Martha to train Ruth but she refused and over time, people stopped talking.

Ruth grew to become a delinquent who had no parental care and she hated her mother. Each day, she would steal Martha's things and ensure that there was unrest in the house. Everyone began to blame Martha for the menace she had caused due to her lack of care for her child. Soon, Martha became tired of the whole matter and took Ruth with her to the bishop so she could be saved.

While there, Martha heard of the signing of the Lateran treaty and immediately changed towards Ruth but it was too late. She organized a party for Ruth but Ruth no longer cared. When Ruth finally met with the pope as an adult, the pope couldn't even remember Martha.

Vocabulary

Papato - Papacy
Distante - Distant
Minaccia - Menace
Degno - Worthy
Delinquente - Delinquent
Trascurato - Neglected
Inquietudine - Unrest
Celebrazione - Celebration
Genitoriale - Parental
Garantire - Ensure

Comprehension Questions

Perché Marta si rifiutò di prendersi cura del suo bambino? Why did Martha refuse to care for her child?

Cosa fece Ruth di conseguenza? What did Ruth do as a result?

Il Papa si ricordò di Marta? Did the Pope remember Martha?

Historical Note

The independence of Vatican City, the world's smallest sovereign state, dates back to February 11, 1929, with the signing of the Lateran Treaty between the Holy See and the Kingdom of Italy. This historic agreement resolved long-standing disputes, granting the Vatican full sovereignty. It recognized the Pope as both the spiritual leader of the Catholic Church and the head of state. Vatican City, a 44-hectare enclave in the heart of Rome, was officially established as an independent city-state. This event marked the end of the Pope's temporal rule and the beginning of a new era of Vatican autonomy, preserving its religious and political significance to this day.

EROI

Giorgio Perlasca era uno degli uomini che procuravano i rifornimenti per l'esercito italiano nei Balcani. Grazie al suo zelo nel lavoro, fu promosso e incaricato di acquistare carne per l'esercito italiano che combatteva contro i russi. Questo ruolo lo spingeva a recarsi nell'Europa orientale per procurare rifornimenti.

Tuttavia, l'esercito si arrese agli Alleati e agli italiani fu data la possibilità di unirsi ai fascisti o di rimanere fedeli al re italiano. Egli decise di rimanere fedele al re e fece parte della resistenza italiana. Questo lo portò all'arresto a Budapest. In seguito, chiese asilo politico all'ambasciata spagnola e divenne un uomo libero.

Lì lavorò con altri diplomatici in Stati neutrali alla guerra. Insieme, fecero uscire clandestinamente gli ebrei dall'Ungheria per proteggerli sotto la guida di vari Stati neutrali. Dopo la guerra, si rifiutò di raccontare la sua storia al pubblico e solo poche persone lo sostennero. Lo raccontò solo ai suoi stretti collaboratori e alla sua famiglia solo anni dopo. Nonostante il suo coraggio, non ricevette mai credito per le sue azioni fino all'ultima parte della sua vita.

Questo è un adattamento del ruolo che Giorgio Perlasca ebbe nella Seconda Guerra Mondiale.

HEROES

Giorgio Pelasca was one of the men who procured supplies for the Italian army in the Balkans. As a result of his zeal at work, he was promoted and charged with the role of buying meat for the Italian army fighting the Russians. This role sent him to Eastern Europe to get supplies.

However, the army surrendered to the Allies and Italians were given the option of joining the fascists or staying loyal to the Italian king. He decided to stay loyal to the king and was part of the Italian resistance. This led to his arrest in Budapest. Later, he applied for political asylum at the Spanish embassy and became a free man.

There, he worked with other diplomats in states neutral in the war. Together, they smuggled the Jews out of Hungary to be protected under the guidance of various neutral states. After the war, he refused to tell his story to the public and only a few people supported him. He told just his close associates and didn't tell his family until years later. Despite his bravery, he never received credit for his actions up until the latter part of his life.

This is an adaptation of the role Georgio Pelasca played in World War II.

Vocabulary

Procurato - Procured
Ultimo - Latter
Promosso - Promoted
Incaricato - Charged
Coraggio - Bravery
Opzione - Option
Asilo - Asylum
Neutrale - Neutral
Associati - Associates
Credito - Credit

Comprehension Questions

In che modo Giorgio Perlasca ha aiutato l'esercito italiano? How did Giorgio Perlasca help the Italian Army?

Come era considerata la sua fedeltà al re? How was his loyalty to the king regarded?

Gli fu riconosciuto il merito del suo coraggio? Did he receive credit for his bravery?

Historical Note

In World War II, Italy, under Benito Mussolini's fascist regime, initially aligned with Nazi Germany. They invaded numerous countries but faced significant defeats, notably in North Africa. By 1943, as Allied forces invaded Sicily, the Italian government, led by King Victor Emmanuel III, ousted Mussolini and sought an armistice with the Allies. This shift marked the fall of fascism in Italy. However, German forces occupied the north, leading to a civil war. The Allies, with local resistance, gradually liberated the country, culminating in the surrender of German troops in May 1945. Italy then abolished the monarchy and established a republic, ending its fascist era.

LA PROFEZIA

Nel 1946, Georgia era una delle donne entusiaste che Umberto II fosse diventato re d'Italia. Sebbene ci fossero state molte controversie, poiché alcuni volevano diventare una repubblica mentre altri amavano il re d'Italia, Georgia non esitò a dichiarare il suo amore per lui.

Progettò di andare nella capitale e incontrare il re per entrare a far parte del gabinetto. La cosa sembrava irreale, perché non si diventa semplicemente membri del gabinetto del re, ma Georgia lo disse con tanta sicurezza che la gente cominciò a credere che conoscesse qualcuno a palazzo.

Questa fede incrollabile derivava da una profezia che Georgia aveva ricevuto da sua nonna quando era più giovane, secondo la quale sarebbe cresciuta fino a lavorare con l'ultimo re regnante d'Italia. La controversia tra la monarchia e i repubblicani ha ulteriormente alimentato la sua fede nel fatto che Umberto II fosse il re con cui avrebbe lavorato.

Presto gli italiani furono chiamati a votare in un referendum per scegliere tra monarchia e repubblica. Per giorni, Georgia andò a convincere la gente a scegliere la monarchia, con la speranza che Umberto II avrebbe regnato per un po'. Purtroppo, la maggioranza votò per l'istituzione di una repubblica ed Georgia concluse che aveva lavorato per il re spingendo la gente a votare per lui.

Si tratta di un adattamento romanzato della storia di Umberto II, l'ultimo re d'Italia in carica.

THE PROPHECY

In 1946, Georgia was one of the women who was elated that Umberto II became king of Italy. Although there had been a lot of controversy as some of the people wanted to become a republic while others loved the king of Italy, Georgia didn't hesitate to declare her love for him.

She planned to go into the capital and meet the king so she could become part of the cabinet. This seemed unreal though, since one didn't just become a member of the king's cabinet but Georgia said this with so much assurance that people began to believe she knew someone in the palace.

This unwavering faith came from a prophecy Georgia had received from her grandmother when she was younger that she would grow to work with the last reigning king of Italy. The controversy between the monarchy and republicans further sparked her faith to believe that Umberto II was the king she would work with.

Soon, Italians were asked to vote in a referendum to choose between a monarchy and a republic. For days, Georgia went about convincing people to choose the monarchy, with the hope that Umberto II would reign for a while. Alas, the majority voted for the establishment of a republic and Georgia concluded that she had worked for the king by prompting people to vote for him.

This is a fictional adaptation of the story of Umberto II, the last reigning king of Italy.

Vocabulary

Felicitante - Elated
Garanzia - Assurance
Monarchia - Monarchy
Polemica - Controversy
Votato - Voted
Referendum - Referendum
Monarchia - Monarchy
Incrollabile - Unwavering
Scintillante - Sparked
Convincente - Convincing

Comprehension Questions

Chi ha fatto la profezia e perché la Georgia ci ha creduto così tanto? Who made the prophecy and why did Georgia believe it so much?

Come votò la maggioranza? How did the majority vote?

In che modo la Georgia servì l'ultimo re? How did Georgia serve the last king?

Historical Note

The Italian institutional referendum of 2016 was a significant event in the country's political history. It aimed to reform the constitution, primarily reducing the power of the Senate and streamlining the legislative process. The proposal, championed by then-Prime Minister Matteo Renzi, faced opposition from various political parties, including the populist Five Star Movement. Ultimately, the referendum resulted in a resounding "no" vote, with around 60% of Italians rejecting the reforms. This outcome led to Renzi's resignation, political instability, and discussions on the future of Italian governance. The referendum underscored the nation's complex political landscape and the desire for change.

LUCAS PROUDO

Dopo la Seconda Guerra Mondiale, il popolo italiano era incerto su molte cose. Anche se la guerra era finita, desideravano ancora una maggiore stabilità e facevano molta pressione sul primo ministro, Alcide De Gasperi. Questo lo spinse a confidarsi con uno dei membri del suo gabinetto, Lucas, un giovane esperto di politica.

Ogni settimana, Lucas si incontrava con il primo ministro e discutevano le questioni del Paese prima di sottoporle al gabinetto. Il primo ministro inviò Lucas in altri Paesi per indagare e strinsero alleanze con diversi Paesi.

Queste attività aiutarono l'Italia a diventare uno dei membri fondatori dell'Organizzazione del Trattato del Nord Atlantico (NATO) nel 1949, contribuendo a consolidare i legami del Paese con le potenze occidentali.

Tuttavia Lucas si lasciò distrarre dal fermento intorno al primo ministro, voleva che l'attenzione fosse rivolta anche a se stesso. Riteneva che gli si dovesse dare più credito, così iniziò a cercare di sabotare il governo. Questo lo portò all'arresto e trascorse il resto dei suoi anni in prigione.

PROUD LUCAS

Post World War II, the people of Italy were unsure about a lot of things. Although the war had ended, they still desired more stability and they put a lot of pressure on the prime minister, Alcide De Gasperi. This pressured the prime minister to confide in one of the people in his cabinet, Lucas, a young man, versed in politics.

Every week, Lucas would meet up with the prime minister and they would discuss matters of the country before tabling them with the cabinet. The prime minister sent Lucas to other countries to investigate and they formed alliances with several countries.

These activities helped Italy to become one of the founding members of the North Atlantic Treaty Organization (NATO) in 1949, which helped them to solidify the country's ties with Western powers.

However Lucas became distracted by the buzz around the prime minister, he wanted the attention to himself as well. He believed he should be given more credit, so he began to try to sabotage the government. This eventually led to his arrest and he spent the rest of his years in prison.

Vocabulary

Stabilità - Stability
Desiderata - Desired
Attività - Activities
Buzz - Buzz
Sabotaggio - Sabotage
Pressione - Pressure
Confidare - Confide
Indagare - Investigate
Alleanze - Alliances
Solidificare - Solidify

Comprehension Questions

Con chi si è confidato il primo ministro? In whom did the prime minister confide?

In che modo Lucas ha aiutato il primo ministro? How did Lucas help the prime minister?

Perché Lucas sabotò il governo? Why did Lucas sabotage the government?

Historical Note

Following World War II, Italy's alliance with NATO and the EU emerged as a critical foundation for post-war stability. Italy, ravaged by the war, joined NATO in 1949, committing to collective defense and deterring potential threats. Concurrently, Italy's involvement in the European Coal and Steel Community in 1951 laid the groundwork for EU membership. These alliances provided Italy security and economic opportunities, helping reconstruct the nation. However, Italy's EU journey has brought challenges as it balances national sovereignty with European integration. Despite occasional tensions, these alliances have shaped Italy's place in the post-war world, fostering peace, prosperity, and cooperation.

LA LAMBORGHINI

Quando Ferruccio Lamborghini fondò la sua azienda di auto sportive, Mattia fu uno di quelli che ne rimase affascinato. Desiderava possedere una di queste auto e aveva intenzione di ottenerla con ogni mezzo. Ma Mattia era solo un contabile di basso livello che poteva permettersi solo una bicicletta.

Chiamò il suo amico Edoardo ed entrambi decisero di avviare un'attività commerciale, approfittando del boom economico, per potersi procurare l'auto sportiva. Compravano pezzi di ricambio per auto e biciclette, li portavano da chi li rendeva più belli e li rivendeva a un prezzo più alto. Quando il capo di Mattia venne a conoscenza dell'attività, fu interessato ad acquistarne alcuni e li presentò a diversi suoi amici.

Alla fine dell'anno, Mattia e il suo amico avevano investito in diverse aziende e avevano iniziato a utilizzare le tecnologie più avanzate per produrre i loro pezzi di ricambio. Inviarono alcuni dei loro prodotti all'estero e crebbero una clientela internazionale. Mattia alla fine si dimise dal suo lavoro e assunse alcuni dei suoi precedenti collaboratori. Quando l'attività crebbe abbastanza, Mattia non volle più comprare l'auto sportiva. Fece costruire la sua auto da zero da un'azienda straniera e fu l'unico uomo a possedere il suo modello.

THE LAMBORGHINI

When Ferruccio Lamborghini started his sports car company, Mattia was one of those who was fascinated. He desired to own one of the cars and he was going to get it by all means. But Mattia was only a low-grade accountant who could only afford a bicycle.

He called his friend Edoardo and they both decided to start a business, taking advantage of the economic boom, so he could eventually get the sports car. They would buy spare parts for cars and bicycles, take them to people who made them look better and sell them at a higher price. When Mattia's boss heard of the business, he was interested in buying some as well and introduced them to several of his friends.

By the end of the year, Mattia and his friend had invested in several businesses and they began to use the latest technology to make their spare parts. They sent some of their products overseas and grew an international clientele. Mattia eventually resigned from his job and employed some of his previous co-workers. When the business grew enough, Mattia no longer desired to buy the sports car. He had a foreign company build his car from scratch and was the only man who owned his model.

Vocabulary

Investito - Invested
Tecnologia - Technology
Società - Company
Estero - Foreign
Biciclette - Bicycles
Affascinato - Fascinated
Contabile - Accountant
Pezzi di ricambio - Spare parts
Diversi - Several
Modello - Model

Comprehension Questions

Qual era il lavoro di Mattia? What was Mattia's job?

Mattia può permettersi l'auto sportiva? Could Mattia afford the sports car?

Quale auto ha acquistato Mattia? What car did Mattia eventually get?

Historical Note

The Italian economic boom, known as the "Italian miracle," was a period of remarkable growth and transformation that occurred in the 1950s and 1960s. Emerging from the devastation of World War II, Italy experienced a surge in industrialization, modernization, and increased living standards. Key factors contributing to this boom included massive infrastructure development, a skilled labor force, and a global demand for Italian goods. Industries like automotive and fashion flourished, with brands like Fiat and Gucci gaining international prominence. The boom transformed Italy from an agrarian society into a modern industrial nation, bringing newfound prosperity and significantly improving the quality of life for its citizens.

LO STRANO LADRO

Michelle era la governante della casa di Aldo Moro. Ogni mattina arrivava al lavoro con il figlio piccolo, Michael, e se ne andava la sera. Ben presto, in casa cominciarono a sparire delle cose. Tutti puntarono il dito contro gli altri lavoratori, ma nessuno pensò a Michelle. La famiglia si fidava di lei e affidò a Michelle le indagini sul furto. La donna indicò come colpevoli due domestici maschi, che vennero immediatamente sollevati dal lavoro.

Michelle fece dei colloqui per trovare nuovi lavoratori e la famiglia tornò ad essere tranquilla. Non appena gli episodi di furto cessarono, ripresero e questa volta furono più gravi. Ogni giorno in casa sparivano soldi e gioielli e nessuno poteva fidarsi dell'altro. Lo statista italiano ed ex primo ministro Aldo Moro non era al corrente degli incidenti. Anche i nuovi operai furono licenziati, ma i furti non si fermarono e tutti cominciarono a puntare il dito contro Michelle.

Alla fine fu sorpresa a rubare da uno dei cuochi e gli operai decisero di denunciarla ad Aldo Moro, visto che era una conoscente. Tuttavia, egli fu rapito e assassinato dalle Brigate Rosse prima che potessero farlo e Michelle fuggì dalla città con il suo bambino.

Si tratta di una storia di fantasia ambientata nella casa di Aldo Moro, ex primo ministro italiano assassinato negli anni di piombo.

THE STRANGE THIEF

Michelle was a housekeeper in the home of Aldo Moro. Every morning, she would come to work with her young son, Michael and leave in the evenings. Soon, things began to go missing in the house. Everyone pointed fingers at the other workers but no one thought of Michelle. The household trusted her and entrusted the investigation of the theft to Michelle. She pointed out two of the male servants as the culprit and they were relieved from work immediately.

Michelle conducted interviews for new workers and the household became peaceful again. Just as soon as the theft incidents stopped, it resumed again and this time, it was worse. Money and jewelry disappeared in the household daily, and no one could trust the other. The Italian statesman and former prime minister, Aldo Moro was not privy to the incidents. The new workers were sacked as well but the theft didn't stop, so everyone began to point fingers at Michelle.

She was eventually caught stealing by one of the cooks and the workers decided to report her to Aldo Moro since she was an acquaintance. However, he was abducted and assassinated by the Red Brigades before they could do so and Michelle fled town with her child.

This is a fictional story set in the home of Aldo Moro, a former prime minister of Italy who was assassinated in the years of lead.

Vocabulary

Governante - Housekeeper
Brigata - Brigade
Conoscente - Acquaintance
Rapito - Abducted
Gioielli - Jewelry
Intervista - Interview
Fiducioso - Trusted
Colpevole - Culprit
Sollevato - Relieved
Affidato - Entrusted

Comprehension Questions

Quanto si fidava la famiglia di Michelle? How much did the family trust Michelle?

Chi era il ladro? Who was the thief?

Cosa è successo ad Aldo Moro? What happened to Aldo Moro?

Historical Note

The "Years of Lead" were characterized by political violence, terrorism, and social conflict in Italy, involving far-left and far-right extremist groups. The Red Brigades, a far-left terrorist organization, carried out high-profile kidnappings and assassinations during this period.

ISOLAMENTO

L'epidemia del virus COVID-19 ha incontrato Victoria nella casa del suo amico Williams. Era andata a casa sua per prendere alcuni libri per il nuovo semestre e, all'improvviso, ha saputo che le scuole erano state chiuse e che stava iniziando una serrata. Avrebbe potuto sapere la notizia giorni prima per prepararsi, ma il suo telefono era guasto e solo dopo il suo arrivo Williams l'ha informata. Pensò di tornare a casa, ma non era sicura di voler passare settimane chiusa in casa con sua madre, con la quale sembrava non essere mai d'accordo su nulla.

Così, quando Williams le offrì di stare a casa sua per tutta la durata dell'isolamento, fu troppo veloce a dire di sì.

Nei giorni successivi, la ragazza imparò subito a conoscere meglio Williams. Lui le raccontò del padre politico che evadeva spesso le tasse e non era mai nel Paese e lei gli disse che sua madre era troppo capricciosa per rimanere sposata. Imparò a cucinare i suoi piatti preferiti e fu in una di quelle sere in cui cucinò che lui alla fine le confessò di amarla.

La settimana di isolamento si trasformò in mesi e alla fine passarono la maggior parte dell'anno 2020 a conoscersi mentre il mondo lottava contro il Coronavirus.

LOCKDOWN

The outbreak of the COVID-19 virus met Victoria in the house of her friend, Williams. She had gone to his house to get some books for the new semester and suddenly, she learnt that schools had been locked and a lockdown was starting. She could have heard the news days before so she could prepare but her phone was bad and only after she arrived did Williams inform her. She thought of going back home but she wasn't sure she wanted to spend weeks locked with her mother who she never seemed to agree with on anything.

So, when Williams offered her his place to stay for the duration of the lockdown, she was too quick to say yes.

Over the next few days, she was quick to know more about Williams. He told her of his politician father who evaded taxes a lot and was never in the country and she told him that her mother was too temperamental to stay married. She learned to cook his favorite meals and it was on one of those nights she cooked that he eventually confessed to loving her.

The week-long lockdown turned to months and eventually, they spent most of the year 2020 getting to know each other while the world battled Coronavirus.

Vocabulary

Epidemia - Outbreak
Semestre - Semester
Isolamento - Lockdown
Durata - Duration
Evaso - Evaded
Temperamento - Temperamental
Tasse - Texes
Bloccato - Locked
Telefono - Phone
Politico - Politician

Comprehension Questions

Perché Victoria esitava a tornare a casa? Why was Victoria reluctant to return home?

Che lavoro faceva il padre di William? What job did William's father do?

Come hanno trascorso Victoria e William il periodo di isolamento? How did Victoria and William spend the period of isolation?

Historical Note

The Second Italian Republic began in 1994 with the collapse of the First Republic due to a corruption scandal. Silvio Berlusconi's conservative coalition dominated politics for much of this period, marked by economic growth but also allegations of corruption. Italy was an active participant in NATO and the European Union.

In recent years, Italy faced economic challenges and political instability. Austerity measures, the European debt crisis, and the rise of populist movements, like the Five Star Movement, characterized the nation's politics. In 2020, Italy was severely hit by the COVID-19 pandemic. Mario Draghi became Prime Minister in 2021, tasked with leading Italy's recovery efforts and navigating its complex political landscape.

Conclusion

L earning the basics of any language is difficult, and the Italian language can feel daunting for many newcomers. With that being said, if you were able to finish all of the lessons in this book, you have built a solid foundation in Italian.

However, learning a language is a long process that rewards consistency. Even just listening and watching Italian shows for 30 minutes a day can go a long way in improving your Italian skills. We sincerely hope that you continue your Italian language journey with the foundation you have built up and reach your goals, whether that be to understand the basics or speak like a native.

Thank you for choosing our book along your path to Italian mastery and we hope that you obtained a lot of useful information! If you have any questions, comments, or even suggestions we would love to hear from you by email at Contact@worldwidenomadbooks.com. We greatly appreciate the feedback and this allows us to improve our books and provide the best language learning experience we can.

Thank you,

Worldwide Nomad Team

Made in the USA
Coppell, TX
07 May 2024